Barron's Review Course Series

Let's Review:

English

5th Edition

Carol Chaitkin, M.S.
Former Director of American Studies
Lycée Français de New York
New York, New York

Former English Department Head
Great Neck North High School
Great Neck, New York

BARRON'S

Acknowledgments

Page 75: "The Pitcher" from *The Orb Weaver* by Robert Francis © 1960, by Robert Francis and reprinted by permission of Wesleyan University Press.

Page 79: "Old Photograph of the Future" by Robert Penn Warren © 1985. Reprinted by permission of Random House, Inc.

Page 81: "Child on Top of a Greenhouse," copyright © 1946 by Editorial Publications, Inc.; from COLLECTED POEMS by Theodore Roethke. Used by permission of Doubleday, an imprint of Knopf Doubleday Publishing Group, a division of Random House LLC. All rights reserved.

Page 81: "The Sleeping Giant" from OLD AND NEW POEMS by Donald Hall. Copyright © 1990 by Donald Hall. Reprinted by permission of Houghton Mifflin Harcourt Publishing Company. All rights reserved.

All inquiries should be addressed to:
Barron's Educational Series, Inc.
250 Wireless Boulevard
Hauppauge, NY 11788
www.barronseduc.com

Library of Congress Control Number: 2015943734
ISBN: 978-1-4380-0626-0

PRINTED IN THE UNITED STATES OF AMERICA
9 8 7 6 5 4 3 2 1

10%
POST-CONSUMER
WASTE
Paper contains a minimum
of 10% post-consumer
waste (PCW). Paper used
in this book was derived
from certified, sustainable
forestlands.

TABLE OF CONTENTS

REGENTS ELA (COMMON CORE) EXAMINATIONS

INDEX

INTRODUCTION

Let's Review is designed as a handbook for high school English courses, including those aligned with the new Common Core Standards, and as a review book for students preparing to take the Regents Exam in English Language Arts (Common Core). Because the English Regents Exam is not a test of specific curriculum but an assessment of skills in reading comprehension, literary analysis, and composition, *Let's Review* offers a comprehensive guide to essential language, literature, and critical reading and writing skills all high school students should seek to demonstrate as they prepare for college and the workplace.

A GUIDE TO THE NEW YORK STATE STANDARDS IN LITERACY (ELA)

Most middle school and high school students in New York State should already be familiar with some key shifts in curriculum and instruction in their English courses. These shifts in emphasis include the following:

- Students will read more informational texts and perhaps fewer literary texts than in the past. Alignment with the Common Core requires a balancing of the two.
- In all academic subjects, students will be expected to build their knowledge primarily through engaging directly with text.
- Throughout secondary school, students will read texts of increasing complexity and will be expected to develop skills in **close reading** in all academic subjects.
- Students will be expected to engage in rich and rigorous **evidence-based** conversations/class discussions about text.
- Student writing will emphasize **use of evidence** from sources to express their understanding and to form and develop argument.
- Students will acquire the **academic vocabulary** they need to comprehend and respond to grade level complex texts. This vocabulary is often relevant to more than one subject.

TERMS TO HELP YOU UNDERSTAND THE STATE STANDARDS

- **ELA/LITERACY**—**English Language Arts** refers to skills in reading, writing, speaking, and listening. Courses and exams once identified as English may also be identified as ELA. **Literacy** refers to the ability to read and write and to use language proficiently. The term also identifies the quality of being knowledgeable in a particular subject or field. For example, we often refer to "digital" or "computer literacy."
- **COMMON CORE LEARNING STANDARDS (CCLS)***—These are the learning standards in ELA and math, also known as **CCSS** (Common Core State Standards), developed and adopted by a consortium of over 40 states. New York State adopted the CCLS in 2010 and continues to implement them in curriculum and assessments (testing).
- **CCR**—The phrase **"college and career ready"** is widely used in discussion of new curriculum and assessments. This refers to the fundamental principle of the Common Core Standards: to reflect the knowledge and skills that all students need for success in college and careers.
- **ASSESSMENT**—You may hear teachers and other educators using the term **assessment** instead of test or examination. An **assessment** is more than a simple test (in vocabulary, say) because it seeks to measure a number of skills at one time. Although we continue to refer to the English Regents as an exam or test, its goal is to be a valid **assessment** of a broad range of reading, thinking, language, and writing skills outlined in the Standards.
- **TEXT**—Broadly, the term text refers to any written material. The Common Core standards use the term to refer to the great variety of material students are expected to be able to read, understand, analyze, and write about. Texts may include **literary** works of fiction, drama, and poetry; and **informational**, or nonfiction, including essays, memoirs, speeches, and scientific and historical documents. The Common Core also emphasizes the use of **authentic texts;** that is, students will read actual historical documents or scientific essays rather than simply read articles about them.
- **CLOSE READING**—Skill in close, analytic reading is fundamental to the CCLS and to the new Regents exam. The Common Core curriculum focuses student attention on the text itself in order to understand not only what the text says and means but also how that meaning is constructed and revealed. Close reading enables students to understand central ideas and key supporting details. It also enables students to reflect on the meanings of individual words and sentences, the order in which sentences unfold, and the development of ideas over the course

2

of the text, which ultimately leads students to arrive at an understanding of the text as a whole.

- **ARGUMENT**—What is an argument? In academic writing, an argument is usually a central idea, often called a **claim** or **thesis statement,** which is backed up with evidence that supports the idea. Much of the writing high school students do in their English courses constitutes essays of argument, in addition to personal essays, descriptive pieces, and works of imagination.
- **SOURCE-BASED/EVIDENCE-BASED**—The ability to compose sound arguments using relevant and specific evidence from a given text is central to the expectations of the Common Core Standards.
- **WRITING STRATEGY**—This is the general term for a literary element, literary technique, or rhetorical device. Examples include characterization, conflict, denotation/connotation, metaphor, simile, irony, language use, point of view, setting, structure, symbolism, theme, and tone. In class discussions and on examinations, students are expected to understand and explain how literary elements and writing strategies contribute to the meaning of a text.

*The Anchor (Common Core) Standards for Grades 11–12 Reading, Writing, and Language are found in the Appendices, pages 223–227.

THE REGENTS ELA (COMMON CORE) EXAM

This 3-hour examination requires students to read, analyze, and write about both literary and informational texts.

PART I—READING COMPREHENSION

This part requires close reading of three texts and will contain at least one literature text, one poem, and one informational text, followed by 24 multiple-choice questions.

PART II—WRITING FROM SOURCES: ARGUMENT

This part includes close reading of four informational texts and may contain some information in graphics; students will compose an essay of argument with a claim based on the sources.

PART III—TEXT ANALYSIS: EXPOSITION

Students will perform a close reading of one informational or one literature text and write a two to three paragraph expository response that identifies a central idea in the text and analyzes how the author's use of one writing strategy develops that central idea.

Note: The ACT and the new SAT (2015) include similar assessments of close reading, text analysis, the rhetoric of arguments, and the use of academic vocabulary.

WAYS TO USE *LET'S REVIEW: ENGLISH*

As a handbook for literature study in high school and college courses, see especially

    Chapter 4—Reading Prose
    Chapter 5—Reading Poetry
    Chapter 6—Writing About Literature: A General Review

As a handbook for reading comprehension and language skills, see especially

    Chapter 1—Reading Comprehension
    Chapter 3—Reading and Writing to Analyze Text
    Chapter 4—Reading Prose
    Chapter 5—Reading Poetry
    Chapter 8—Vocabulary

As a handbook for writing and proofreading, see especially

    Chapter 2—Writing from Sources
    Chapter 3—Reading and Writing to Analyze Text
    Chapter 6—Writing About Literature: A General Review
    Chapter 9—Grammar and Usage for the Careful Writer
    Chapter 10—Punctuation: Guidelines and Reminders

As a review text for the ELA (Common Core) Regents exam, the SAT, and the ACT, see especially

    Chapter 1—Reading Comprehension
    Chapter 2—Writing from Sources
    Chapter 3—Reading and Writing to Analyze Text
    Chapter 8—Vocabulary
    Appendices—The New York State Common Core Learning Standards
    for English Language Arts

Chapter 1

READING COMPREHENSION

Throughout your schooling, you have been developing skills in the ability to read and comprehend works of literature as well as informational texts in nearly every subject, including history and social studies, science, and technical studies. Because the ability to understand, interpret, and make use of a wide range of texts is central to learning, it is a skill students are regularly asked to demonstrate. Assessment of students' reading comprehension skills may be informal or indirect, as in a class discussion or short quiz, or through formal testing.

Students at Regents level—11th and 12th grades—are expected to have the ability to understand and interpret both literary and informational texts of significant complexity: that is, Regents-level students understand literary texts with multiple levels of meaning, with structures that may be complex or unconventional, and with elements of figurative or deliberately ambiguous language that are integral to its meaning. The expectations for reading informational texts include the ability to interpret and analyze personal essays, speeches, opinion pieces, and memoir and autobiographical works as well as official documents and historical, scientific, and technical material for subject courses other than English. This increased emphasis on a wide range of informational texts is one of the key shifts in high school curriculum and should already be familiar to most students. It is also helpful to know that both the ACT and new SAT (2015) exams include a similar variety of texts and primary source documents.

CLOSE READING

One useful way to think about what we mean by "close reading" is to think about what you are doing when you can annotate something you are reading; that is, what do you underline? circle? check in the margins? You are probably checking off main ideas and conclusions, underlining the most important details, and circling significant or unfamiliar words. Whether or not you actually mark up a text, that process of checking, underlining, and circling is the thinking process of close reading.

In-class discussions of literary works are often exercises in what is meant by close reading—Where are we? Which details give us an image of the set-

5

ting? What just happened? What is this character thinking now? What does the story lead us to expect? What is surprising? How were we prepared? How does the author/narrator guide our understanding of characters and their actions? Why is this incident important in the plot? What does this character's remark really mean? Was the ending convincing?

The most satisfying "close reading," however, is what we are doing when our imaginations are fully engaged in a story, a play, a poem, or a film(!) Then it is not an academic exercise or assessment but the pleasure of experiencing a good story.

Reading for information in history, social studies, or science requires careful attention to the sequence of ideas, to how general statements are supported with relevant details. This kind of reading may also require familiarity with specialized language. (See Academic Language in Chapter 8 — Vocabulary.)

On exams, you will exercise this same kind of thinking and engagement with the text on your own. The multiple-choice questions are designed to assess your close reading skills and the depth of your understanding.

QUESTIONS TO KEEP IN MIND AS YOU READ

If you are reading a literary passage, ask yourself

What is this piece about? What is the narrative point of view?
What do we understand about the setting?
What do we understand about the narrator? Other characters?

In reading a poem, consider

What experience, memory, or dramatic situation is the poem about?
Who and where is the narrator/speaker?
How does the organization of lines and stanzas affect the meaning?
How are language and imagery used?

In passages of memoir and personal essay, ask

What experience is meant to be shared and understood?
What does the author say? Describe? Suggest? Reveal?

If you are reading an informational text, ask yourself

What is the subject? What do I already know about this subject?
What main idea or theme is being developed? What phrases or terms signal that?
What is the purpose? To inform? To persuade? To celebrate? To guide? To show a process? To introduce a new or unfamiliar subject?

READING COMPREHENSION PASSAGES AND QUESTIONS FOR REVIEW

The following passages and questions are from actual tasks on Regents ELA exams.

21st oct 2017

PASSAGE ONE—LITERATURE *Author*

This passage is from a classic Sherlock Holmes story by Sir Arthur Conan Doyle. Many of the expressions are unfamiliar but can be understood in context. High school students may already be familiar with the character of Sherlock Holmes, both through reading of the original stories and through modern retelling in popular American and British television series. On the Regents ELA exam, you are expected to read and analyze texts from works of American literature as well as works from British and world literatures.

It was upon the 4th of March, as I have good reason to remember, that I rose somewhat earlier than usual, and found that Sherlock Holmes had not yet finished his breakfast. The landlady had become so accustomed to my late habits that my place had not been laid nor my coffee prepared. With the unreasonable petulance[1] of
(5) mankind I rang the bell and gave a curt intimation that I was ready. Then I picked up a magazine from the table and attempted to while away the time with it, while my companion munched silently at his toast. One of the articles had a pencil-mark at the heading, and I naturally began to run my eye through it. ...

"From a drop of water," said the writer, "a logician could infer the possibility
(10) of an Atlantic or a Niagara without having seen or heard of one or the other. So all life is a great chain, the nature of which is known whenever we are shown a single   *topic* link of it. Like all other arts, the Science of Deduction and Analysis is one which can only be acquired by long and patient study, nor is life long enough to allow any mortal to attain the highest possible perfection in it. Before turning to those
(15) moral and mental aspects of the matter which present the greatest difficulties, let the inquirer begin by mastering more elementary problems. Let him, on meeting a fellow-mortal, learn at a glance to distinguish the history of the man and the trade or profession to which he belongs. Puerile[2] as such an exercise may seem, it sharpens the faculties of observation and teaches one where to look and what to look for. By
(20) a man's fingernails, by his coat-sleeve, by his boot, by his trouser-knees, by the callosities of his forefinger and thumb, by his expression, by his shirt-cuffs—by each of these things a man's calling is plainly revealed. That all united should fail to enlighten the competent inquirer in any case is almost inconceivable."

---

[1]petulance — a quality or state of being rude
[2]puerile — childish

"What ineffable twaddle!" I cried, slapping the magazine down on the table; "I
(25) never read such rubbish in my life."

"What is it?" asked Sherlock Holmes.

"Why, this article," I said, pointing at it with my egg-spoon as I sat down to my
breakfast. "I see that you have read it, since you have marked it. I don't deny that
it is smartly written. It irritates me, though. It is evidently the theory of some arm-
(30) chair lounger who evolves all these neat little paradoxes in the seclusion of his own
study. It is not practical. I should like to see him clapped down in a third-class carriage on the Underground and asked to give the trades of all his fellow-travellers. I
would lay a thousand to one against him."

"You would lose your money," Sherlock Holmes remarked, calmly. "As for the
(35) article, I wrote it myself."

"You?"

"Yes, I have a turn both for observation and for deduction. The theories which
I have expressed there, and which appear to you to be so chimerical, are really
extremely practical—so practical that I depend upon them for my bread-and-
(40) cheese."

"And how?" I asked, involuntarily.

"Well, I have a trade of my own. I suppose I am the only one in the world. I'm a
consulting detective, if you can understand what that is. Here in London we have
lots of government detectives and lots of private ones. When these fellows are at
(45) fault they come to me, and I manage to put them on the right scent. They lay all
the evidence before me, and I am generally able, by the help of my knowledge of the
history of crime, to set them straight. There is a strong family resemblance about
misdeeds, and if you have all the details of a thousand at your finger-ends, it is odd
if you can't unravel the thousand and first. Lestrade is a well-known detective. He
(50) got himself into a fog recently over a forgery case, and that was what brought him
here."

"And these other people?"

"They are mostly sent out by private inquiry agencies. They are all people who are
in trouble about something, and want a little enlightening. I listen to their story,
(55) they listen to my comments, and then I pocket my fee."

"But do you mean to say," I said, "that without leaving your room you can
unravel some knot which other men can make nothing of, although they have seen
every detail for themselves?"

"Quite so. I have a kind of intuition that way. Now and again a case turns up
(60) which is a little more complex. Then I have to bustle about and see things with my
own eyes. You see, I have a lot of special knowledge which I apply to the problem,
and which facilitates matters wonderfully. Those rules of deduction laid down in
that article which aroused your scorn are invaluable to me in practical work. Obser-

vation with me is second nature. You appeared to be surprised when I told you, on
(65) our first meeting, that you had come from Afghanistan."

"You were told, no doubt."

"Nothing of the sort. I *knew* you came from Afghanistan. From long habit the
train of thought ran so swiftly through my mind that I arrived at the conclusion
without being conscious of intermediate steps. There were such steps, however. The
(70) train of reasoning ran: 'Here is a gentleman of a medical type, but with the air of a
military man. Clearly an army doctor, then. He has just come from the tropics, for
his face is dark, and that is not the natural tint of his skin, for his wrists are fair. He
has undergone hardship and sickness, as his haggard face says clearly. His left arm
has been injured. He holds it in a stiff and unnatural manner. Where in the tropics
(75) could an English army doctor have seen much hardship and got his arm wounded?
Clearly in Afghanistan.' The whole train of thought did not occupy a second. I then
remarked that you came from Afghanistan, and you were astonished." ...

I was still annoyed at his bumptious style of conversation. I thought it best to
change the topic.

(80) "I wonder what that fellow is looking for?" I asked, pointing to a stalwart,
plainly dressed individual who was walking slowly down the other side of the street,
looking anxiously at the numbers. He had a large, blue envelope in his hand, and
was evidently the bearer of a message.

"You mean the retired sergeant of marines," said Sherlock Holmes.

(85) "Brag and bounce!" thought I to myself. "He knows that I cannot verify his
guess." The thought had hardly passed through my mind when the man whom we
were watching caught sight of the number on our door, and ran rapidly across the
roadway. We heard a loud knock, a deep voice below, and heavy steps ascending
the stair.

(90) "For Mr. Sherlock Holmes," he said, stepping into the room and handing my
friend the letter.

Here was an opportunity of taking the conceit out of him. He little thought of
this when he made that random shot. "May I ask, my lad," I said, blandly, "what
your trade may be?"

(95) "Commissionnaire, sir," he said, gruffly. "Uniform away for repairs."

"And you were?" I asked, with a slightly malicious glance at my companion. "A
sergeant, sir, Royal Marine Light Infantry, sir. No answer? Right, sir." He clicked
his heels together, raised his hand in a salute, and was gone.

—A. Conan Doyle
excerpted from *A Study in Scarlet*, 1904
Harper & Brothers Publishers

Questions for Comprehension

This passage, narrated by the character of Dr. Watson, reveals the differences in character and personality of the two men. The discussion of the magazine article leads to a dramatic demonstration of Holmes's powers of observation and deduction. At the end, Watson's doubts are erased, and he is left speechless.

1 The phrase "with the unreasonable petulance of mankind" (lines 4–5) emphasizes the narrator's

   (1) frustration with himself for missing sleep
   (2) irritation about not finding his breakfast ready
   (3) concern regarding the pencil-mark on the newspaper
   (4) impatience with Sherlock Holmes's silence   1____

2 How do the words "logician" (line 9), "deduction" (lines 12, 37, and 62), and "analysis" (line 12) advance the author's purpose?

   (1) by indicating the relationship between science and art
   (2) by suggesting the reasons why private inquiry agencies seek outside help
   (3) by highlighting the complexity of the crimes encountered by Sherlock Holmes
   (4) by emphasizing the systematic nature of Sherlock Holmes's approach to solving crimes   2____

3 What is the effect of withholding the identity of Sherlock Holmes as the author of the article (lines 9 through 35)?

   (1) It creates a somber mood.
   (2) It foreshadows an unwelcome turn of events.
   (3) It allows the reader to learn the narrator's true feelings.
   (4) It leads the reader to misunderstand who the writer is.   3____

10

4 In this passage, the conversation between Holmes and the narrator (lines 24 through 40) serves to

(1) reinforce the narrator's appreciation for deduction
(2) establish a friendship between the narrator and Holmes
(3) reveal how Holmes makes his living
(4) expose some of Holmes's misdeeds

4____

5 As used in line 38, the word "chimerical" most nearly means

(1) unfair   (3) aggravating
(2) unrealistic   (4) contradictory

5____

6 Which analysis is best supported by the details in lines 45 through 58 of the text?

(1) Private detectives base their analyses on an understanding of human nature.
(2) Sherlock Holmes's association with other well-known detectives improves his crime-solving abilities.
(3) Government detectives are mostly ineffective at solving complicated crimes.
(4) Sherlock Holmes's intuition relies on his ability to detect similarities among various crimes.

6____

Strong family resemblance about misdeeds

11

Looking at the Questions and the Standards

- Questions 1, 2, and 5 ask you to determine the meaning of words and phrases as they are used in context and to understand how they contribute to the meaning of the text.
- Question 3 asks you to recognize how the author uses one element or detail to structure the plot. Holmes deliberately allows Watson to think someone else wrote the article, which then creates the situation in which he can show how skilled and clever he is.
- Questions 4 and 6 ask you to recognize how specific details contribute to character development and plot structure.

Answers

(1) **2**   (2) **4**   (3) **3**   (4) **3**   (5) **2**   (6) **4**

(See Chapter 4—Reading Prose for a detailed review of the elements of fiction.)

PASSAGE TWO—POEM

Money Musk

Listen, you upstate hillsides (nothing
Like the herb-strewn fields of Provence[1])
Which I have loved
So loyally, your wood lots
(5)   And trailers and old farmhouses,
Your satellite dishes—

Haven't I driven
Past the strip malls and country airports,
The National Guard armories and even
(10)   That abandoned missile depot
Clutched in the lake's fingers
Past the tattered billboards.
The barns spray-painted with praise,

───────────
[1]Provence—a region of southern France

12

Past the farm tools, fiddles,
(15)   And fishing lures, the sprung bellows
Of accordions on the tables of flea markets,
Just to catch a glimpse of you as you once were,
Like the brass showing, raw and dull,
Where the silver plate has worn off
(20)   The frame around this mirror, and the silver
Gone too, the only reflection as faint

As light on dusty glass,
And beyond it, tarnished, dim, the rafters
And beams of the attic where I climbed
(25)   To take out my grandmother's mandolin
And play on the three or four unbroken strings
With a penny for a pick.
                          Listen,
Wasn't that offering enough, a life
(30)   Of playing half-badly on an antique instrument,
Trying to catch a tune you'd long ago
Forgotten even the name of, *Money Musk*
Or *Petronella*.[2] Wasn't it enough
To take my vows of poverty of spirit
(35)   Before the plain geometry of a 19th-century
Farmhouse, and praise no other goods
Than this rectitude,[3] this stillness,
This clarity you have spurned now, oh
Landscape I have sung
(40)   Despite my voice, despite the stubborn
Silence behind your tawdry,[4] best intentions.

—Jordan Smith
from *The Cortland Review*
Issue Eight, August 1999

---

[2]Money Musk or Petronella—classic old American dances
[3]rectitude—honesty
[4]tawdry—cheap

Questions for Comprehension

The opening line establishes the dramatic situation and the speaker in this poem: we hear the voice of someone who once lived in the area he is now driving through and who now regrets the changes he sees. The poem is a song to the landscape he has loved and been loyal to.

1 The details presented in lines 4 through 13 emphasize the landscape's

  (1) historical significance
  (2) beauty
  (3) economic possibilities
  (4) transformation   1____

2 What shift in focus occurs from lines 7 through 27?

  (1) from social conflict to personal conflict
  (2) from external description to childhood memory
  (3) from the narrator's feelings to his family's feelings
  (4) from the narrator's thoughts to the narrator's actions   2____

3 What is the effect of the simile used in lines 21 and 22?

  (1) It suggests how the narrator has changed.
  (2) It conveys the narrator's lack of awareness.
  (3) It indicates the darkness of the setting.
  (4) It emphasizes the diminishing of the past.   3____

4 Which word best describes the narrator's tone in lines 28 through 38 of the poem?

  (1) frustrated   (3) contentment
  (2) embarrassed   (4) respectful   4____

5 Lines 33 through 37 contribute to a central theme in the poem by describing the narrator's

(1) wish to live in a suburban setting
(2) obligation to continue a past tradition
(3) commitment to the values of a past era
(4) reluctance to accept different points of view   5____

Looking at the Questions and the Standards

- Questions 1 and 3 focus on the significance of key details. The importance of the landscape to the narrator is the central theme of the poem. The simile in these lines reflects the changes in the landscape the narrator so regrets.
- Question 4 asks you to recognize how the meaning of a word or phrase establishes tone, that is, the attitude of the narrator is revealed throughout the poem.
- Questions 2 and 5 ask you to recognize key elements in the structure of the poem, through a shift in focus and in the narrator's final address to the landscape.

Answers

(1) **4**   (2) **2**   (3) **4**   (4) **1**   (5) **3**

(See Chapter 5—Reading Poetry for a detailed review of the elements of poetry.)

PASSAGE THREE—INFORMATIONAL

This passage is an engaging and effective presentation for a general reader of a challenging question in modern physics and cosmology: Is there "a theory of everything"? Readers familiar with the highly successful film *The Theory of Everything* (2014) will recognize some of the ideas explored in the article.

A few years ago the City Council of Monza, Italy, barred pet owners from keeping goldfish in curved fishbowls. The sponsors of the measure explained that it is cruel to keep a fish in a bowl because the curved sides give the fish a distorted view of reality. Aside from the measure's significance to the poor goldfish, the story raises
(5) an interesting philosophical question: How do we know that the reality we perceive is true?

The goldfish is seeing a version of reality that is different from ours, but can we be sure it is any less real? For all we know, we, too, may spend our entire lives staring out at the world through a distorting lens.

(10) In physics, the question is not academic. Indeed, physicists and cosmologists are finding themselves in a similar predicament to the goldfish's. For decades we have strived to come up with an ultimate theory of everything—one complete and consistent set of fundamental laws of nature that explain every aspect of reality. It now appears that this quest may yield not a single theory but a family of intercon-
(15) nected theories, each describing its own version of reality, as if it viewed the universe through its own fishbowl.

This notion may be difficult for many people, including some working scientists, to accept. Most people believe that there is an objective reality out there and that our senses and our science directly convey information about the material world.
(20) Classical science is based on the belief that an external world exists whose properties are definite and independent of the observer who perceives them. In philosophy, that belief is called realism.

Do Not Attempt to Adjust the Picture

The idea of alternative realities is a mainstay of today's popular culture. For example, in the science-fiction film *The Matrix* the human race is unknowingly liv-
(25) ing in a simulated virtual reality created by intelligent computers to keep them pacified and content while the computers suck their bioelectrical energy (whatever that is). How do we know we are not just computer-generated characters living in a Matrix-like world? If we lived in a synthetic, imaginary world, events would not necessarily have any logic or consistency or obey any laws. The aliens in control
(30) might find it more interesting or amusing to see our reactions, for example, if everyone in the world suddenly decided that chocolate was repulsive or that war was not

16

an option, but that has never happened. If the aliens did enforce consistent laws, we would have no way to tell that another reality stood behind the simulated one. It is easy to call the world the aliens live in the "real" one and the computer-generated

(35) world a false one. But if—like us—the beings in the simulated world could not gaze into their universe from the outside, they would have no reason to doubt their own pictures of reality.

The goldfish are in a similar situation. Their view is not the same as ours from outside their curved bowl, but they could still formulate scientific laws governing

(40) the motion of the objects they observe on the outside. For instance, because light bends as it travels from air to water, a freely moving object that we would observe to move in a straight line would be observed by the goldfish to move along a curved path. The goldfish could formulate scientific laws from their distorted frame of reference that would always hold true and that would enable them to make predictions

(45) about the future motion of objects outside the bowl. Their laws would be more complicated than the laws in our frame, but simplicity is a matter of taste. If the goldfish formulated such a theory, we would have to admit the goldfish's view as a valid picture of reality.

Glimpses of the Deep Theory

In the quest to discover the ultimate laws of physics, no approach has raised higher hopes—or more controversy—than string theory. String theory was first

(50) proposed in the 1970s as an attempt to unify all the forces of nature into one coherent framework and, in particular, to bring the force of gravity into the domain of quantum[1] physics. By the early 1990s, however, physicists discovered that string theory suffers from an awkward issue: there are five different string theories. For

(55) those advocating that string theory was the unique theory of everything, this was quite an embarrassment. In the mid-1990s researchers started discovering that these different theories—and yet another theory called supergravity—actually describe the same phenomena, giving them some hope that they would amount eventually to a unified theory. The theories are indeed related by what physicists call duali-

(60) ties, which are a kind of mathematical dictionaries for translating concepts back and forth. But, alas, each theory is a good description of phenomena only under a certain range of conditions—for example at low energies. None can describe every aspect of the universe.

String theorists are now convinced that the five different string theories are just

(65) different approximations to a more fundamental theory called M-theory. (No one seems to know what the "M" stands for. It may be "master," "miracle" or "mystery," or all three.) People are still trying to decipher the nature of M-theory, but it seems that the traditional expectation of a single theory of nature may be untenable[2]

---

[1]quantum—a small, indivisible unit of energy
[2]untenable—indefensible

(70) and that to describe the universe we must employ different theories in different situations. Thus, M-theory is not a theory in the usual sense but a network of theories. It is a bit like a map. To faithfully represent the entire Earth on a flat surface, one has to use a collection of maps, each of which covers a limited region. The maps overlap one another, and where they do, they show the same landscape. Similarly, the different theories in the M-theory family may look very different, but they can all be (75) regarded as versions of the same underlying theory, and they all predict the same phenomena where they overlap, but none works well in all situations.

Whenever we develop a model of the world and find it to be successful, we tend to attribute to the model the quality of reality or absolute truth. But M-theory, like the goldfish example, shows that the same physical situation can be modeled (80) in different ways, each employing different fundamental elements and concepts. It might be that to describe the universe we have to employ different theories in different situations. Each theory may have its own version of reality, but according to model-dependent realism, that diversity is acceptable, and none of the versions can be said to be more real than any other. It is not the physicist's traditional expecta- (85) tion for a theory of nature, nor does it correspond to our everyday idea of reality. But it might be the way of the universe.

—Stephen Hawking and Leonard Mlodinow
excerpted from "The (Elusive) Theory of Everything,"
Scientific American, October 2010

Questions for Comprehension

The topic is highly complex, but the narrative of description and explanation is composed in language that is highly readable and developed through a series of vivid images and analogies, beginning with the anecdote about goldfish in curved bowls.

1 The authors' anecdote about pet owners in Monza, Italy, serves to introduce a

(1) proof of a universal world view
(2) measure that is objectionable to scientists
(3) central question about the way we see
(4) philosophical question about what we value   1____

2 The primary purpose of lines 10 through 16 is to clarify the

(1) need for a single theory
(2) role of the senses in understanding
(3) possibility of other life in the universe
(4) origin of alternative theories   2____

3 How do lines 17 through 22 develop a claim?

(1) by providing details about a philosophical challenge faced by scientists
(2) by showing how scientists should handle alternate realities
(3) by arguing for an approach that scientists have always followed
(4) by explaining how scientists should view a philosophical approach   3____

4 The reference to *The Matrix* in lines 24 through 28 is used to emphasize the questioning of our

(1) virtues
(2) perception
(3) education
(4) ideals   4____

5 The references to goldfish in lines 39 through 49 contribute to the authors' purpose by suggesting that

(1) people's theories are influenced by their viewpoints
(2) nature's mysteries are best left undiscovered
(3) reality can only be determined by an outside perspective
(4) light must be viewed under similar circumstances   5____

6 As used in lines 51 and 52 of the text, what does the word "coherent" mean?

(1) balanced
(2) indisputable
(3) popular
(4) understandable   6____

7 The authors' reference to "a collection of maps" (line 72) is used to help clarify

 (1) a complex theory
 (2) a historical concept
 (3) the representation of space
 (4) the limitations of previous theories   7____

8 The function of lines 77 through 84 is to

 (1) argue for a specific theory
 (2) suggest that theories relate to expectations
 (3) describe the way differing theories should co-exist
 (4) evaluate theories based on specific needs   8____

9 With which statement would the authors most likely agree?

 (1) The perception of the universe can never be questioned.
 (2) There is a single, agreed upon theory of reality.
 (3) There are multiple realities that are possible to prove.
 (4) The understanding of the universe continues to change.   9____

10 The authors attempt to engage the audience through the use of

 (1) absolute statements
 (2) real-world examples
 (3) detailed descriptions
 (4) simple questions   10____

Looking at the Questions and the Standards

- Questions 1 and 10 call your attention to how rhetorical elements are part of the structure.
  The anecdote at the beginning and the real-world examples used throughout the article help the reader understand key ideas.
- Question 6 is an example of determining the meaning of a term in context, and question 7 calls attention to how a specific image clarifies the meaning of a central idea.
- Questions 2–5 and 7–9 focus on the need to determine the central ideas and analyze how they are developed over the course of a text.

Answers

(1) **3**	(4) **2**	(7) **1**	(10) **2**
(2) **4**	(5) **1**	(8) **3**	
(3) **1**	(6) **4**	(9) **4**	

(See Chapter 4—Reading Prose for a detailed review of elements of nonfiction.)

Chapter 2

WRITING FROM SOURCES

Most high school students already have experienced writing essays of opinion and personal experience; these are likely to have been on topics the writer was interested in. The shift in the new standards is to source-based argument, where the writer must first do research to understand a topic before trying to develop an opinion.

In the second part of the Regents ELA exam, you will demonstrate your ability to comprehend and analyze several documents on a substantive, even controversial topic. The topics raise questions that have a variety of legitimate answers or present problems with alternative solutions. You then must take a position on that topic and develop a coherent essay of argument, which is supported by specific evidence in the texts; the final essay must include references to at least three of the sources. These are, in fact, the skills you use when you do any kind of research and writing project.

Close reading in this part means first reading to understand the issue and then to analyze the information in the texts to see how they support various points of view. As you read the following documents, keep in mind the process of annotation: note central ideas and themes, key details, and important terms and phrases. On an actual exam, you are permitted to take notes in the margins, and you will have scrap paper to plan your essay.

STEP ONE—READING FOR INFORMATION AND UNDERSTANDING

Here are the texts from a recent Regents ELA Exam.

Topic: Should companies be allowed to track consumers' shopping or other preferences without their permission?

Text 1

Cell Phone Carrier Marketing Techniques:
An Invasion of Privacy?

BOSTON (CBS) – Your cell phone may be spying on you.

Every time you download an app, search for a website, send a text, snap a QR code or drive by a store with your GPS on, you are being tracked by your cell phone company.

(5) "They know you were playing Angry Birds. They know that you drove by Sears. They know you drove by Domino's Pizza. They can take that and take a very unique algorithm[1] that can focus on your behavior," explained marketing expert Mark Johnson. "It's very impactful."

According to Johnson, your data trail is worth big money to the cell phone com-
(10) panies.

Details about your habits, your age and gender are compiled and can be sold to third parties. The information is predominantly used as a marketing tool so adver-tisers can target you with products or services that you are more likely to use or want.

(15) The idea does not sit well with smartphone user Harrine Freeman. "It does seem creepy that companies are collecting all this information about consumers," she said.

Freeman is so uneasy; she turns off her GPS when she is not using it. She also clears her browser history.

(20) "I think it is an invasion of privacy," she said.

All of the major cell phone carriers admit to collecting information about its customers. Some in the industry argue it benefits consumers because they get ads that are relevant to them. Cell phone companies do notify customers about the data they collect, but critics say the notices are often hard to understand and written in
(25) fine print.

Rainey Reitman of the Electronic Frontier Foundation doesn't like the fact that those who don't want to be tracked have to go out of their way to get the company to stop.

"This is something that consumers are automatically opted into," Reitman said.
(30) To find out how your cell phone company might be monitoring you, be sure to carefully read the privacy policy.

---

[1]algorithm — process or set of rules followed in calculations

Change the way of track

Also, make sure you read all of the updates your carrier might send you because this tracking technology keeps changing.

—Paula Ebben
http://boston.cbslocal.com, January 16, 2012

Text 2

EyeSee You and the Internet of Things: Watching You While You Shop

what it is.

Why they use it?

...Even the store mannequins have gotten in on the gig. According to the *Washington Post*, mannequins in some high-end boutiques are now being outfitted with cameras that utilize facial recognition technology. A small camera embedded in the eye of an otherwise normal looking mannequin allows storekeepers to keep
(5) track of the age, gender and race of all their customers. This information is then used to personally tailor the shopping experience to those coming in and out of their stores. As the *Washington Post* report notes, "a clothier introduced a children's line after the dummy showed that kids made up more than half its mid-afternoon traffic... Another store found that a third of visitors using one of its
(10) doors after 4 p.m. were Asian, prompting it to place Chinese-speaking staff members by the entrance."

How much?

New Feature

At $5,072 a pop, these EyeSee mannequins come with a steep price tag, but for store owners who want to know more—*a lot more*—about their customers, they're
(15) the perfect tool, able to sit innocently at store entrances and windows, leaving shoppers oblivious to their hidden cameras. Itaian mannequin maker Almax SpA, manufacturer of the EyeSee mannequins, is currently working on adding ears to the mannequins, allowing them to record people's comments in order to further tailor the shopping experience. ...

Selling Info

It's astounding the amount of information—from the trivial to the highly per-
(20) sonal—about individual consumers being passed around from corporation to corporation, all in an effort to market and corral potential customers. Data mining companies collect this wealth of information and sell it to retailers who use it to gauge your interests and tailor marketing to your perceived desires.

How they use it?

All of the websites you visit collect some amount of information about you,
(25) whether it is your name or what other sites you have visited recently. Most of the time, we're being tracked without knowing it. For example, most websites now include Facebook and Twitter buttons so you can "like" the page you are viewing or "Tweet" about it. Whether or not you click the buttons, however, the companies can still determine which pages you've visited and file that information away for
(30) later use. ...

As the EyeSee mannequins show, you no longer even have to be in front of your computer to have your consumer data accessed, uploaded, stored and tracked. In August 2012, for example, data mining agency Redpepper began testing a service known as Facedeals in the Nashville, Tennessee area. Facial recognition cameras set *(35)* at the entrances of businesses snap photos of people walking in, and if you've signed up to have a Facedeals account via your Facebook, you receive instant coupons sent to your smartphone. Similarly, a small coffee chain in San Francisco, Philz Coffee, has installed sensors at the front door of their stores in order to capture the Wi-Fi signal of any smartphone within 60 yards. Jacob Jaber, president of Philz Coffee, *(40)* uses the information gleaned from these sensors to structure his stores according to the in-store behavior of customers. ...

Not even politicians are immune to the lure of data mining. In the run-up to the 2012 presidential election, the Romney and Obama campaigns followed voters across the web by installing cookies on their computers and observing the *(45)* websites they visited in an attempt to gather information on their personal views. CampaignGrid, a Republican affiliated firm, and Precision Network, a Democratic affiliated firm, both worked to collect data on 150 million American Internet users, or 80% of the registered voting population. ...

—John W. Whitehead
excerpted *https://www.rutherford.org*, December 17, 2012

Text 3

Where Will Consumers Find Privacy Protection from RFIDs?: A Case for Federal Legislation

What Are RFIDs? How Do RFIDs Work?

...RFID [Radio Frequency Information Device] technology is an automatic identification system that identifies objects, collects data, and transmits information about the object through a "tag." A device called a reader extracts and processes the information on the tag. Experts characterize RFIDs as devices "that can be sensed *(5)* at a distance by radio frequencies with few problems of obstruction or misorientation."[1] In essence, RFIDs are wireless barcodes. However, unlike typical barcodes, which are identical for all common products, each RFID has a unique identification. Therefore, every individually tagged item has a different barcode sequence.

---

[1]KATHERINE ALBRECHT & LIZ MCINTRYE, SPYCHIPS 13 (Nelson Current 2005) quoting Raghu Das, *RFID Explained: An Introduction to RFID and Tagging Technologies,* ID TECHEX (2003).

Typical barcodes also require unobstructed paths for scanning, whereas RFIDs can
(10) be scanned through solid objects.[2] RFIDs have communication signals that facilitate
data storage on RFID tags and enable the stored information to be gathered elec-
tronically—hypothetically permitting, for example, Coca-Cola to have a database
storing information about the life cycle of a Coke can. The database would contain
tracking details from the moment the can is manufactured through its processing at a
(15) garbage dump—since RFID readers can be attached to garbage trucks. Between the
birth and death of a customer's Coke can, the RFID tags would tell the Coca-Cola
Company where and when the Coke was purchased, what credit card the Coke was
purchased with, and, in turn, the identity of the purchaser. Even if the customer did
not purchase the Coke with a credit card, state issued ID cards equipped with RFID
(20) technology could relay the customer's identity to RFID readers as he or she leaves
the store. Coca-Cola's final product of the RFIDs' communications is a database of
the life cycles of individual cans of Coke and personal information about their pur-
chasers. With this myriad of information, Coca-Cola has the ability to individually
market to each of the 1.3 billion daily Coca-Cola consumers. ...

How Are RFIDs Used?

(25) RFIDs are currently used in many ways, including, "livestock management[,]
24 hour patient monitoring[,] authentication of pharmaceuticals[,] tracking con-
signments in a supply chain[,] remote monitoring of critical components in aircraft
[, and] monitoring the safety of perishable food."[3] Advocates of RFID technology,
including retailers and manufacturers, praise the increased functionality and effi-
(30) ciency that will likely ensue from using RFIDs. Once all products are individually
tagged, shoppers are expected to be able to purchase items without checking-out.
This should be possible since RFID readers will be able to scan every item as the
customer exits the store and charge an RFID credit card, thereby simultaneously
increasing efficiency and possibly reducing shoplifting. Other RFID uses include
(35) easy monitoring of product recalls, tracking lobsters for conservation purposes,
and purchasing products with transaction-free payment systems.[4] Additionally,
in October 2003, the Department of Defense set standards mandating suppliers to
place RFID tags on all packaging for the Department of Defense.[5] Thus, RFIDs can
be used to increase efficiency and safety. ...

---

[2]*Id.*
[3]Viviane Reding, Member of the European Commission responsible for Information
Society and Media, Address at EU RFID 2006 Conference: Heading for the Future, RFID:
WHY WE NEED A EUROPEAN POLICY, 1,3 (Oct. 16, 2006).
[4]David Flint, *Everything with Chips!*, BUS. L. REV., Mar. 2006, 73, 73.
[5]PRESS RELEASE, US DEP. OF DEFENSE, DOD ANNOUNCES RADIO FREQUENCY IDENTIFICATION
POLICY, UNITED STATES DEPARTMENT OF DEFENSE NEWS RELEASE, (Oct. 23, 2003).

Do Consumers Have a Right to Privacy
from RFIDs under Tort Law?[6]

(40)   …In the context of RFIDs, there are some situations where gathering information from RFID tags violates consumers' privacy expectations. For example, a consumer does not have a reasonable expectation of privacy when carrying RFID equipped items in a transparent shopping cart. However, once the items are placed in an opaque bag, a right to privacy immediately arises. If a business or third-party *(45)* gathers data about the items once the items are no longer visible to the naked eye, there is an objective invasion of privacy. Gathering information stored in the RFID tag in a winter jacket worn in public is also not an invasion of privacy, yet pulling data off undergarments is intrusive. However, since the home is always considered a private place, once an active RFID tag enters the home, any information gathered, *(50)* including information from the winter jacket, immediately offends the principles of privacy. Protecting consumers from unreasonably intrusive actions of businesses requires that RFID tags become unreadable once they enter private places. However, the fundamental nature of the technology does not harmonize with this privacy goal because RFID readers do not scrutinize whether the information is *(55)* considered private before it gathers data from the tag. …

With new technologies come new methods of consumer tracking and changing parameters for what may be considered highly offensive. These new methods of tracking are not considered intrusive simply because the nature of the technology requires consumer purchases to be recorded. If individuals make active decisions to *(60)* use a credit card instead of cash—a voluntary act—their purchases can be tracked. Similarly, the gathering of information stored on RFID technology in consumer goods may not be deemed highly offensive depending on changing consumer expectations. …

—Serena G. Stein excerpted and adapted
Duke Law & Technology Review, 2007, No.3

---

[6]Tort Law — covers civil wrongs resulting in an injury or harm constituting the basis for a claim by the injured person

Text 4

RFID Consumer Applications and Benefits

...One of the first consumer applications of RFID was automated toll collection systems, which were introduced in the late 1980s and caught on in the 1990s. An active transponder is typically placed on a car's or truck's windshield. When the car reaches the tollbooth, a reader at the booth sends out a signal that wakes up the
(5) transponder on the windshield, which then reflects back a unique ID to the reader at the booth. The ID is associated with an account opened by the car owner, who is billed by the toll authority. Consumers spend less time fumbling for change or waiting on lines to pay their toll fee.

In the late 1990s, ExxonMobil (then just Mobil) introduced Speedpass, an RFID
(10) system that allows drivers who have opened an account to pay for gas automatically. Drivers are given a small, passive 13.56 MHz transponder in a small wand or fob that can be put on a key chain. To pay for gas, they just wave the key fob by a reader built into the gas pump. Seven million people in the United States use the system, and it has increased the number of cars each gas station can serve during
(15) rush periods. ...

RFID has other consumer applications, besides being a convenient payment system. One is the recovery of lost or stolen items. A company called Snagg in Palo Alto, Calif., has created an electronic registry for musical instruments. It provides an RFID tag that can be affixed to a classic guitar or priceless violin and keeps a
(20) record of the serial number in the tag. If the instrument is recovered by the police after being lost or stolen, they can call Snagg, which can look up the rightful owner. ...

Merloni Elettrodomestici, an Italian appliance maker, has created a smart washing machine. When you drop your clothes in the machine, an RFID reader in the
(25) appliance can read the tags in the clothes (if your clothes have tags) and wash the clothes based on instructions written to the tag.

Whether smart appliances with RFID readers catch on depends on how long it takes for RFID tags to become cheap enough to be put into packaging for items. It also depends on whether consumers find RFID-enabled products convenient
(30) enough to accept the potential invasion of privacy that comes with having RFID tags in products. But RFID will certainly have a positive impact on people's lives in less direct ways.

One area of importance is product recalls. Today, companies often need to recall all tires, meat or drugs if there is a problem to ensure people's safety. But
(35) they can never be sure they recovered all the bad goods that were released into the supply chain. With RFID, companies will be able to know exactly which items are bad and trace those through to stores. Customers that register their products

could be contacted individually to ensure they know something they bought has been recalled. ...

(40)   And RFID should enable consumers to get more information about the products they want to purchase, such as when the items were made, where, whether they are under warrantee and so on. When RFID tags are eventually put on the packaging of individual products, consumers will be able to read the tag with a reader embedded in a cell phone or connected to a computer and download data
(45) from a Web site. They'll be able to learn, for example, whether the steak they are about to buy is from an animal that was raised organically in the United States. Some companies will be reluctant to share this information, but smart companies will provide it to their customers to build trust and loyalty.

RFID could also have an [sic] positive impact on our environment by greatly
(50) reducing waste. The main reason many companies want to use RFID is to better match supply and demand and to make sure that products are where they are supposed to be. If successful, there should be fewer products that are thrown away because no one wants to buy them or they pass their sell-by date (it's estimated that 50 percent of all food harvested in the United States is never eaten).

(55)   RFID tags could also help improve our environment by identifying hazardous materials that should not be dumped in landfills. One day, robots at landfills might be equipped with RFID tags, and they might be able to quickly sort through garbage to locate batteries and other items that contain toxic materials. ...

—Bob Violino
excerpted *http://www.rfidjournal.com*, January 16, 2005

LOOKING AT THE TEXTS

Text 1—*Cell Phone Carrier Marketing Techniques: An Invasion of Privacy?*

This document opens with a dramatic assertion: "Your cell phone may be spying on you." The rest of the short article, from a television news report, gives a general description of data collection by cell phone companies and provides a useful introduction to the issue.

Text 2—*EyeSee You and the Internet of Things: Watching You While You Shop*

This article, from a website devoted to issues of civil liberties, presents several detailed examples of how retailers, Internet providers, and political campaigns make use of data mining. This text is an excellent source of material to support an argument opposed to tracking consumers' behavior without their permission.

Text 3—*Where Will Consumers Find Privacy Protection from RFIDs?: A Case for Federal Legislation*

This article, from a university law review, is the most challenging: The article offers a detailed technical description of what RFIDs are and how they operate. It also offers an analysis of the complex legal issues they raise. Finally, the last paragraph seems to suggest that if consumers are aware of this new technology, its use might not be considered intrusive.

Text 4—*RFID Consumer Applications and Benefits*

The title of this document, from a journal that promotes development and use of RFIDs, is a clear statement of the content and point of view. What follows is a list of various applications of RFID technology in language that is technical but readily understood, and the examples are presented as only beneficial for consumers.

STEP TWO—COMPOSING A SOURCE-BASED ARGUMENT

Because the issues presented for argument will be relevant and may already be familiar to high school students, you should be able to choose a position (claim) that you can make convincing. Here are the Guidelines for Part 2 of the Regents ELA (Common Core) Exam:

BE SURE TO:

- Establish your claim regarding companies being allowed to track consumers' shopping or other preferences without their permission
- Distinguish your claim from alternate or opposing claims
- Use specific, relevant, and sufficient evidence from at least **three** of the texts to develop your argument
- Identify each source that you reference by text number and line number(s) or graphic (for example: Text 1, line 4 or Text 2, graphic)
- Organize your ideas in a cohesive and coherent manner
- Maintain a formal style of writing
- Follow the conventions of standard written English

PLANNING THE ESSAY

First, consider who your audience is. You should assume a reader who is interested in the subject but who has not yet formed a strong opinion about the issue. Your reader is interested in what you have to say and can be convinced by a sound and well-documented argument.

Establishing a claim and distinguishing it from an alternate or opposing claim means that you are taking a particular position on the issue, you are not just offering a description or explanation of the subject. In each of the following examples, there is a reference to at least one of the issues the topic raises, and there is an indication of how the writer's argument is going to be developed.

Supporting the claim with specific and relevant evidence is part of any effective argument; supporting the claim with **sufficient** evidence means the writer has included not only several examples from different sources but has also used analysis of the texts to determine which evidence **best supports** the argument. Remember, too, that showing faulty or weak reasoning in examples from documents with opposing views is one of the most effective strategies in argument. Identifying references is, of course, part of any source-based writing.

The organization (structure) of the essay should be determined by the logic of the argument. An effective essay moves from establishing the claim through a series of examples (evidence) to a persuasive conclusion. In a **coherent** essay, the reader should understand how each new section extends the ideas that have come before and leads to the ideas that follow and to a convincing conclusion. **Cohesive** writing means that the connection of your ideas within each sentence and at the paragraph level is clear and that the writing follows the conventions of standard written English.

LOOKING AT A VARIETY OF EFFECTIVE CLAIMS

Here are several examples of how students established effective claims for arguments on the topic of data mining and consumer privacy:

Technology is changing, allowing companies and other interests . . . to track our location any given time and collect information about what we buy, all without our consent. There should be a limit to what these entities can gather on us . . .

Companies should be permitted to have access to consumers' spending habits without their permission. The companies may seem like they are invading our privacy, but they are simply finding better and more efficient ways to help their customers and profit their businesses.

Under most circumstances, consumers should not be tracked without permission for sole benefit of companies. However, if the consumer does authorize its use by way of contract, companies should have right to track them.

Companies should not be permitted to track consumers' shopping and other activities without their consent. Without informing people of new tracking devices and methods and letting them decide, companies invade people's personal privacy . . .

Technology has made major improvements all over the world; however, these improvements have made it much easier for companies to track consumers without their permission. I support the view that the tracking of a customer's habits and preferences is an invasion of privacy.

New innovations in technology have enabled companies to monitor cell phone usage, the goods bought by consumers, or the places that people travel. In some cases, this is seen as an invasion of privacy. However, for the majority of the time, this new technology should be seen as a benefit to both consumers and the companies involved.

(See also Chapter 7—Writing on Demand for more discussion.)

Chapter 3

READING AND WRITING TO ANALYZE TEXT

TEXT ANALYSIS: EXPOSITION

Text analysis requires first doing a close reading of a passage to identify a central idea and then analyzing how the author develops that central idea. This means understanding the author's purpose and seeing how the author's choice of literary techniques or a specific rhetorical strategy serves that purpose. In this part of the Regents ELA exam, you may read a literary passage of autobiography or memoir, a speech of historical significance, or a personal essay on a historical or scientific subject or on a philosophical idea.

SAMPLE TEXT AND EXPOSITORY RESPONSE

...It turned out to be true. The face of the water [Mississippi River], in time, became a wonderful book—a book that was a dead language to the uneducated passenger, but which told its mind to me without reserve, delivering its most cherished secrets as clearly as if it uttered them with a voice. And it was not a book to be
(5)   read once and thrown aside, for it had a new story to tell every day. Throughout the long twelve hundred miles there was never a page that was void of interest, never one that you could leave unread without loss, never one that you would want to skip, thinking you could find higher enjoyment in some other thing. There never was so wonderful a book written by man; never one whose interest was
(10) so absorbing, so unflagging, so sparklingly renewed with every reperusal. The passenger who could not read it was charmed with a peculiar sort of faint dimple on its surface (on the rare occasions when he did not overlook it altogether); but to the pilot that was an *italicized* passage; indeed, it was more than that, it was a legend of the largest capitals, with a string of shouting exclamation points at
(15) the end of it, for it meant that a wreck or a rock was buried there that could tear the life out of the strongest vessel that ever floated. It is the faintest and simplest expression the water ever makes, and the most hideous to a pilot's eye. In truth, the passenger who could not read this book saw nothing but all manner of pretty pictures in it, painted by the sun and shaded by the clouds, whereas to the trained

35

(20) eye these were not pictures at all, but the grimmest and most dead-earnest of reading matter.

Now when I had mastered the language of this water, and had come to know every trifling feature that bordered the great river as familiarly as I knew the letters of the alphabet, I had made a valuable acquisition. But I had lost something, too. I (25) had lost something which could never be restored to me while I lived. All the grace, the beauty, the poetry, had gone out of the majestic river! I still kept in mind a certain wonderful sunset which I witnessed when steamboating was new to me. A broad expanse of the river was turned to blood; in the middle distance the red hue brightened into gold, through which a solitary log came floating, black and (30) conspicuous; one place a long, slanting mark lay sparkling upon the water; in another the surface was broken by boiling, tumbling rings, that were as many-tinted as an opal; where the ruddy flush was faintest, was a smooth spot that was covered with graceful circles and radiating lines, ever so delicately traced; the shore on our left was densely wooded, and the sombre shadow that fell from this forest (35) was broken in one place by a long, ruffled trail that shone like silver; and high above the forest wall a clean-stemmed dead tree waved a single leafy bough that glowed like a flame in the unobstructed splendor that was flowing from the sun. There were graceful curves, reflected images, woody heights, soft distances; and over the whole scene, far and near, the dissolving lights drifted steadily, enriching it every passing (40) moment with new marvels of coloring.

I stood like one bewitched. I drank it in, in a speechless rapture. The world was new to me, and I had never seen any thing like this at home. But as I have said, a day came when I began to cease from noting the glories and the charms which the moon and the sun and the twilight wrought upon the river's face; another (45) day came when I ceased altogether to note them. Then, if that sunset scene had been repeated, I should have looked upon it without rapture, and should have commented upon it, inwardly, after this fashion:"This sun means that we are going to have wind to-morrow; that floating log means that the river is rising, small thanks to it; that slanting mark on the water refers to a bluff reef which is going to (50) kill somebody's steamboat one of these nights, if it keeps on stretching out like that; those tumbling 'boils' show a dissolving bar and a changing channel there; the lines and circles in the slick water over yonder are a warning that that troublesome place is shoaling up dangerously; that silver streak in the shadow of the forest is the 'break' from a new snag, and he has located himself in the very best place he could (55) have found to fish for steamboats; that tall dead tree, with a single living branch, is not going to last long, and then how is a body ever going to get through this blind place at night without the friendly old landmark?"

No, the romance and the beauty were all gone from the river. All the value any feature of it had for me now was the amount of usefulness it could furnish toward (60) compassing the safe piloting of a steamboat. Since those days, I have pitied doc-

Author personality changed became more serious about Life

educated about nature

36

tors from my heart. What does the lovely flush in a beauty's cheek mean to a doctor but a "break" that ripples above some deadly disease? Are not all her visible charms sown thick with what are to him the signs and symbols of hidden decay? Does he ever see her beauty at all, or doesn't he simply view her professionally, and comment *(65)* upon her unwholesome condition all to himself? And doesn't he sometimes wonder whether he has gained most or lost most by learning his trade?

—Mark Twain
excerpted and adapted from *Life on the Mississippi*, 1901
Harper & Brothers Publishers

RESPONSE

In this excerpt, Twain introduces the central idea as a metaphor: "The face of the water {Mississippi River}…became a wonderful book."

Throughout the passage he uses vivid imagery to convey the beauty of the river and to convey how the acquisition of knowledge means losing that beauty. Before the author learned to see the signs of danger in navigating the river, he saw only beauty. When Twain was new to steam boating, he witnessed a particularly magnificent sunset. The sky was red, which reflected on the water and slowly transitioned to gold. He noticed delicate rings growing from a spot in the water. He noticed a dead tree rising above the wall of forest, with a bough of leaves that shone with brightness of flames. He was in a state of "speechless rapture."

Later on, the beauty faded as he learned the signals behind what he saw. Twain tells us that the river was a "wonderful book"; but it was also "the grimmest and most dead-earnest of reading matter." That beautiful red hue in his surroundings would mean wind the next day. The growing ripples marked a dangerous obstacle that could kill a steamboat. The dead tree, whose leaves were like fire, was a "friendly landmark" and would be lost after it fell. In learning to read the book of the river, Twain loses forever the ability to see the beauty and grace of the Mississippi and regrets what he has lost in learning his trade: "No, the romance and beauty were all gone from the river… all it had for me now was the amount of usefulness it could furnish. . . ."

This is an excellent example of an expository response: In the opening sentence, this writer expresses the central idea of the passage and identifies Twain's use of vivid imagery as key to understanding its meaning. The analysis is developed in two paragraphs, each of which cites several specific and relevant examples from the text. In the first paragraph, the images recall Twain's delight in the beauty of the river; in the second, these images become examples of how the knowledge Twain acquires destroys his ability to see beauty in them. This organization in parallel details is both sophisticated and effective. The incorporation of quoted phrases enhances development of the central idea and meets the requirement for an evidence-based analysis.

ADDITIONAL TEXTS FOR ANALYSIS AND REVIEW

PASSAGE ONE

This passage is an excerpt from a speech given by Red Jacket, Chief of the Seneca Nation, to the United States acting secretary of war in Washington, D.C., on February 10, 1801.

...Brother, the business on which we are now come is to restore the friendship that has existed between the United States and the Six Nations, agreeably to the direction of the commissioner from the fifteen fires[1] of the United States. He assured us that whensoever, by any grievances, the chain of friendship should become rusty, we might have it brightened by calling on you. We dispense with the usual formality of having your speech again read, as we fully comprehended it yesterday, and it would therefore be useless to waste time in a repetition of it.

(10)   Brother, yesterday you wiped the tears from our eyes, that we might see clearly; you unstopped our ears that we might hear; and removed the obstructions from our throats that we might speak distinctly. You offered to join with us in tearing up the largest pine-tree in our forests, and under it to bury the tomahawk. We gladly join with you, brother, in this work, and let us heap rocks and stones on the root of this tree that the tomahawk may never again be found. ...

---

[1]fires—fires refers to states

Brother, we observe that the men now in office are new men, and, we fear, not
(15) fully informed of all that has befallen us. In 1791 a treaty was held by the com-
missioners of Congress with us at Tioga Point, on a similar occasion. We have lost
seven of our warriors, murdered in cold blood by white men, since the conclusion
of the war. We are tired of this mighty grievance and wish some general arrangement to prevent it in future. The first of these was murdered on the banks of
(20) the Ohio, near Fort Pitt. Shortly after two men belonging to our first families
were murdered at Pine Creek; then one at Fort Franklin; another at Tioga Point;
and now the two that occasion this visit, on the Big Beaver. These last two had
families. The one was a Seneca; the other a Tuscarora. Their families are now desti-
tute of support, and we think that the United States should do something toward
(25) their support, as it is to the United States they owe the loss of their heads.

Brother, these offences are always committed in one place on the frontier
of Pennsylvania. In the Genesee country we live happy and no one molests
us. I must therefore beg that the President will exert all his influence with
all officers, civil and military, in that quarter, to remedy this grievance, and
(30) trust that he will thus prevent a repetition of it and save our blood from being
spilled in future.

Brother, let me call to mind the treaty between the United States and the Six
Nations, concluded at Canandaigua. At that treaty Colonel Pickering, who was
commissioner on behalf of the United States, agreed that the United States should
(35) pay to the Six Nations four thousand five hundred dollars per annum, and that this
should pass through the hands of the superintendent of the United States, to be
appointed for that purpose. This treaty was made in the name of the President of
the United States, who was then General Washington; and, as he is now no more,
perhaps the present President would wish to renew the treaty. But if he should
(40) think the old one valid and is willing to let it remain in force we are also willing.
The sum above mentioned we wish to have part of in money, to expend in more
agricultural tools and in purchasing a team, as we have some horses that will do
for the purpose. We also wish to build a sawmill on the Buffalo creek. If the President, however, thinks proper to have it continue as heretofore, we shall not be very
(45) uneasy. Whatever he may do we agree to; we only suggest this for his consideration.

Brother, I hand you the above-mentioned treaty, made by Colonel Pickering,
in the name of General Washington, and the belt that accompanied it; as he is now
dead we know not if it is still valid. If not, we wish it renewed—if it is, we wish it
copied on clean parchment. Our money got loose in our trunk and tore it. We also
(50) show you the belt which is the path of peace between our Six Nations and the
United States. ...

Brother, the business that has caused this our long journey was occasioned by
some of your bad men; the expense of it has been heavy on us. We beg that as so

39

(55) great a breach has been made on your part, the President will judge it proper that the United States should bear our expenses to and from home and whilst here.

Brother, three horses belonging to the Tuscarora Nation were killed by some men under the command of Major Rivardi, on the plains of Niagara. They have made application to the superintendent and to Major Rivardi, but get no redress. You make us pay for our breaches of the peace, why should you not pay also? A white
(60) man has told us the horses were killed by Major Rivardi's orders, who said they should not be permitted to come there, although it was an open common on which they were killed. Mr. Chapin has the papers respecting these horses, which we request you to take into consideration.

—Red Jacket
excerpted from *Orations from Homer to William McKinley,*
Vol. VII, 1902
P.F. Collier and Son

Looking at the Text

The repetition of "Brother, . . ." at the beginning of each point is the most obvious rhetorical element in this speech. Careful analysis will show how that not only establishes the speaker's attitude toward his audience (the tone of the speech) but also structures the various examples as reminders of past history and treaty obligations and establishes the legitimacy of the Chief's demands for compensation and justice.

PASSAGE TWO

Here is an example of a classic essay form, in which a specific aspect of human nature or conduct is explored. First made popular by the French writer Michel de Montaigne in the 16th century, this kind of essay is relatively brief, offers intellectual insight, and often includes anecdotes or analogies as illustrations. In "Of Suspicion," Sir Francis Bacon, a contemporary of Shakespeare, first offers his observations on how suspicion clouds the mind and then suggests ways to avoid its corrosive effects.

corrosive
anecdotes
analogy
intellectual

Of Suspicion

SUSPICIONS amongst thoughts are like bats amongst birds, they ever fly by twilight. Certainly they are to be repressed, or at least well guarded: for they cloud the mind; they leese [lose] friends; and they check with [hinder, restrain] business, whereby business cannot go on currently and constantly. They dispose [lead]
(5) kings to tyranny, husbands to jealousy, wise men to irresolution [indecisiveness] and melancholy. They are defects, not in the heart, but in the brain; for they take place in the stoutest [bravest] natures; as in the example of Henry the Seventh of England. There was not a more suspicious man, nor a more stout. And in such a composition they do small hurt. For commonly they are not admitted, but [unless]
(10) with examination, whether they be likely or no. But in fearful natures they gain ground too fast. There is nothing makes a man suspect much, more than to know little; and therefore men should remedy suspicion by procuring to know more, and not to keep their suspicions in smother [suppressed]. What would men have? Do they think those they employ and deal with are saints? Do they not think they will
(15) have their own ends, and be truer to themselves than to them? Therefore there is no better way to moderate suspicions, than to account upon such suspicions as true and yet to bridle them as false. For so far a man ought to make use of suspicions, as to provide, as if that should be true that he suspects, yet it may do him no hurt. Suspicions that the mind of itself gathers are but buzzes; but suspicions that are
(20) artificially nourished, and put into men's heads by the tales and whisperings of others, have stings. Certainly, the best mean [strategy] to clear the way in this same wood of suspicions is frankly to communicate them with the party that he suspects; for thereby he shall be sure to know more of the truth of them than he did before; and withal shall make that party more circumspect not to give further cause of sus-
(25) picion. But this would not be done to men of base [dishonorable, corrupt] natures; for they, if they find themselves once suspected, will never be true. . . . (c 1625)

Looking at the Text

This is a passage that requires careful, slow reading. The essay begins with a simile that establishes the tone of what is to follow: suspicions are creatures of twilight; they are elusive, ambiguous, and potentially dangerous. Bacon then insists that suspicions must be kept under control and offers guidance on how best to "clear the way in…the wood of suspicions." Note how condensed the development of ideas is and how each sentence balances two or three assertions. The meanings of some unfamiliar terms have been inserted here, but the language of Bacon is also the language of Shakespeare and should be accessible to high school students at Regents level.

(There is a list of Archaic and Unfamiliar terms in Chapter 8 — Vocabulary.)

PASSAGE THREE

In 1858, Abraham Lincoln and Stephen Douglas were campaigning in Illinois for the U.S. Senate seat then held by Douglas. They held a series of debates throughout the state, which were widely and often raucously attended. Douglas argued that it was an absolute right of self-government for residents of a territory to permit or to prohibit slavery. Here is a passage from an eyewitness account of the seventh and final of the Lincoln-Douglas debates*.

. . . Douglas had been theatrical and scholarly, but this tall, homely man [Lincoln] was creating by his very looks what the brilliant lawyer and experienced Senator had failed to make people see and feel. The Little Giant [Douglas] had assumed striking attitudes, played tricks with his flowing white hair, mimicking
(5) the airs of authority, with patronizing allusions, but these affectations, usually so effective when he addressed an audience alone, went for nothing when brought face to face with realities. Lincoln had no genius for gesture and no desire to produce a sensation. The failure of Senator Douglas to bring conviction to critical minds was caused by three things: a lack of logical sequence in argument, a lack of
(10) intuitional judgment, and a vanity that was caused by too much intellect and too little heart. Douglas had been arrogant and vehement, Lincoln was now logical and penetrating. . . .
The enthusiasm created by Douglas was wrought out of smart epigram thrusts and a facile, superficial eloquence. . . . His weight in the political balance was
(15) purely materialistic; his scales of justice tipped to the side of cotton, slavery, and popular passions, while the man who faced him now brought to the assembly cold logic in place of wit, frankness in place of cunning, reasoned will and judgment in place of chicanery and sophistry . . . His looks, his words, his voice, his attitude, were like a magical essence dropped into the seething cauldron of politics, reacting
(20) against the foam, calming the surface and letting the people see to the bottom. It did not take him long:

"Is it not a false statesmanship," he asked, "that undertakes to build up a system of policy upon the basis of caring nothing about the very thing that everybody does care the most about? Judge Douglas may say
(25) he cares not whether slavery is voted up or down, but he must have a choice between a right thing and a wrong thing. He contends that whatever community wants slaves has a right to have them. So they have, if it is not a wrong; but if it is a wrong he cannot say people have a right to do wrong. He says that upon the score of equality slaves should be
(30) allowed to go into a new Territory like other property. This is strictly logi-

42

*cal if there is no difference between it [slaves] and other property. If it
and other property are equal his argument is entirely logical; but if you
insist that one is wrong and the other right there is no use to institute a
comparison between right and wrong."*

(35)   This was the broadside. The great duel on the high seas of politics was over.
The Douglas ship of State Sovereignty was sinking. The debate was a triumph
that would send Lincoln to Washington as President in a little more than two years
from that date.

—Francis Grierson, *The Valley of Shadows*

Looking at the Text

In this passage, we can see how the observer uses various rhetorical elements to recreate the experience of hearing the two famous men, and within
this account, we see how Lincoln himself revealed the morally flawed logic
in Douglas's position on slavery.

The observer sets the stage with a series of balanced and contrasting
images: Douglas is theatrical and vain, a man of "too much intellect and too
little heart." Lincoln "had no genius for gesture" or sensational language;
Lincoln was ". . . now logical and penetrating." He introduces Lincoln's
words with a vivid image of an alchemist calming intense passions—the
seething cauldron of politics—with the "magical essence" of clear, moral
argument.

Lincoln attacks Douglas for "caring nothing about" slavery, that is, for
being neutral on the issue, when it is the issue the nation most cares about.
Douglas contends that slavery is an issue of property and rights of States,
but Lincoln says that is a logical fallacy: the issue is not about property,
it is about right and wrong; " . . . *he cannot say people have a right to do
wrong.*" The passage ends with another strong metaphor: Douglas's ship of
State Sovereignty has been sunk in a battle on the [political] high seas by the
cannon shot of Lincoln's words.

(The Lincoln-Douglas Debates, Twain's memoir, and Red Jacket's speech
are examples of what is meant by "seminal U.S. texts" in the State Standards.
Analyzing and evaluating the reasoning in these and other "foundational
U.S. documents of historical and literary significance" can be expected on
the Regents ELA exam and on the new SAT (2015). See the Appendices,
pages 223–227, to review the standards.)

43

Chapter 4

READING PROSE
ESSAY

One of the characters in Moliere's satire *Le Bourgeois Gentilhomme* (*The Bourgeois Gentleman*) makes an astonishing discovery: "For over forty years I have been speaking prose without knowing it!" Prose writing is composed in the rhythms and patterns of spoken discourse. When we read novels and short stories, essays and reports, journals and letters, we are usually reading prose. In our daily lives and as students, we read prose that varies widely in purpose, in method of development, and in tone. Prose serves the purposes of personal expression, persuasion, literary effect, and information.

WHAT WRITERS DO: A LIST OF USEFUL TERMS

A group of high school juniors recently was asked to list all the verbs they could think of to denote what writers *do*. Here is the list they came up with:

address	declare	imply	refine
affirm	defend	infer	reflect
alert	define	influence	refute
amuse	delineate	inform	remind
analyze	depict	inspire	reveal
appraise	describe	interpret	revise
argue	discern	invent	scrutinize
assert	discover	judge	see
assess	dramatize	note	select
capture	edit	observe	shock
caution	emphasize	offer	show
censure	enhance	persuade	suggest
cite	enrich	play	summarize
clarify	establish	ponder	support
classify	evaluate	portray	symbolize
comment	examine	present	teach
conclude	explain	probe	theorize
condemn	explore	produce	uncover
conjecture	expose	propose	view
convey	expound	provoke	work(!)
create	forewarn	question	
create images	formulate	reassure	
criticize	illustrate	recreate	

As you consider these terms, you will note that they are not separated by categories; many of them denote both purpose and tone, and many suggest a method of development as well. While this list may not include everything writers "do," it is a useful reminder of the great variety in written expression. (Because command of this vocabulary will also help you to express your understanding and appreciation of what you read, you will find examples showing how many of these words are applied to discussions of nonfiction and, in Chapter 6, writing about literature. Note also that most of these terms are part of the vocabulary that is considered Academic Language. (See Chapter 8—Vocabulary.)

To read well you must be listening actively to the narrator's voice, thinking with the author. If you are reading a piece for information or direction, ask questions; expect them to be answered. If you are reading a work of argument or persuasion, question it; actively agree or disagree; follow how the argument is developed. If you are reading a piece of personal expression, try to imagine, even share, the experience. If you are reading a piece of vivid description, recreate the images and feelings for yourself. Reading well offers us the entire range of human history and experience expressed in language.

Works of fiction are usually narrative in form. They tell us stories of what *happened* in the lives of the characters and, more important, *why it happened.* Nonfiction takes many forms, and its subjects touch on nearly everything in the human and natural worlds.

READING FICTION

When we speak of fiction, we are generally referring to narrative works— works in which events are recounted, are *told,* and have been imagined and structured by the author. (Although not narrative in form, drama shares many of the essential characteristics of fiction.) The subjects of fiction, however, are no less real than those of history or of what we call the actual or real world. In *Aspects of the Novel*, E. M. Forster shows how "fiction is truer than history." He reminds us that only in narrative fiction and drama can we truly know what is in a character's heart or mind; that is, only in a novel, short story, or play can we fully understand the motives, desires, and reasons for characters' actions. The historian draws conclusions from records of the past; the psychologist interprets interviews and tests; a jury weighs evidence and testimony; and our experience indicates that these are highly reliable ways to understand people and their lives. But only the author of a fictional work can offer an absolutely reliable account of what a character feels, believes, and desires, of why things happen as they do.

Plot and Story

The primary pleasure for most readers of narrative fiction is the story. The reason we become involved in a novel or short story is that we want to know how it turns out; we want to know what is going to happen to those characters. An author creates a **plot*** when he or she gives order and structure to the action: in a plot, the incidents, or episodes, of the story have meaningful relationships to one another. A story becomes a plot when we understand not only *what happened* but also *why*. In good fiction we are *convinced* of the causal relationship among incidents, and we are convinced by the relationship of characters' motives and feelings to the action.

For most readers of fiction, the first response is to keep track of the plot. We do this spontaneously. If you are preparing a novel or story for class discussion, one of the first things your instructor will expect you to know is, "What happens in . . . ?" This is not a trivial question, because you cannot fully understand the significance of character, theme, or structure if you do not first understand the action as it is presented. Understanding plot, of course, requires memory, and remembering the major incidents of a plot is usually a natural and relatively easy response. The more extensively you read, however, the more skilled you become in remembering and relating the key incidents in a complex plot and in recalling details when their full significance becomes evident—sometimes well after the incidents themselves occur. Keeping notes on the development of a complex plot is very useful, especially for students whose reading of a novel is broken up over days or weeks.

For a class, or as part of your preparation for the Regents exam questions on literature, practice summarizing the plots of works you know or are reading. Be able to tell the story of a novel or play to someone who does not know it in a narrative of your own words, including all the major incidents and their consequences. Be able to tell the story in the same way you would retell a familiar children's story or narrate a significant experience of your own.

Plot and Conflict

At the end of any meaningful story, something has *happened;* something is significantly different in the world and lives of the characters from what it was at the beginning. **Conflict** in the most general sense refers to the forces that move the action in a plot. Conflict in plot may be generated from a search or pursuit, from a discovery, from a deception or misunderstanding, from opportunities to make significant choices, or from unexpected consequences of an action. Although the term *conflict* connotes an active struggle

---

*Terms in bold are featured in A Glossary of Literary Terms and Techniques at the end of the chapter.

between opposing or hostile forces, conflict in fiction may refer to any progression, change, or discovery. The resolution of conflict in a plot may be subtle and confined to the inner life of a character or it may be dramatic and involve irreversible change, violent destruction, or death.

This term may identify an actual struggle between characters, anything from dominance or revenge to simple recognition or understanding. A plot may also focus on conflict between characters and the forces of nature or society. These are essentially **external conflicts**. A work may also center on **internal conflicts**, characters' struggle to know or change themselves and their lives. Most works of fiction and drama contain more than one aspect of conflict.

In Shakespeare's *Romeo and Juliet*, the most dramatic conflicts are external, vivid, and literal: the street brawls between followers of the rival Capulets and Montagues, the fatal fight with Tybalt that leads to Romeo's banishment, and the tragic deaths of the young lovers. In *Macbeth*, however, the primary interest is in the internal conflict between Macbeth's ambitious desires and his understanding of the moral consequences of the actions he takes to achieve those desires. The action in Edith Wharton's most famous story, "Roman Fever," is ironically serene and pleasant: two middle-aged women, longtime friends now both widowed, sit on a terrace overlooking the splendors of Rome and reflect on their common experiences and lifelong friendship. At the end of the conversation—and the story—their actual feelings of rivalry have surfaced, and one of the two learns something that reveals how little she truly knew her husband or understood her marriage or the life of her friend. The conflict between the two women emerges almost imperceptibly, and its meaning is fully understood only in the completely unexpected revelation of the last line.

Plot and Chronology

Narrative is not necessarily presented in chronological order, but it does have a chronology. In other words, incidents may be presented out of the order in which they actually occurred, but by the end of the work the reader understands their order and relationship and appreciates why the story was structured as it was. Plots that are narrated in flashback or from different points of view are common examples.

The Great Gatsby, by F. Scott Fitzgerald, and *Ethan Frome,* by Edith Wharton, are novels in which the narrators first introduce themselves and their interest in the story, then tell the story in a narrative flashback whose full significance to the narrator (and reader) is revealed only at the end. Tennessee Williams's play *The Glass Menagerie* has a similar structure, in which the character of Tom serves both as a narrator in the present and as a principal character in the series of memory scenes that make up the drama. The memory scenes in Arthur Miller's play *Death of a Salesman,* however, are not flashbacks in the same way. Willy Loman relives incidents from the past while the other characters and the action of the play continue in the present. As the play progresses, the shifts in time occur only within Willy's mind.

Shakespeare's tragedies are dramas in which normal chronology is preserved, as it is in such familiar novels as William Golding's *Lord of the Flies* and Mark Twain's *Huckleberry Finn*.

Plot and Time

Related to understanding of chronology is appreciation of how an author creates understanding of *elapsed time*. In the several hours required to read a novel, the two to three hours for a full-length play, and the half-hour to an hour for a one-act play or short story, how much time in the lives of the characters has been accounted for? In one-act plays and many short stories, the time covered by the action is equal to the time to read them. In Wharton's "Roman Fever," for example, the action of the story is contained in a few hours of one afternoon—little more time than it takes to read the story. That conversation, however, completely transforms the women's, and the reader's, understanding of their lives over twenty-five years. The time required for the action in Shirley Jackson's widely read story "The Lottery" is also roughly equal to the time required to read it, yet the plot accounts indirectly for events that have taken place for longer than anyone in the story can even remember. Miller's play *Death of a Salesman* takes place over a period of only twenty-four hours, but the plot and Willy's memories tell us the story of an entire lifetime. Awareness of how an author uses and accounts for time adds considerably to the reader's appreciation of a work.

Narrative Point of View

The **narrator** of a work is the character or author's **persona** that tells a story. **Point of view** is the standpoint, perspective, and degree of understanding from which the narrator speaks. For many students and scholars, how a story is told is one of the most interesting questions. What is the narrative point of view? Is the narration **omniscient**, essentially the point of view of the author? If not, who is the narrator? What is the narrator's relationship to the story? What is the narrator's understanding of the story? How much does the narrator really know? Appreciating how, or by whom, a story is told is often essential to understanding its meaning.

One of the most easily discerned narrative points of view is the first person (*I*), in which either the central character or another directly involved in the action tells the story. J. D. Salinger's novel *The Catcher in the Rye* is a vivid and popular example of such narration. Fitzgerald's *The Great Gatsby* is also

49

told in the first person. In each of these works, the fundamental meaning of the novel becomes apparent only when the reader understands the character of the narrator. In each of these works, what the narrator experiences and what he learns about himself and the world are the novel's most important themes.

In first-person narration, the incidents of the plot are limited to those that the narrator himself experiences. First-person narrators can, however, report what they learn from others. In Wharton's *Ethan Frome,* the engineer who narrates tells us that he has "pieced together the story" from the little he has been able to learn in the town of Starkfield, from his limited conversations with Frome himself, and from his brief visit to the Frome house. Wharton's method, of course, dramatizes Frome's inability to express or fulfill the desires of his heart and reveals the reluctance of the people of Starkfield to fully understand the lives of those around them.

Authors may also use first-person narration to achieve an ironic or satiric effect. In Ring Lardner's well-known story "Haircut," a barber in a small midwestern town narrates a story about a local fellow who kept the town entertained with his practical jokes on people. As the story progresses, the reader understands how cruel and destructive the fellow's pranks were, but the barber does not. The narrative method in this story reveals, indirectly, a story of painful ignorance and insensitivity in the "decent" citizens of a small town. Mark Twain's masterpiece, *Huckleberry Finn*, is told by Huck himself. Through the morally naive observations of Huck, Twain satirizes the evils of slavery, fraud, hypocrisy, and virtually every other kind of corrupt human behavior. Edgar Allan Poe's story "The Tell-Tale Heart" is the confession of a cunning madman.

In third-person narration (*he, she, it, they*) a story is reported. The narrative voice may be *omniscient* and, therefore, able to report everything from everywhere in the story; this voice can also report on the innermost thoughts and feelings of the characters themselves. In many novels of the eighteenth and nineteenth centuries, the omniscient narrator even speaks directly to the reader, as if taking him or her into the storyteller's confidence. In Nathaniel Hawthorne's *The Scarlet Letter,* the narrator pauses from time to time to share personal feelings with the reader, as does Nick Carraway, the narrator of *The Great Gatsby*.

A widely used narrative method is the **limited omniscient** point of view. The narrative is in the third person but is focused on and even may represent the point of view of a central character. The actions and feelings of other characters are presented from the perspective of that character. Hawthorne's short story "Young Goodman Brown" is an excellent example.

Some third-person narration is dramatically **objective** and detached; it simply reports the incidents of the plot as they unfold. This narrative method, too, can be used for intensely **ironic** effect. Jackson's "The Lottery" is one of the best examples. The real horror of the story is achieved through the utterly detached, nonjudgmental unfolding of the plot.

In some plays, too, there is a character who serves a narrative role: the Chorus in Shakespeare's *Henry V*, the character of Tom in Williams's *The Glass Menagerie,* and the Stage Manager in Thornton Wilder's *Our Town* are familiar examples.

In each of the works discussed here, the narrative method is not simply a literary device; it is an intrinsic part of the meaning of the work.

Setting

The setting of a work includes the time and places in which the action is played out; setting may also include a significant historical context. In drama, setting may be presented directly in the set, costumes, and lighting. In narrative fiction, it is usually presented directly through description. In some works, the physical setting is central to the plot and developed in great detail; in other works, only those details necessary to anchor the plot in a time or place will be developed. Regardless of detail, responsive readers recreate images of setting as they read.

In addition to the physical and natural details of the fictional world, setting also includes mood and **atmosphere**. In some works, social or political realities constitute part of the setting. *The Scarlet Letter* is not only set in Puritan Boston, it is also *about* that society; and *The Great Gatsby* presents a vivid picture of life in New York during Prohibition and the roaring twenties.

For some works, the author may create specific details of setting to highlight a theme. In Golding's novel *Lord of the Flies*, the island on which the story takes place has everything essential for basic survival: food and water are available, and the climate is temperate. In order to explore the moral questions of the boys' regression into savagery, Golding carefully establishes a setting in which survival itself is not a primary issue. In *Ethan Frome,* details of the harsh winter and of the isolation of a town "bypassed by the railroad" intensify the story of a man's desperately cold and isolated life.

Character

We understand characters in fiction and drama, as we do the people in our own lives, by what they say and do and by what others say about them. Because characters are imagined and created by an author, we can even understand them more reliably and fully than we can many of the people around us. Many students find their greatest satisfaction in reading works about characters to whom they can relate, characters whose struggles are recognizable and whose feelings are familiar.

Understanding character in fiction means understanding a person's values and **motivation**, beliefs and principles, moral qualities, strengths and weaknesses, and degree of self-knowledge and understanding. To fully

51

appreciate a work, the reader must understand what characters are searching for and devoting their lives to.

Literature also seeks to account for the forces outside individuals that influence the directions and outcomes of their lives. These "forces" range from those of nature and history to the demands of family, community, and society. The response of characters to inner and outer forces is what literature depicts and makes comprehensible.

Any meaningful or convincing plot stems from human thought, motive, and action. Depending on the narrative point of view (see page 49), a character's thoughts and feelings may be presented directly through omniscient narrative or first-person commentary. In "Young Goodman Brown," the narrator tells us directly what the title character is thinking and feeling; in "Roman Fever," the reader discovers the most important revelations of character simultaneously with the two central characters. Character in drama is revealed directly in dialogue and action, but it may be expanded through soliloquies and asides. In Shakespeare's *Othello*, for example, the full extent of Iago's evil is revealed through the variety of methods Iago uses to manipulate different characters and through his **soliloquies**.

In some works, the author's primary purpose is to reveal character gradually through plot; in others, the author establishes understanding of character from the beginning in order to account for what happens. In the opening pages of *The Great Gatsby*, the narrator, Nick, who is also a character in the novel, introduces himself and declares his judgment of the moral quality of the people and events he is about to narrate. With Nick's own character and motives clearly established, the reader then shares his *gradual* discovery of the truth about Gatsby and his life.

Theme

The subjects of literature may come from any aspect of human experience: love, friendship, growing up, ambition, family relationships, conflicts with society, survival, war, evil, death, and so on. **Theme** in a work of literature is the understanding, insight, observation, and presentation of such subjects. Theme is what a work *says about* a subject. Themes are the central ideas of literary works.

One way to think about theme is to consider it roughly analogous to the topic or thesis of an expository essay. If the author of a novel, story, or play had chosen to examine the subjects of the work in an essay, what might be the topic assertions of such an essay? The student is cautioned, however, not to overinterpret the analogy. Themes in literature are rarely "morals," such as those found at the end of a fable, but neither are they "hidden meanings." Although scholars and critics often express thematic ideas in phrases, students are often required to state themes in full sentences. In the next paragraph are some examples of statements about theme.

Macbeth is a play about the temptation to embrace evil forces and about the power of ambition to corrupt; Macbeth himself makes one of the most important statements of theme in the play when he says, "I do all that becomes a man/who does more is none." *Ethan Frome* and Lardner's "Haircut" both illustrate that people in small towns do not truly understand the innermost needs and desires of other people they *think* they know. William Golding's novel *Lord of the Flies* illustrates the bleak view that human beings' savage nature will prevail without external forces of authority, that human beings are not civilized in their fundamental natures. In contrast, in *Adventures of Huckleberry Finn,* Twain presents civilization as the source of corruption and finds truly moral behavior only in the runaway slave, Jim, and the ignorant boy, Huck.

In Chapter 6 you will find an extensive list of literature topics, many of which are expressed in terms of theme.

READING NONFICTION

Fiction and nonfiction share many common elements; they also make similar demands and offer comparable rewards to the thoughtful reader. In broad contrast to fiction, where characters and plot are imaginative creations of the author, nonfiction is about actual persons, experiences, and phenomena. The texts reviewed in Chapter 3 are good examples of how nonfiction speculates on abstract and philosophical questions of history and politics, ethics and religion, culture and society, as well as the natural world. In biography and autobiography, the writer focuses on what is meaningful and interesting in the life of an individual. The purpose of this section is to review some of the distinctive features of formal and informal essays and to illustrate some of the methods authors use to develop arguments in persuasive writing. The glossary at the end of the chapter also features extended definitions and examples of many important terms.

Questions for the Critical Reader

Here again are the questions you are urged to keep in mind as you prepare for the reading comprehension and text analysis sections of the Regents ELA exam:

What is the purpose of this piece? Its tone or mood? Its overall effect?

What does the author say? believe? recall? value? assert?

What does the author mean? imply? suggest? agree with? disagree with?

How are language and imagery used?

What conclusions or inferences is the reader led to?

What experience is meant to be shared and understood?

Purpose

In speaking of fiction, the central ideas of a work are identified as its themes. In essays, purpose refers both to the central ideas and to their intended effect on the reader. For example, many authors of essays develop a thesis with a view to influencing opinion or urging action. We encounter such writing daily on the editorial and Op-Ed pages of a newspaper. Many of the verbs on the list of "what writers do" (page 45) identify such purposes: *affirm, alert, argue, assert, caution, censure, condemn, criticize, declare, defend, evaluate, expose, forewarn, imply, inspire, judge, persuade, propose, provoke, reveal, scrutinize, support.*

Much nonfiction, of course, has as its purpose to explain and inform. The verbs used to identify informative writing include *analyze, assess, clarify, define, describe, explore, formulate, illustrate, interpret, recreate, summarize.*

Other purposes may be likened to conversations between the author and the reader; these "conversations" may be about anything from the most personal experiences to reflections on the nature of life and the universe. Some useful verbs here might be *address, amuse, capture, comment, conjecture, depict, discover, enhance, enrich, examine, explore, invent, observe, offer, ponder, probe, propose, question, recreate, reflect, shock.*

Methods of Development and Patterns of Organization

The ability to use a variety of methods to organize and express ideas is one of the most important skills a student writer learns, and the thoughtful reader should also be able to appreciate how a writer develops material. Informational texts are part of the reading comprehension and text analysis parts of the Regents ELA exam and the new SAT (2015); reviewing the following methods of organization is also useful preparation for composing essays of argument.

FROM ABSTRACT TO CONCRETE/FROM GENERAL TO SPECIFIC

Going from the general to the specific is the most common and natural pattern for explanation, illustration, and reasoning. A passage by author and playwright Sandy Asher is an especially good example:

> **As a child, I sensed there was something I desperately needed from books. As a writer for young readers, I've tried to figure out what that something was. It turned out to be a combination of three things: companionship, a sense of control, and magic.**

In her essay, Asher goes on to develop a paragraph about each of the three things that make up the "something" she is explaining.

Here is how journalist Ernie Pyle begins his explanation of what "The awful waste and destruction of war" really means:

> **I walked for a mile and a half along the water's edge of our many-miled invasion beach. I walked slowly, for the detail on the beach was infinite.**
>
> **The wreckage was vast and startling. The awful waste and destruction of war, even aside from the loss of human life, has always been one of its outstanding features to those who are in it. Anything and everything is expendable. And we did expend on our beachhead in Normandy during those first few hours.**
>
> **For a mile out from the beach there were scores of tanks and trucks and boats that were not visible, for they were at the bottom of the water—swamped by overloading, or hit by shells, or sunk by mines.**

His description of a Normandy beach following the D-Day invasion in 1944 is developed in a series of vivid images and poignant details that make the waste and destruction of war comprehensible to those who have not experienced it.

FROM CONCRETE TO ABSTRACT/FROM SPECIFIC TO GENERAL

Reversing the more common pattern, going from the specific to the general can also be a very effective way to develop understanding of a general concept. This is the pattern author William Kittredge uses in the **anecdote** about his boyhood encounter with a sage grouse. The passage recounts a specific experience, which leads to the closing general observation:

> **For that childhood moment I believed the world to be absolutely inhabited by an otherness which was utterly demonic and natural, not of my own making. But soon as that bird was enclosed in a story which defined it as a common-place prairie chicken, I was no longer frightened. It is a skill we learn early, the art of inventing stories to explain away the fearful sacred strangeness of the world. Storytelling and make-believe, like war and agriculture, are among the arts of self-defense, and all of them are ways of enclosing otherness and claiming ownership.**

Here is how the passage by Stephen Hawking in Chapter 1 (page 16) begins:

> **A few years ago the City Council of Monza, Italy, barred pet owners from keeping goldfish in curved fishbowls. The sponsors of the measure explained that it is cruel to keep a fish in a bowl because the curved sides give the fish a distorted view of reality. Aside from the measure's significance to the poor goldfish, the story raises an interesting philosophical question: How do we know that the reality we perceive is true?**
>
> **The goldfish is seeing a version of reality that is different from ours, but can we be sure it is any less real? For all we know, we, too, may spend our entire lives staring out at the world through a distorting lens.**

FROM QUESTION TO ANSWER

Another method of developing **argument** and explanation is to pose a question, which the paragraph or essay then answers. Here is an example from the conclusion of Thoreau's *Walden:*

> **Why should we be in such desperate haste to succeed, in such desperate enterprises? If a man does not keep pace with his companions, perhaps it is because**

he hears a different drummer. Let him step to the music which he hears, however measured or far away.

And here is a passage from "The Almost Perfect State," an essay by Don Marquis:

You have seen the tall towers of Manhattan, wonderful under the stars. How did it come about that such growths come from such soil—that a breed lawless and prosaic has written such a mighty hieroglyphic against the sky? How is it that this hideous, half-brute city is also beautiful and a fit habitation for demi-gods? How come? . . . It comes about because the wise and subtle deities permit nothing worthy to be lost. It was with no thought of beauty that the builders labored . . . the baffled dreams and broken visions and the ruined hopes and the secret desires of each one labored with him . . . the rejected beauty, the strangled appreciation, the inchoate art, the submerged spirit—these groped and found each other and gathered themselves together and worked themselves into the tiles and mortar of the edifice and made a town that is a worthy fellow of the sunrise and the sea winds.

This passage by Sandy Asher is also an example of this method; the final paragraph reveals that the essay is an answer to the question, "Why do I write for children?"

Magic, companionship, a sense of control. The wonder of ourselves, of each other, and of life—this is the true subject matter of all novels. The best children's literature speaks not only to children but to the human condition. Writing for children simply means writing for human beings in the beginning, when you can still take part in creation, before habit, cynicism and despair have set in, and while there is still hope and energy, a willingness to learn, and a healthy sense of humor. These qualities I find irresistible in the young people I write about and for, qualities I want to hang onto and to cultivate in myself. So I write for children, not just for their sakes—but for my own.

CHRONOLOGICAL ORDER/NARRATION

Although narration is the primary mode of development for fiction, it is also widely used in **exposition** and argument. The historian uses narration and chronology in recounting significant events; the scientific writer may use narration to explain a process. Narration is also an essential part of biography and the personal essay. The passage from *Life on the Mississippi* (page 60) is a classic example of personal narrative. Here, author Annie Dillard, in a passage that appeared on a past Regents exam, uses narration to explain what she means by the "unwrapped gifts and free surprises" of Nature.

I walked up to a tree, an Osage orange, and a hundred birds flew away. They simply materialized out of the tree. I saw a tree, then a whisk of color, then a tree again. I walked closer and another hundred blackbirds took flight. Not a branch, not a twig budged: the birds were apparently weightless as well as invisible. Or, it was as if the leaves of the Osage orange had been freed from a spell in the form of red-winged blackbirds; they flew from the tree, caught my eye in the sky, and vanished. When I looked again at the tree, the leaves had reassembled as if nothing had happened. Finally I walked directly to the trunk of the tree and a final hundred, the real diehards, appeared, spread, and vanished. How could so many hide in the tree without my seeing them? The Osage orange, unruffled, looked just as it had looked from the house, when three hundred red-winged blackbirds cried from its crown. I looked upstream where they flew, and they were gone. Searching, I couldn't spot one. I wandered upstream to force them to play their hand, but they'd crossed the creek and scattered. One show to customer. These appearances catch at my throat; they are the free gifts, the bright coppers at the roots of trees.

CAUSE AND EFFECT

Formal development of cause and effect arguments is essential to the historian, the scientist, and the lawyer. It also serves as a basic method for much of the expository writing students do. This paragraph from a speech by former governor Madeleine Kunin offers a good example of explanation through cause and effect:

> **In my own case, most essential to my political evolution was a strong desire to have an effect on events around me, whether that was a flashing red light at the railroad crossing in my neighborhood, to protect my children on their way to school, or whether it was a new environmental law for the state of Vermont. The fact that I succeeded in obtaining the flashing red light, as a private citizen, enabled me to change the environmental laws as governor. Each step builds a new self-image, enabling us to move from the passive to the active voice.**

Here is a brief example from the Text on RFID technology (page 26) in Chapter 2:

> **All of the websites you visit collect some amount of information about you, whether it is your name or what other sites you have visited recently. Most of the time, we're being tracked without knowing it. For example, most websites now include Facebook and Twitter buttons so you can "like" the page you are viewing or "Tweet" about it. Whether or not you click the buttons, however, the companies can still determine which pages you've visited and file that information away for later use. . . .**

COMPARISON AND CONTRAST

In these paragraphs, historian Bruce Catton in "Lee and Grant: A Study in Constrasts," brings to a close his extended discussion of the contrasts between Ulysses S. Grant and Robert E. Lee and introduces the discussion of how the two men were alike:

So Grant and Lee were in complete contrast, representing two diametrically opposed elements in American life. Grant was the modern man emerging; beyond him, ready to come on the stage, was the great age of steel and machinery, of crowded cities and a restless burgeoning vitality. Lee might have ridden down from the old age of chivalry, lance in hand, silken banner fluttering over his head. Each man was the perfect champion of his cause, drawing both his strengths and his weaknesses from the people he led.

Yet it was not all contrast, after all. Different as they were—in background, in personality, in underlying aspiration—these two great soldiers had much in common. Under everything else, they were marvelous fighters. Furthermore, their fighting qualities were really very much alike.

Here, from *Life on the Mississippi* (1883), is Mark Twain's comparison of how the North and South treated the Civil War as a topic of conversation, years after it ended:

In the North one hears the war mentioned, in social conversations, once a month; sometimes as often as once a week; but as a distinct subject for talk, it has long ago been relieved of duty. There are sufficient reasons for this. Given a dinner company of six gentlemen to-day, it can easily happen that four of them—and possibly five—were not in the field at all. So the chances are four to two, or five to one, that the war will at no time during the evening become the topic of conversation; and the chances are still greater that if it becomes the topic it will remain so but a little while. If you add six ladies to the company, you have added six people who saw so little of the dread realities of the war that they ran out of talk concerning them years ago, and now would soon weary of the topic if you brought it up.

The case is very different in the South. There, every man you meet was in the war; and every lady you meet saw the war. The war is the great chief topic of conversation. The interest in it is vivid and constant; the interest in other topics is fleeting. Mention of the war will wake up a dull company and set their tongues going, when nearly any other topic would fail. In the South, the war is what A.D. is elsewhere: they date from it . . . . It shows how intimately every individual was visited, in his own person, by the tremendous episode. It gives the inexperienced stranger a better idea of what a vast and comprehensive calamity invasion is than he can ever get by reading books at the fireside.

DEVELOPMENT THROUGH EXTENDED METAPHOR

An extended metaphor or **analogy** is a very effective way to develop an argument or illustrate a concept. It uses the known and familiar to explain the unfamiliar. The excerpt from *Life on the Mississippi* is also a vivid example of how a writer relates an experience through extended metaphor. Here is the introduction to an essay written by a student on the topic "All the World's a Stage."

All the world is indeed a stage. And we are the performers. Everything we do in life is a production, and we must constantly perform our best because, in life, there are no rehearsals. Each of us performs on a separate stage, some for a larger audience than others. But each performance, regardless of the size of the audience, is of equal importance, and each performer must meet the standard of life's most important critic—himself.

Here is a passage from Stephen Crane's novel *The Red Badge of Courage:*

The ground was cluttered with vines and bushes, and the trees grew close and spread out like bouquets. The creepers, catching against his legs, cried out harshly as their sprays were torn from the barks of trees. The swishing saplings tried to make known his presence to the world. He could not conciliate the forest. As he made his way, it was always calling out protestations. When he separated embraces of trees and vines the disturbed foliage waved their arms and turned their face leaves toward him.

Here is an illustrative passage from *The Education of Henry Adams*, published in 1918:

For convenience as an image, the [dynamic theory of history] may liken man to a spider in its web, watching for chance prey. Forces of nature dance like flies before the net, and the spider pounces on them when it can; but it makes many fatal mistakes, though its theory of force is sound. The spider-mind acquires a faculty of memory, and, with it, a singular skill of analysis and synthesis, taking apart and putting together in different relations the meshes of its trap. Man had in the beginning no power of analysis or synthesis approaching that of the spider, or even of the honey-bee; he had acute sensibility to the higher forces. Fire taught him secrets that no other animal could learn; running water probably taught him even more, especially in his first lessons of mechanics; the animals helped to educate him, trusting themselves into his hands merely for the sake of their food, and carrying his burdens or supplying his clothing; the grasses and grains were academies of study. With little or no effort on his part, all these forces formed his thought, induced his action, and even shaped his figure.

DEFINITION OR CLASSIFICATION

In this paragraph from a speech by Madeleine Kunin, she develops a key term by classifying its component parts:

Political courage stems from a number of sources: anger, pain, love, hate. There is no lack of political motivation within women. We feel it all. Anger at a world which rushes toward saber-rattling displays of power. Pain at a world which ignores the suffering of its homeless, its elderly, its children. Hatred toward

the injustice which occurs daily as the strong over-
power the weak. And love for the dream of peace on
earth.

Here is a brief passage from *The Federalist #10* by James Madison:

... The two great points of difference between a
democracy and a republic are: first, the delegation
of the government, in the latter, to a small number
of citizens elected by the rest; secondly, the greater
number of citizens, and greater sphere of country,
over which the latter may be extended.

The effect of the first difference is, on the one hand,
to refine and enlarge the public views, by passing
them through the medium of a chosen body of citizens, whose wisdom may best discern the true interest of their country, and whose patriotism and love of
justice will be least likely to sacrifice it to temporary
or partial considerations. Under such a regulation, it
may well happen that the public voice, pronounced
by the representatives of the people, will be more consonant to the public good than if pronounced by the
people themselves, convened for the purpose.

EXAMPLES IN ORDER OF IMPORTANCE

The most persuasive arguments are those in which the reasoning has a
cumulative effect. The skilled writer does not present the supporting details
of a thesis in random order; rather, the skilled writer presents details in
an order that stresses importance and significance. Here is how Abraham
Lincoln concluded his speech marking the celebration of Independence Day
in 1858:

... So I say in relation to the principle that all men
are created equal, let it be as nearly reached as we
can. If we cannot give freedom to every creature, let
us do nothing that will impose slavery upon any other
creature. Let us then turn this government back into
the channel in which the framers of the Constitution
originally placed it.

... Let us discard all this quibbling about this man and the other man—this race and that race and the other race being inferior, and therefore they must be placed in an inferior position—discarding our standard that we have left us. Let us discard all these things, and unite as one people throughout this land, until we shall once more stand up declaring that all men are created equal.

This excerpt is from one of the best-known speeches in Shakespeare's *Hamlet*. The character of Polonius is advising his son on how to conduct himself honorably as a university student in Paris:

> ... Give thy thoughts no tongue,
> Nor any unproportioned thought his act.
> Be thou familiar, but by no means vulgar.
> Those friends thou hast, and their adoption tried,
> Grapple them to thy soul with hoops of steel;
> But do not dull thy palm with entertainment
> Of each new-hatch'd, unfledged comrade. Beware
> Of entrance to a quarrel, but being in,
> Bear't that the opposed may beware of thee.
> Give every man thy ear, but few thy voice;
> Take each man's censure, but reserve thy
>   judgment.
> Costly thy habit as thy purse can buy,
> But not express'd in fancy; rich, not gaudy;
> For the apparel oft proclaims the man,
> And they in France of the best rank and station
> Are of a most select and generous chief in that.
> Neither a borrower nor a lender be;
> For loan oft loses both itself and friend,
> And borrowing dulls the edge of husbandry.
> This above all: to thine ownself be true,
> And it must follow, as the night the day,
> Thou canst not then be false to any man.
> Farewell: my blessing season this in thee!

These models offer examples of only some of the ways in which writers develop ideas. As you read more widely, you will appreciate the extent to which every writer, especially the writer of essays, creates a form best suited to the subject and purpose. When you find a piece of writing you especially admire or find convincing, note how the author developed the ideas.

Tone

When we speak of **tone** in writing we are referring to the attitude of the writer toward the subject and/or toward the reader. It is closely related to what we mean when we refer to someone's "tone of voice." Tone may range from *harsh* and *insistent* to *gentle* and *reflective*. There is as much variety of tone in writing as there is in human feeling. Some pieces—essays of opinion, for example—usually have a very distinct tone; other works, especially in fiction or personal expression, may have a more subtle and indirect tone.

Here is a list of adjectives to help you identify the tone or mood of a prose passage. Many have been gathered by students in their reading of Op-Ed page essays. These terms are part of the academic language you are expected to comprehend in reading and to use appropriately in discussing works of nonfiction. Each reflects a distinctive feeling; be sure to look up in a dictionary any that you are not sure about.

admiring	cautious	informed	provocative
advisory	challenging	inquiring	questioning
affectionate	concerned	instructive	reasoned
alarmed	credible	intense	reflective
amused	critical	ironic	sad
anguished	curious	knowledgeable	sarcastic
appalled	cynical	melancholy	satirical
apprehensive	defensive	mocking	sentimental
argumentative	disappointed	mysterious	skeptical
arrogant	dismayed	nonchalant	surprised
assured	eerie	nostalgic	thoughtful
(with) awe	frank	objective	troubled
bewildered	grateful	offended	understanding
bitter	haughty	optimistic	whimsical
boastful	humorous	outraged	wondering
candid	indifferent	peaceful	
cautionary	indignant	probing	

The Op-Ed pages of most newspapers offer daily examples of essays on current topics, representing widely varied methods of argument, style, and tone. *Harper's Magazine*, *The Atlantic Monthly*, and *The New Yorker* include excellent selections of essays and other examples of literary non-fiction. National magazines such as *Time* and *Sports Illustrated* also offer examples of feature writing and reporting on current issues. The list of Recommended Reading on page 215 also offers titles of books of nonfiction available in paperback.

A GLOSSARY OF LITERARY TERMS AND TECHNIQUES

abstract In contrast to the *concrete,* abstract language expresses general ideas and concepts apart from specific examples or instances. Very formal writing is characterized by abstract expression. An *abstract* (n.) is a brief summary of the key ideas in a scientific, legal, or scholarly piece of writing.

analogy An expression of the similarities between things that are not wholly alike or related. (See, for example, the student essay on page 61.) See *metaphor* in A Glossary of Poetic Terms and Techniques, Chapter 5.

anecdote A very brief, usually vivid, story or episode. Often humorous, anecdotes offer examples of typical behavior or illustrate the personality of a character. Writers of biography and autobiography make extensive use of anecdote to reveal the lives of their subjects.

antithesis In formal argument, a statement that opposes or contrasts with a *thesis* statement. Informally, we use the term to refer to any expression or point of view completely opposed to another. In literature, even an experience or feeling may be expressed as the *antithesis* of another. See also *thesis.*

argument In persuasive writing or speaking, the development of reasons to support the writer's position; also the method of reasoning used to persuade. Informally, we may use the term to describe the development of a topic in any piece of exposition. Historically, it has also denoted a summary of a literary work's plot or main ideas.

atmosphere Closely related to *tone* or mood, it refers to a pervasive feeling in a work. Atmosphere often stems from setting and from distinctive characters or actions. For example, the atmosphere in many of Poe's stories is mysterious, troubling, even sinister, and Hawthorne's "Young Goodman Brown" reflects the threatening and ambiguous world of its Puritan setting.

autobiography A formally composed account of a person's life, written by that person. While we must trust, or be skeptical of, the reliability of the account, we often appreciate the firsthand narration of experience. Autobiography is also a rich source of information and insight into an historical period or into literary or artistic worlds. Autobiography, like the novel, has *narrative* and chronology. (See also *journal*.) We describe literary works that are closely based on the author's life as "auto-biographical." Eugene O'Neill's *Long Day's Journey into Night* and Tennessee Williams's *The Glass Menagerie* are plays that reflect many details of their authors' lives.

biography A narrative, historical account of the life, character, and significance of its subject. Contemporary biography is usually researched in detail and may not always paint an admiring portrait of its subject. A critical biography of a literary figure includes discussion of the writer's works to show the writer's artistic development and career. Biographies of figures significant in history or public affairs also offer commentary on periods and events of historical importance.

character Characters are the imagined persons, created figures, who inhabit the worlds of fiction and drama. E. M. Forster distinguished between *flat* and *round* characters: Flat are those, like stereotypes, who represent a single and exaggerated human characteristic; round are those whose aspects are complex and convincing, and who change or develop in the course of a work. In good fiction, plot must develop out of character. The desires, values, and motives of characters account for the action and conflict in a plot.

characterization The method by which an author establishes character; the means by which personality, manner, and appearance are created. It is achieved directly through description and dialogue and indirectly through observations and reactions of other characters.

concrete Refers to the particular, the specific, in expression and imagery. That which is concrete can be perceived by the senses. Concrete also refers to that which is tangible, real, or actual, in contrast to the *abstract,* which is intangible and conceptual.

conflict In the most general sense, it identifies the forces that give rise to a plot. This term may identify an actual struggle between characters, anything from revenge to simple recognition or understanding. A plot may focus on conflict between characters and the forces of nature or society. These are essentially **external conflicts**. A work may also center on **internal conflicts**, characters' struggles to know or change themselves and their lives. Most works of fiction and drama contain more than one aspect of conflict. (See the discussion on page 47.)

denouement A French term meaning "untying a knot," it refers to the way the complications or conflict of a plot are finally resolved. It also refers to what is called the "falling action" in a drama, that part of the play that follows the dramatic climax and reveals the consequences of the main action for minor characters; it also accounts briefly for what happens in the world of the play after the principal drama is resolved. In Arthur Miller's *Death of a Salesman*, the "Requiem" may be considered a denouement; it accounts for the response to Willy's death by his wife, sons, and only friend. In Shakespeare's *Macbeth,* the climax is in the scene following the death of Lady Macbeth in which Macbeth understands that he has destroyed all capacity for feeling and has rendered his life meaningless; the denouement includes the battle in which Macbeth comprehends the treachery of the witches and is killed by MacDuff, thus restoring the throne to the rightful heir, Malcolm.

determinism The philosophical view that human existence is determined by forces over which humans have little or no control. The concept that fate predestines the course of a character's life or a tragic figure's downfall is a form of determinism.

episode A series of actions or incidents that make up a self-contained part of a larger narrative. Some novels are structured so that each chapter is a significant episode. Fitzgerald's *The Great Gatsby* and Mark Twain's *Huckleberry Finn* are good examples of this structure. A *scene* in a play is often analogous to an episode in a narrative. Many television series are presented in weekly episodes.

essay A general term (from French *essai,* meaning an attempt, a trying out of something) to denote an extended composition, usually expository, devoted to a single topic. Essays may be composed to persuade, to reflect on philosophical questions, to analyze a subject, to express an opinion, or to entertain. As a literary form, the essay dates from the sixteenth century and remains a popular and widely practiced form. The essay by Francis Bacon on page 41 is a classic example. See *formal/ informal* essay.

exposition Writing whose purpose is to inform, illustrate, and explain. In literature, exposition refers to those passages or speeches in which setting, offstage or prior action, or a character's background is revealed. In *The Great Gatsby,* Nick Carraway pauses in the narrative to give the reader additional information about Gatsby's background. The prologue to Shakespeare's *Romeo and Juliet* is an example of exposition.

flashback A presentation of incidents or episodes that occurred prior to the beginning of the narrative itself. When an author or filmmaker uses flashback, the "present" or forward motion of the plot is suspended. Flashback may be introduced through the device of a character's memory or through the narrative voice itself. William Faulkner's "Barn Burning" and *Light in August* include vivid passages of memory and narrative flashback. Jack Burden's recounting of the Cass Mastern story in Robert Penn Warren's *All the King's Men* is also a form of flashback.

foreshadowing A technique in which an author establishes details or mood that will become more significant as the plot of a work progresses. Thoughtful readers usually sense such details and accumulate them in their memories. In one of the opening scenes of *Ethan Frome*, Ethan and Mattie talk about the dangers of sledding down Starkfield's steepest hill; and, in the second paragraph of "The Lottery," the boys are stuffing their pockets with stones or making piles of them on the edge of the square.

form The organization, shape, and structure of a work. Concretely, form may refer to *genre* (see below), for example, the sonnet form, the tragic form. More abstractly, form also refers to the way we sense inherent structure and shape.

formal/informal essay The formal essay emphasizes organization, logic, and explanation of ideas, whereas the informal essay emphasizes the voice and perspective of the writer. In the latter, also called a *personal essay*, the reader is aware of the author's *persona* and is asked to share the author's interest in the subject.

genre A type or form of literature. Examples include *novel, short story, epic poem, essay, sonnet, tragedy.*

image Although the term suggests something that is visualized, an image is an evocation through language of *any* experience perceived directly through the senses. See also A Glossary of Poetic Terms and Techniques, Chapter 5.

irony In general, a tone or figure of speech in which there is a discrepancy (a striking difference or contradiction) between what is expressed and what is meant or expected. Irony achieves its powerful effect indirectly: in satire, for example, which often uses *understatement* or *hyperbole* to express serious criticism of human behavior and social institutions. We also speak of *dramatic irony* when the narrator or reader understands more than the characters do.

journal A diary or notebook of personal observations. Many writers use journals to compose personal reflection and to collect ideas for their works; the journals of many writers have been published. Students are often urged to keep journals as a way to reflect on their reading, compose personal pieces, and practice writing free of concern for evaluation.

melodrama A plot in which incidents are sensational and designed to provoke immediate emotional responses. In such a plot, the "good" characters are pure and innocent and victims of the "bad" ones, who are thoroughly evil. The term refers to a particular kind of drama popular in the late nineteenth century and, later, in silent films and early Westerns. A work becomes melodramatic when it relies on improbable incidents and unconvincing characters for strong emotional effect.

memoir A form of autobiographical writing that reflects on the significant events the writer has observed and on the interesting and important personalities the writer has known.

monologue In a play, an extended expression or speech by a single speaker that is uninterrupted by response from other characters. A monologue is addressed to a particular person or persons, who may or may not actually hear it. Ring Lardner's short story "Haircut" is an example of monologue as a method of narration. In it, a barber tells the story to a customer (the reader) who is present but does not respond. See also *dramatic monologue* in A Glossary of Poetic Terms and Techniques, Chapter 5.

motivation The desires, values, needs, or impulses that move characters to act as they do. In good fiction the reader understands, appreciates, and is convinced that a character's motivation accounts for the significant incidents and the outcome of a plot.

narrative point of view The standpoint, perspective, and degree of understanding from which a work of narrative fiction is told. See *omniscient point of view, objective point of view.*

narrator The character or author's *persona* that tells a story. It is through the perspective and understanding of the narrator that the reader experiences the work. In some works, the narrator may inhabit the world of the story or be a character in it. In other works, the narrator is a detached but knowledgeable observer.

naturalism Closely related to *determinism,* naturalism depicts characters who are driven not by personal will or moral principles but by natural forces that they do not fully understand or control. In contrast to other views of human experience, the naturalistic view makes no moral judgments on the lives of the characters. Their lives, often bleak or defeating, simply *are* as they are, determined by social, environmental, instinctive, and hereditary forces. Naturalism was in part a reaction by writers against the nineteenth century Romantic view of man as master of his own fate. It is important to note, however, that none of the Naturalistic writers in America (Crane, Dreiser, London, Anderson, and Norris chief among them) presented a genuinely deterministic vision. Several of these authors began their careers in journalism and were drawn to the Naturalistic view of life as a result of their own experience and observation of life in the United States. See also *realism.*

objective point of view In fiction or nonfiction, this voice presents a story or information, respectively, without expressed judgment or qualification. A fundamental principle of journalism is that news *reports* should be objective. Ernest Hemingway's short story "The Killers" is an example of fiction rendered in a completely detached, objective point of view.

omniscient point of view Spoken in third person (*she, he, it, they*), this is the broadest narrative perspective. The omniscient narrator speaks from outside the story and sees and knows everything about the characters and incidents. Omniscient narration is not limited by time or place. In **limited omniscient** point of view, the author may choose to reveal the story through full understanding of only one character and limit the action to those incidents in which this character is present.

persona A term from the Greek meaning "mask," it refers in literature to a narrative voice created by an author and through which the author speaks. A narrative persona usually has a perceptible, even distinctive, personality that contributes to our understanding of the story. In Nathaniel Hawthorne's *The Scarlet Letter,* the omniscient narrator has a distinctive persona whose attitudes toward Puritan society and the characters' lives are revealed throughout the novel.

plot The incidents and experiences of characters selected and arranged by the author to create a meaningful narrative. A good plot is convincing in terms of what happens and why.

poetic justice The concept that life's rewards and punishments should be perfectly appropriate and distributed in just proportions. In Ring Lardner's short story "Haircut," Jim Kendall's ironic fate is an example of poetic justice: He is a victim of one of his own crude and insensitive practical jokes.

point of view In nonfiction, this denotes the attitudes or opinions of the writer. In narrative fiction, it refers to how and by whom a story is told: the perspective of the narrator and the narrator's relationship to the story. Point of view may be *omniscient,* where the narrator knows everything about the characters and their lives; or it may be *limited* to the understanding of a particular character or speaker. Point of view may also be described as *objective* or *subjective. Third-person* narrative refers to characters as "he, she, it, they." *First-person* narrative is from the "I" point of view. J. D. Salinger's *The Catcher in the Rye* and Twain's *Huckleberry Finn* are told in the first person. *Second-person* narrative, the "you" form, is rare but is found in sermons addressed to a congregation or in essays of opinion addressed directly to a leader or public figure: "You, Mr. Mayor (Madame President), should do the following . . ." Thomas Friedman and Gail Collins occasionally write pieces in the second-person voice for the Op-Ed page of *The New York Times.*

prologue An introductory statement of the dramatic situation of a play or story. Shakespeare's *Romeo and Juliet* begins with a brief prologue. The first two pages of Fitzgerald's *The Great Gatsby* are a prologue to the story Nick Carraway will tell.

prose Most of what we write is prose, the expression in sentences and phrases that reflect the natural rhythms of speech. Prose is organized by paragraphs and is characterized by variety in sentence length and rhythm.

protagonist A term from Ancient Greek drama, it refers to the central character, the hero or heroine, in a literary work.

realism The literary period in the United States following the Civil War is usually called the Age of Realism. Realism depicts the directly observable in everyday life. Realistic writers seek to *present* characters and situations as they would appear to a careful observer, not as they are imagined or created by the author. After 1865, American writers became increasingly interested in the sources of power and force, and in the means to survival and success, in an increasingly materialistic society. For writers of this period, realism was a literary mode to express a *naturalistic* philosophy. See also *naturalism, verisimilitude.*

rhetoric From Ancient Greece, the art of persuasion in speech or writing achieved through logical thought and skillful use of language.

rhetorical question A question posed in the course of an *argument* to provoke thought or to introduce a line of reasoning.

romance A novel or tale that includes elements of the supernatural, heroic adventure, or romantic passion. Hawthorne's *The Scarlet Letter* is a romance, not because it is a love story but because it goes beyond *verisimilitude* in dramatizing elements of demonic and mystical forces in the characters and their lives.

satire A form or style that uses elements of irony, ridicule, exaggeration, understatement, sarcasm, humor, or absurdity to criticize human behavior or a society. All satire is **ironic** (see above) in that meaning or theme is conveyed in the discrepancy between what is said and what is meant, between what is and what should be, between what appears and what truly is. While satire is often entertaining, its purpose is serious and meant to provoke thought or judgment. The verses of Alexander Pope are often extended satire, and many poems by e. e. cummings are satiric. In prose, much of the writing of Mark Twain is satire; *Huckleberry Finn* is the most striking example. Other American writers of satire include Sinclair Lewis, Dorothy Parker, Edith Wharton, Joseph Heller, and Tom Wolfe. On television, *Saturday Night Live*, and *The Simpsons* are good examples of contemporary satire, as was *The Colbert Report.*

short story This form is distinguished from most novels not simply by length but by its focus on few characters and on a central, revealing incident. In short stories, however, there is as much variety in narrative point of view, subject, and technique as there is in novels. Edgar Allan Poe characterized the short story as "a short prose narrative, requiring from a half-hour to one or two hours in its perusal."

soliloquy A form of *monologue* in which a character expresses thoughts and feelings aloud but does not address them to anyone else or intend other characters in the work to hear them. In essence, the audience for a play is secretly listening in on a character's innermost thoughts. Macbeth's reflection on "Tomorrow, and tomorrow, and tomorrow . . . " is the best-known soliloquy in the play.

speaker The narrative voice in a literary work (see *persona*). Also, the character who speaks in a *dramatic monologue.*

symbol Most generally, anything that stands for or suggests something else. Language itself is symbolic; sounds and abstract written forms may be arranged to stand for virtually any human thought or experience. In literature, symbols are not Easter eggs or mushrooms—they are not "hidden meanings." Symbols are real objects and *concrete* images that lead us to *think about* what is suggested. They organize a wide variety of ideas into single acts of understanding. They embody not single "meanings" but suggest whole areas of meaning.

theme Roughly analogous to thesis in an essay, this is an observation about human experience or an idea central to a work of literature. The *subject* of a work is in the specific setting, characters, and plot. Theme in a work of fiction is what is meaningful and significant to human experience generally; themes are the ideas and truths that transcend the specific characters and plot. Shakespeare's *Macbeth* is about an ambitious nobleman who, encouraged by his equally ambitious wife, murders the king of Scotland in order to become king himself. The themes in *Macbeth* include the power of ambition to corrupt even those who are worthy and the mortal consequences of denying what is fundamental to one's nature.

thesis The central point, a statement of position in a formal or logical argument. Also used to refer to the topic, or controlling, idea of an essay. Use of the term *thesis* implies elaboration by reasons and examples. See *antithesis*.

tone The attitude of the writer toward the subject and the reader. See also A Glossary of Poetic Terms and Techniques, Chapter 5.

transition A transition is a link between ideas or sections in a work. In prose arguments, single words such as *first, second . . . moreover,* and *therefore* or phrases such as *in addition, on the other hand,* and *in conclusion* serve as transitions. In fiction, a brief passage or chapter may serve as a transition. In *The Great Gatsby,* the narrator pauses from time to time to "fill in" the reader and to account for the passage of time between the dramatic episodes that make up the novel's main plot.

turning point In drama and fiction, the moment or episode in a plot when the action is moved toward its inevitable conclusion.

verisimilitude A quality in fiction and drama of being "true to life," of representing that which is real or actual. Verisimilitude in fiction is often achieved through specific, vivid description and dialogue; first-person narration also creates the effect of verisimilitude. In drama it may be enhanced through means of set, costumes, and lighting that are realistic in all their details.

(See also, in Chapter 5 — A Glossary of Poetic Terms and Techniques.)

Chapter 5

READING POETRY

INTRODUCTION

How to Read a Poem

How should you read a poem? Aloud. Several times. And never quickly. Here is a short poem about baseball. As you read, pay attention first to what the poem by Robert Francis says.

Pitcher

His art is eccentricity, his aim
How not to hit the mark he seems to aim at,
His passion how to avoid the obvious,
His technique how to vary the avoidance.
The others throw to be comprehended. He
Throws to be a moment misunderstood.
Yet not too much. Not errant, arrant, wild,
But every seeming aberration willed.
Not to, yet still, still to communicate
Making the batter understand too late.

Now, read the poem again, with particular attention to the varied length of the statements; read from comma to comma or period to period as you would in prose. When you reach the end of the first and fifth lines, for example, pause very slightly—but do not stop. After several readings, you will not only appreciate what Robert Francis undertands about the art of pitching but also feel the way in which the rhythm of the poem is also the rhythm of pitching.

In poetry we are meant to sense a structure and to feel the rhythm. (See **meter*** and **rhythm**.) The structure and rhythm of poetry may be formal, informal, even "free." Poetry is also characterized by its directness of effect and by its concentration—ideas and feelings are expressed in relatively few words. Karl Shapiro says, "Poems are what ideas *feel like*." Robert Francis's poem is about what good pitching *feels like*.

---

*Terms in bold type are defined in A Glossary of Poetic Terms and Techniques at the end of the chapter.

This poem, by Emily Dickinson (1830–1886), recalls the feeling of mourning:

> After great pain, a formal feeling comes—
> The nerves sit ceremonious, like Tombs—
> The stiff Heart questions was it He, that bore,
> and Yesterday, or Centuries before?
>
> The Feet, mechanical, go round—
> Of Ground, or Air or Ought—
> A Wooden way
> Regardless grown,
> A Quartz contentment, like a stone—
>
> This is the Hour of Lead—
> Remembered, if outlived,
> As Freezing persons, recollect the Snow—
> First—Chill—then Stupor—then the letting go—

In this poem, Dickinson recreates what it feels like suddenly to encounter a snake in the grass:

> A narrow Fellow in the Grass
> Occasionally rides—
> You may have met Him—did you not
> His notice sudden is—
> The Grass divides as with a Comb—
> A spotted shaft is seen—
> And then it closes at your feet
> And opens further on—
>
> He likes a Boggy Acre
> A Floor too cool for corn—
> Yet when a boy, and Barefoot—
> I more than once at Noon
> Have passed, I thought, a Whip lash
> Unbraiding in the Sun
> When stooping to secure it
> It wrinkled, and was gone—

Several of Nature's People
I know, and they know me—
I feel for them a transport
Of cordiality—

But never met this Fellow
Attended, or alone
Without a tighter breathing
And Zero at the Bone—

Where the writer of prose may seek immediate clarity of meaning above all, the poet often seeks **ambiguity**, not to create "confusion," but to offer multiplicity of meaning, in single words, in images, in the meaning of the poem itself. Look again at "Pitcher." Might this poem also be a reflection on the art of poetry itself? It is because of such richness in meaning that poems often require several readings.

The experience of poetry is conveyed in vivid **imagery**, which appeals to the mind and to the senses. It is often expressed in **figurative language**, that is, words and comparions that are not literal but that imaginatively create original, vivid, and often unexpected images and associations. (See **metaphor** and **simile**.) Finally, in poetry there is particular significance in the way words and lines sound. The story or experience is enhanced through musical effects. A poem must be felt and heard!

In this poem by Laurence Binyon, a boy kept home from school with a fever, is dazzled by the light of the sun as it comes out after rain, and he no longer regrets being "...a captive/Apart from his schoolfellows."

The rain was ending, and light

THE rain was ending, and light
Lifting the leaden skies.
It shone upon ceiling and floor
And dazzled a child's eyes.

Pale after fever, a captive
Apart from his schoolfellows,
He stood at the high room's window
With face to the pane pressed close,

And beheld an immense glory
Flooding with fire the drops
Spilled on miraculous leaves
Of the fresh green lime-tree tops.

Washed gravel glittered red
To a wall, and beyond it nine
Tall limes in the old inn yard
Rose over the tall inn sign.

And voices arose from beneath
Of boys from school set free,
Racing and chasing each other
With laughter and games and glee.

To the boy at the high room-window,
Gazing alone and apart,
There came a wish without reason,
A thought that shone through his heart.

I'll choose this moment and keep it,
He said to himself, for a vow,
To remember for ever and ever
 As if it were always now.

A note on reading this poem: do not read to emphasize regular meter and rhyming pattern; remember, read from comma to comma, period to period. For example, the second and third stanzas should be read with only slight pauses at the commas and through the third stanza, where there is no end punctuation, in as few breaths as possible. The fourth stanza completes the vivid image of the "immense glory" the boy sees as he looks out the window.

STRUCTURE AND LANGUAGE IN POETRY

All the traditional poetic forms stem from an oral tradition, in which poetry was sung or recited. The **epic** and the **ballad** are the oldest forms of **narrative poetry**, but modern poets also tell stories in narrative verse. (Robert Frost's "Out, Out—" is a well-known example.) Most of the poetry we read today, however, is **lyric** poetry.

Think of the lyric poem as a song; in the Ancient Greek tradition, the lyric poem was meant to be sung to the accompaniment of a lyre, a small harplike instrument. Indeed, we speak of the words for a song as its lyrics. The ancient form is evident in the songs for Shakespeare's plays, in the tradition of the nineteenth-century art song, and in the twentieth-century ballads and songs. The ancient form is evident in the songs for Shakespeare's plays, in the tradition of the nineteenth-century art song, and in the twentieth-century ballads and songs we associate, for example, with Rodgers and Hart, Cole Porter, and Stephen Sondheim and sung by Frank Sinatra, Barbra Streisand, among many others, including Tony Bennett in his duets with Lady Gaga.

Lyric poems are relatively brief and are expressed in the voice (that is, from the point of view) of a single speaker. They express a powerful emotion, usually captured in a significant experience or dramatic situation. A lyric poem, like a song, often tells a story, but it does so in nonnarrative form. The **speaker** (or "poet") may recall an experience, or render it directly, in order to understand its meaning and then reveal it to the reader. Thus, many lyric poems are *meditations, reflections,* or *recollections* of experience that lead to a *discovery*, to an emotionally powerful *recognition* of the meaning of the experiences. The effect of the poem is to convey that meaning directly, to engage readers in such a way that they share the experience, feel the emotion, with the speaker. The poems by Robert Francis, Emily Dickinson, and Laurence Binyon on the previous pages are examples of lyrics.

This poem by Robert Penn Warren appeared on a past Regents ELA exam.

Old Photograph of the Future

That center of attention—an infantile face
That long years ago showed, no doubt, pink and white—
Now faded, and in the photograph only a trace
Of grays, not much expression in sight.

(5) That center of attention, swathed in a sort of white dress,
Is precious to the woman who, pretty and young,
Leans with a look of surprised blessedness
At the mysterious miracle forth-sprung.

In the background somewhat, the masculine figure
(10) Looms, face agleam with achievement and pride.
In black coat, derby at breast, he is quick to assure
You the world's in good hands—lay your worries aside.

The picture is badly faded. Why not?
Most things show wear around seventy-five,
(15) And that's the age this picture has got.
The man and woman no longer, of course, live.

79

> **They lie side by side in whatever love survives**
> **Under green turf, or snow, and that child, years later,**
>   **stands there**
> **While old landscapes blur and he in guilt grieves**
> *(20)* **Over nameless promises unkept, in undefinable despair.**

In this poem, the speaker expresses the profound feelings of guilt and despair he feels in looking at an old photograph of himself and his parents when he was an infant. The **tone** of the poem is reflective, that of an elegy. The mood at the end is one of regret and loss as the speaker recalls his dead parents, confronts his own age, "the age this picture has got," and grieves at the "nameless promises unkept." Although the narrator speaks of "that child, years later" who "stands there . . . and . . . in guilt grieves," the intensity and privacy of feeling at the end indicate that the speaker is that child. The narrative voice and the lack of specific identification of the characters serve to emphasize the passage of time and underscore the fact that looking at the photograph leads the "child," now old, to reflect on his entire life.

The structure is simple and easy to observe: five **quatrains** with alternating **rhyme**; each quatrain is self-contained—ends with a period—and tells a part of the story. The first fifteen lines of the poem describe the picture and the "characters" in it. Note that the final section of the poem begins with the last line of the fourth quatrain, the description having concluded in line 15. Line 16 both ends the narrator's rendering of the photograph and also begins the "conclusion," which is the significance of the experience of looking at the photograph.

The rhythm within lines is varied and often broken by dashes or other pauses; this rhythm allows us to share the speaker's questions and reflections. The rhythm of the fourth stanza slows as each line completes a thought. In contrast, the final stanza should be heard as a single, long gesture of recognition and regret.

The experience of looking at the picture—in which he is the "center of attention"—leads the speaker to reflect on whether he has satisfied the "promises" that the "mysterious miracle" of his birth meant to his awed and proud parents. The photograph also leads the speaker to reflect on the unfulfilled promises of his own life.

There is little in the way of figurative language in this poem. The imagery, however, reveals more than a description of a photograph, and the paradox in the title reveals one of the poem's central **themes**, the cycle of birth, life, and death. On rereading Warren's poem, with our appreciation of the poet's experience in mind, we see how the third and fourth lines are more than a description of the photograph—they also suggest the speaker's age. He sees himself (in the photo and metaphorically) as "faded . . . only a trace of grays, not much expression in sight." The repetition of the fact that he was the "center of attention" (in the photograph and in his parents' lives) makes more poignant the grief over "promises unkept" at the end.

80

The poet offers only a few details of the photograph, but they are the details we all recognize from our own photographs of grandparents and great-grandparents: the father "In the background somewhat" and in formal pose—"in black coat, derby at breast"—the child (girl or boy) in "a sort of white dress." It is, of course, such widely shared experience that is both the poem's form and its theme.

In this poem by Theodore Roethke, the speaker recalls a significant experience from childhood:

Child on Top of a Greenhouse

The wind billowing out of the seat of my britches,
My feet crackling splinters of glass and dried putty,
The half-grown chrysanthemums staring up like accusers,
Up through the streaked glass, flashing with sunlight,
A few white clouds all rushing eastward,
A line of elms plunging and tossing like horses,
And everyone, everyone pointing up and shouting!

Try repeating just the verbs of this poem, feeling their dramatic energy. The repetition of "-ing" forms also creates what is called **internal rhyme**, while the words "like," "sunlight," "white," "line" form the pattern of sound called **assonance**.

In this poem by Donald Hall the speaker also recalls an important childhood experience:

The Sleeping Giant
(A Hill, So Named, in Hamden, Connecticut)

The whole day long, under the walking sun
That poised an eye on me from its high floor,
Holding my toy beside the clapboard house
I looked for him, the summer I was four.

I was afraid the waking arm would break
From the loose earth and rub against his eyes
A fist of trees, and the whole country tremble
In the exultant labor of his rise;

Then he with giant steps in the small streets
Would stagger, cutting off the sky, to seize
The roofs from house and home because we had
Covered his shape with dirt and planted trees;

And then kneel down and rip with fingernails
A trench to pour the enemy Atlantic
Into our basin, and the water rush,
With the streets full and the voices frantic.

That was the summer I expected him.
Later the high and watchful sun instead
Walked low behind the house, and school began,
And winter pulled a sheet over his head.

In this poem, a child's fearful and vivid imagination is sparked by **personification** of the hill near his house. This poem is particularly effective because it recalls for us the fact that small children are literal and that they tend to give names and human character to inanimate things. This child actually sees—and fears—the sleeping giant. Note too how the images of the sun in the first and last stanzas both unify the poem and denote the passage of time. Finally, there is a gentle **irony** in the final line that suggests that the child, no longer fearful, can now "play" with the metaphor of the sleeping giant, as "winter pulled a sheet over his head."

Shakespeare's Sonnet 30 illustrates several of the formal aspects of verse:

When to the sessions of sweet silent thought

When to the sessions of sweet silent thought
I summon up remembrance of things past
I sigh the lack of many a thing I sought
And with old woes new wail my dear time's waste:

(5) Then can I drown an eye, unused to flow,
For precious friends hid in death's dateless night,
And weep afresh love's long-since-canceled woe,
And moan th'expense of many a vanished sight;

Then can I grieve at grievances forgone,
(10) And heavily from woe to woe tell o'er
The sad account of fore-bemoaned moan,
Which I new pay as if not paid before.
  But if the while I think on thee, dear friend,
  All losses are restored and sorrows end.

The structure of the Shakespearean **sonnet** is three **quatrains** and a closing **couplet**. The **rhyme scheme** is *abab/cdcd/efef/gg*. This pattern allows us to hear the structure of the poem, to hear the development of the ideas. The couplet, with its similar end rhyme and self-contained thought, contrasts the feelings expressed in the previous 12 lines and concludes the poem.

We find in this Shakespearean sonnet, as well, examples of **alliteration** and assonance: In the first quatrain, we hear alliteration in the many words that begin with "s." In lines 7 through 12 we hear assonance in the repetition of "oh" sounds, which are also examples of **onomatopoeia**—that is, the sounds reflect the meanings of the words. Lines 4 and 10 also illustrate what is called internal rhyme.

THEME IN POETRY

Some lyric poems may assert a belief. Others may be a comment on the nature of human experience—love, death, loss or triumph, mystery and confusion, conflict and peace, on the humorous and the ironic, on the imagined and the unexpected in all its forms. Some poems reflect on the nature of time, of existence. Many lyrics are about poetry itself. These aspects of human experience are what we refer to as the themes of poetry.

In this well-known sonnet, Number 55, Shakespeare asserts that poetry confers immortality, that it can prevail over the most powerful forces of time. Note how the central idea is developed in the three quatrains and how the couplet—in its thought and its rhyme—concludes the development of that idea.

Not marble, nor the gilded monuments

Not marble, nor the gilded monuments
Of princes, shall outlive this pow'rful rhyme;
But you shall shine more bright in these contents
Than unswept stone besmeared with sluttish time.

When wasteful war shall statues overturn,
And broils root out the work of masonry,
Nor Mars his sword nor war's quick fire shall burn
The living record of your memory.

'Gainst death and all-oblivious enmity
Shall you pace forth; your praise shall still find room
Even in the eyes of all posterity
That wear this world out to the ending doom.
  So, till the judgment that yourself arise,
  You live in this, and dwell in lovers' eyes.

In this lyric by Carl Sandburg, the poet suggests that poetry is "about" the meaning in life itself.

Last Answers

I WROTE a poem on the mist
And a woman asked me what I meant by it.
I had thought till then only of the beauty of the mist,
    how pearl and gray of it mix and reel,
And change the drab shanties with lighted lamps
    at evening into points of mystery quivering with
    color.
  I answered:
The whole world was mist once long ago and some
    day it will all go back to mist,
Our skulls and lungs are more water than bone and
    tissue
And all poets love dust and mist because all the last
    answers
Go running back to dust and mist.

The best-known lyrics, however, are probably love poems—Sonnet 116 of Shakespeare, for example:

Let me not to the marriage of true minds

Let me not to the marriage of true minds
Admit impediments. Love is not love
which alters when it alteration finds,
Or bends with the remover to remove.

O, no, it is an ever-fixed mark
That looks on tempests and is never shaken;
It is the star to every wand'ring bark,
Whose worth's unknown, although his height be taken.

Love's not Time's fool, though rosy lips and cheeks
Within his bending sickle's compass come;
Love alters not with his brief hours and weeks,
But bears it out even to the edge of doom.
  If this be error and upon me proved,
  I never writ, nor no man ever loved.

In this lyric by Claude McKay, the poet is overcome with longing for his homeland on the island of Jamaica.

The Tropics in New York

Bananas ripe and green, and ginger-root,
  Cocoa in pods and alligator pears,
And tangerines and mangoes and grape fruit,
  Fit for the highest prize at parish fairs,

Set in the window, bringing memories
  Of fruit-trees laden by low-singing rills,
And dewy dawns, and mystical blue skies
  In benediction over nun-like hills.

My eyes grew dim, and I could no more gaze;
  A wave of longing through my body swept,
And, hungry for the old, familiar ways,
  I turned aside and bowed my head.

TONE

Tone in poetry, as in prose and all forms of human communication, expresses the *attitude* of the speaker toward the reader or listener and toward the subject. Tone in literature is as varied as the range of human experience and feeling it reflects. When we speak of the *mood* of a piece of writing, we are also speaking of tone, of an overall feeling generated by the work.

Here are some terms to help you recognize and articulate tone or mood:

ambiguous*	insistent	reconciled
amused	ironic*	reflective
angry	melancholy	regretful
bitter	mournful	reminiscent
celebratory	mysterious	satiric*
elegiac (from elegy*)	nostalgic	sorrowful
grateful	optimistic	thoughtful
harsh	paradoxical*	understated*
humorous	questioning	

WRITING ABOUT POETRY/EXPLICATION

When you are asked to *explicate* a poem, you are being asked to look closely at it and "unfold" its meaning, line by line, idea by idea. Explication combines paraphrase with close reading of form. You are explaining both the content *and* the form: the ideas and meaning as well as the structure and poetic elements.

To begin an explication, read the poem several times to discover what it says. Who is the speaker? What is the subject? the dramatic situation? What theme or experience is central to the poem? What is the tone or mood? Try to summarize or paraphrase the poem as a whole. Then note the formal details: What is the pattern of organization? What is the movement of ideas and feeling? of images and metaphors? How do stanzas or arrangement of lines reveal that? How do rhyme, meter, and rhythm contribute to the experience, to the meaning of the poem? (The commentary that follows Robert Penn Warren's "Old Photograph of the Future" on page 79 is an example of explication.)

---

*These terms are defined in A Glossary of Poetic Terms and Techniques.

POETRY ON EXAMINATIONS

On examinations, such as the Regents ELA exam and the AP Literature and Composition exam, the multiple-choice questions are designed to measure your skill at close reading and *explication*. You are expected to recognize and identify the elements of poetry. (See A Glossary of Poetic Terms and Techniques.) In addition, you are usually required to compose an essay/explication of a poem on the AP Literature and Composition exam, and such essays are commonly assigned in high school and college literature courses. *Analysis,* which requires detailed examination of particular elements of a poem or passage, is usually reserved for course assignments. The thoughtful student will, of course, develop skill in both explication and analysis.

A HANDFUL OF POEMS FOR FURTHER READING

In this excerpt from an extended essay in verse, Alexander Pope reflects on how poets express meaning through sound and rhythm.

An Essay on Criticism

True ease in writing comes from art, not chance,
As those move easiest who have learned to dance.
'Tis not enough no harshness gives offense,
The sound must seem an echo to the sense:
Soft is the strain when Zephyr gently blows,
And the smooth stream in smoother numbers flows;
But when loud surges lash the sounding shore,
The hoarse, rough verse should like the torrent roar.

The horror and loss of war are often expressed through irony. Here is Stephen Crane's reflection on war:

Do Not Weep, Maiden, for War Is Kind

Do not weep, maiden, for war is kind.
Because your lover threw wild hands against the sky
And the affrighted steed ran on alone,
Do not weep.
War is kind.

    Hoarse, booming drums of the regiment
    Little souls who thirst for fight
    These men were born to drill and die.
    The unexplained glory flies above them,
    Great is the battle-god, great, and his kingdom—
    A field where a thousand corpses lie.

Do not weep, babe, for war is kind.
Because your father tumbled in the yellow trenches,
Raged at his breast, gulped and died,
Do not weep.
War is kind.

    Swift blazing flag of the regiment,
    Eagle with crest of red and gold,
    These men were born to drill and die.
    Point for them the virtue of slaughter,
    Make plain to them the excellence of killing
    And a field where a thousand corpses lie.

Mother whose heart hung humble as a button
On the bright splendid shroud of your son,
Do not weep.
War is kind.

In this poem, by Walt Whitman (1819–1892), the speaker moves from the observation of a spider to a reflection on the soul's search to understand all existence.

A Noiseless Patient Spider

A noiseless patient spider,
I mark'd where on a little promontory it stood isolated,
Mark'd how to explore the vacant vast surrounding,
It launch'd forth filament, filament, filament, out of itself,
Ever unreeling them, ever tirelessly speeding them.

And you O my soul where you stand,
Surrounded, detached, in measureless oceans of space,
Ceaselessly musing, venturing, throwing, seeking the
    spheres to connect them,
Till the bridge you will need be form'd, till the ductile
    anchor hold,
Till the gossamer thread you fling catch somewhere,
    O my soul.

In this brief poem by Alfred, Lord Tennyson (1809–1892) the language and imagery convey the experience of both the observer and of the eagle itself.

The Eagle

He clasps the crag with crooked hands;
Close to the sun in lonely lands,
Ringed with the azure world, he stands.

The wrinkled sea beneath him crawls;
He watches from his mountain walls,
And like a thunderbolt he falls.

Here, in free verse, is Whitman's vision of eagles:

The Dalliance of Eagles

Skirting the river road, (my forenoon walk, my rest,)
Skyward in air a sudden muffled sound, the dalliance
      of the eagles,
The rushing amorous contact high in space together,
The clinching interlocking claws, a living, fierce,
      gyrating wheel,
Four beating wings, two beaks, a swirling mass tight
      grappling,
In tumbling turning clustering loops, straight downward
      falling.
Till o'er the river pois'd, the twain yet one, a moment's
      lull,
A motionless still balance in the air, then parting, talons
      loosing,
Upward again on slow-firm pinions slanting, their
      separate diverse flight,
She hers, he his, pursuing.

And here is a poet, Katharine Lee Bates, who takes delight in playing with the names and characters of various fish; the result is a collection of puns, wordplay, and forms of internal and external rhyme.

Don't You See?

THE day was hotter than words can tell,
So hot the jelly-fish wouldn't jell.
The halibut went all to butter,
And the catfish had only force to utter
A faint sea-mew—aye, though some have doubted,
The carp he capered and the horn-pout pouted.
The sardonic sardine had his sly heart's wish
When the angelfish fought with the paradise fish.
'T was a sight gave the bluefish the blues to see,
But the seal concealed a wicked glee—
The day it went from bad to worse,
Till the pickerel picked the purse-crab's purse.

And the crab felt crabedder yet no doubt,
Because the oyster wouldn't shell out.
The sculpin would sculp, but hadn't a model,
And the coddlefish begged for something to coddle.
But to both the dolphin refused its doll,
Till the whale was obliged to whale them all.

In the first of these two poems by Robert Browning (1812–1889) the rich
and varied imagery recreates the journey of a lover to his beloved and, in
the second, his return to the "world of men."

Meeting at Night

The grey sea and the long black land;
And the yellow half-moon large and low;
And the startled little waves that leap
In fiery ringlets from their sleep,
As I gain the cove with pushing prow,
And quench its speed i' the slushy sand.

Then a mile of warm sea-scented beach;
Three fields to cross till a farm appears;
A tap at the pane, the quick sharp scratch
And spurt of a lighted match,
And a voice less loud, through its joys and fears,
Than the two hearts beating each to each.

Parting at Morning

Round the cape of a sudden came the sea,
And the sun looked over the mountain's rim:
And straight was a path of gold for him,
And the need of a world of men for me.

In this sonnet, George Meredith (1828–1909) imagines the desire of this fallen angel, now Satan, to return to the heavens he once inhabited.

Lucifer in Starlight

On a starred night Prince Lucifer uprose.
Tired of his dark dominion swung the fiend
Above the rolling ball in cloud part screened,
Where sinners hugged their spectre of repose.
Poor prey to his hot fit of pride were those.
And now upon his western wing he leaned,
Now his huge bulk o'er Afric's sands careened,
Now the black planet shadowed Arctic snows.
Soaring through wider zones that pricked his scars
With memory of the old revolt from Awe,
He reached a middle height, and at the stars,
Which are the brain of heaven, he looked, and sank.
Around the ancient track marched, rank on rank,
The army of unalterable law.

In this well-known sonnet by Percy Bysshe Shelley (1792–1822) we experience the ironic fate of a once proud and arrogant king.

Ozymandias

I met a traveler from an antique land
Who said: Two vast and trunkless legs of stone
Stand in the desert. Near them, on the sand,
Half sunk a shattered visage lies, whose frown,
And wrinkled lip, and sneer of cold command,
Tell that its sculptor well those passions read
Which yet survive, stamped on these lifeless things,
The hand that mocked them and the heart that fed;
And on the pedestal these words appear:
"My name is Ozymandias, king of kings:
Look on my works, ye Mighty, and despair!"
Nothing beside remains. Round the decay
Of that colossal wreck, boundless and bare,
The lone and level sands stretch far away.

Romantic poets and painters were fond of celebrating sunsets. Here is an excerpt from "Enough Has Been Said of Sunset," by Iris Barry.

LIGHT—imperceptible as
One thin veil drawn across blackness:
Is it dawn? . . .
Comes the twitter-whistle of sleepy birds
Crescendo . . .
Now bright grayness creeping
Drowns the dark; and waves of sea-wind
Rock the thin leaves . . .
A door bangs; sharp barks from dogs released,
    scampering.
After some silence, footsteps.
And the rising bustle of people
Roused by the day-break.

Here is what dawn "feels like" to William Carlos Williams:

Metric Figure

THERE is a bird in the poplars—
It is the sun!
The leaves are little yellow fish
Swimming in the river;
The bird skims above them—
Day is on his wings.
Phoenix!
It is he that is making
The great gleam among the poplars.
It is his singing
Outshines the noise
Of leaves clashing in the wind.

These poems represent only a few examples of the great variety of expression in verse. Your own textbooks and anthologies offer many more examples; and the list of Recommended Reading at the end of the book includes titles of collections readily available in paperback. You will also find the addresses of some excellent websites devoted to poetry. You should read as widely as possible, and always read aloud!

A GLOSSARY OF POETIC
TERMS AND TECHNIQUES

allegory A narrative, in prose or verse, in which abstract ideas, principles, human values or states of mind, are *personified*. The purpose of the allegory is to illustrate the signficance of the ideas by dramatizing them. *Parable* and *fable* are particular kinds of allegory, in which a moral is illustrated in the form of a story.

alliteration The repetition of initial consonant sounds in words and syllables. This is one of the first patterns of sound a child creates (for instance "ma-ma," "pa-pa"). The children's stories of Dr. Seuss use alliteration and assonance. Poets use alliteration for its rich musical effect: "Fish, flesh, and fowl commend all summer long/Whatever is begotten, born, and dies" (Yeats); for humor: "Where at, with blade, with bloody, blameful blade/He bravely broached his boiling bloody breast" (Shakespeare); and to echo the sense of the lines: "The iron tongue of midnight hath told twelve" (Shakespeare).

allusion A reference to a historical event, to Biblical, mythological, or literary characters and incidents with which the reader is assumed to be familiar. Allusion may, with few words, enrich or extend the meaning of a phrase, idea, or image. Allusion may also be used for ironic effect. In his poem "Out, out . . ." Robert Frost expects the reader to recall from Macbeth's final soliloquy the line, "Out, out brief candle!" Such expressions as "a Herculean task" or "Achilles heel" are also forms of allusion.

ambiguity Denotes uncertainty of meaning. In literature, however, especially in poetry, we speak of *intentional* ambiguity, the use of language and images to suggest more than one meaning at the same time.

assonance The repetition of vowel sounds among words that begin or end with different consonants. Sonnet 30 of Shakespeare (page 82) and "Child on Top of a Greenhouse" by Theodore Roethke (page 81), for example, are rich in assonance. Some poets may vary end rhymes with assonance; for example, Emily Dickinson (page 76) does it here: "The Feet, mechanical, go round—Of Ground, or Air, or Ought—."

ballad Narrative poem, sometimes sung, that tells a dramatic story.

blank verse Unrhymed *iambic pentameter,* usually in "paragraphs" of verse instead of stanzas. Shakespeare's plays are composed primarily in blank verse. For example, from *Macbeth* (Act I, Scene 5):

> Your face, my Thane, is as a book where men
> May read strange matters. To beguile the time,
> Look like the time; bear welcome in your eye,
> Your hand, your tongue; look like the innocent flower,
> But be the serpent under't . . .

connotation The feelings, attitudes, images, and associations of a word or expression. Connotations are usually said to be "positive" or "negative." See also discussion on page 148 in Chapter 8—Vocabulary.

couplet Two lines of verse with similar meter and end rhyme. Couplets generally have self-contained ideas as well, so they may function as stanzas within a poem. In the English (Shakespearean) *sonnet,* the couplet concludes the poem. (See the sonnets on pages 82–84.) Also many scenes in Shakespeare's plays end with rhymed couplets: "Away, and mock the time with fairest show/False face must hide what the false heart doth know" (*Macbeth* Act I, Scene 7).

denotation That which a word actually names, identifies, or "points to." Denotation is sometimes referred to as "the dictionary definition" of a word.

dramatic monologue A poem in which a fictional character, at a critical or dramatic point in life, addresses a particular "audience," which is identifiable but silent. In the course of the monologue, we learn a great deal, often ironically, about the character, who is speaking and the circumstances that have led to the speech. Robert Browning is the best-known nineteenth-century poet to compose dramatic monologues; "My Last Duchess" is a famous example. In the twentieth century, such poets as Kenneth Fearing, E. A. Robinson, T. S. Eliot ("The Love Song of J. Alfred Prufrock"), Robert Frost, and Amy Lowell have composed well-known dramatic monologues.

elegy A meditative poem mourning the death of an individual.

epic A long narrative poem often centering on a heroic figure who represents the fate of a great nation or people. *The Iliad* and *The Odyssey* of Homer, *The Aeneid* of Vergil, and the Anglo-Saxon *Beowulf* are well-known epics. Milton's *Paradise Lost* and Dante's *The Divine Comedy* are examples of epic narratives in which subjects of great human significance are dramatized. *Omeros,* by Derek Walcott, is a contemporary example of an epic poem.

figurative language The intentional and imaginative use of words and comparisons that are not literal but that create original, vivid, and often unexpected images and associations. Figurative language is also called *metaphorical language.* See *metaphor* and *simile.*

free verse A poem written in free verse develops images and ideas in patterns of lines without specific metrical arrangements or formal rhyme. Free verse is distinguished from prose, however, because it retains such poetic elements as assonance, alliteration, and figurative language. The poetry of Walt Whitman offers striking examples.

hyperbole An exaggerated expression (also called overstatement) for a particular effect, which may be humorous, satirical, or intensely emotional. Hyperbole is the expression of folk tales and legends and, of course, of lovers: Romeo says to Juliet, "there lies more peril in thine eye/Than twenty of their swords." Hyperbole is often the expression of any overwhelming feeling. After he murders King Duncan, Macbeth looks with horror at his bloody hands: "Will all great Neptune's ocean wash this blood/Clean from my hand . . . ?" In her sleepwalking scene, Lady Macbeth despairs that "All the perfumes of Arabia will not sweeten this little hand." And every one of us has felt, "I have mountains of work to do!"

iambic pentameter The basic meter of English speech: "I think I know exactly what you need/and yet at times I know that I do not." Formally, it identifies verse of ten syllables to the line, with the second, fourth, sixth, eight, and tenth syllables accented. There is, however, variation in the stresses within lines to reflect natural speech—and to avoid a "singsong" or nursery rhyme effect. Most of the dialogue in Shakespeare's plays is composed in this meter. See *blank verse*.

image Images and imagery are the heart of poetry. Although the term suggests only something that is visualized, an image is the recreation through language of *any* experience perceived directly through the senses. For example, Tennyson's "The Eagle" (page 89) is composed of striking visual images. The feelings of fear and of mourning in Emily Dickinson's poems are also images. In "Pitcher" (page 75) we feel the motion of pitching.

internal rhyme A pattern in which a word or words within a line rhyme with the word that ends it. Poets may also employ internal rhyme at irregular intervals over many lines. The verbs in Theodore Roethke's poem "Child on Top of a Greenhouse" (page 81) create the effect of internal rhyme.

irony In general, a tone or figure of speech in which there is a discrepancy—(a striking difference or contradiction)—between what is expressed and what is meant or expected. Irony may be used to achieve a powerful effect indirectly. In satire, for example, it may be used to ridicule or criticize. Stephen Crane's poem "Do Not Weep, Maiden, for War Is Kind" (page 88) is intensely ironic, both in the stanzas apparently seeking to comfort those whose lovers, fathers, and sons have died and in the contrasting stanzas of apparent celebration of the glories of war. We also speak of *dramatic irony* in fiction in which the reader understands more than the characters do. Ring Lardner's short story "Haircut" is an excellent example.

lyric A general term used to describe poems that are relatively brief and expressed in the voice of a single *speaker* (narrative voice). Lyric poems express a powerful emotion revealed in a significant experience or observation. (See discussion on page 78.)

metaphor A form of analogy. Through metaphor, a poet discovers and expresses a similarity between dissimilar things. The poet use metaphors to imaginatively find common qualities between things we would not normally or literally compare. As a figure of speech, metaphor is said to be implicit or indirect. This contrasts to *simile* (see page 98), where the comparison is expressed directly. In his final soliloquy, Macbeth uses a series of metaphors to express the meaninglessness of his own life: "Life's but a walking shadow, a poor player . . . it is a tale told by an idiot . . . ."

meter and **rhythm** Rhythm refers to the pattern of movement in a poem. As music has rhythm, so does poetry. Meter refers to specific patterns of stressed and unstressed syllables. See *iambic pentameter.*

ode A meditation or celebration of a specific subject. Traditional odes addressed "elevated" ideas and were composed in elaborate stanza forms. Keats's "Ode to a Nightingale" and "Ode to Autumn" are particularly fine examples. Modern odes may address subjects either serious or personal. One well-known contemporary ode is Pablo Neruda's "Ode to My Socks."

onomatopoeia The use of words whose sound reflects their sense. "Buzz," "hiss," and "moan" are common examples. Shakespeare's Sonnet 30 shows how the sounds and rhythm of whole lines may be onomatopoetic.

oxymoron Closely related to *paradox,* oxymoron is a figure of speech in which two contradictory or sharply contrasting terms are paired for emphasis or ironic effect. Among students' favorite examples are "jumbo shrimp" and "army intelligence." Poets have written of the "wise fool," a "joyful sadness," or an "eloquent silence."

paradox An expression, concept, or situation whose literal statement is contradictory, yet which makes a truthful and meaningful observation. Consider the widely used expression "less is more," for example. Shakespeare's play *Macbeth* opens with a series of paradoxes to establish the moral atmosphere in which "foul is fair." John Donne's famous poem "Death Be Not Proud" ends with the paradox "Death thou shalt die," and the title of Robert Penn Warren's poem "Old Photograph of the Future" is a paradox.

personification A form of metaphor or simile in which nonhuman things— objects, plants and animals, forces of nature, abstract ideas—are given human qualities; for example, "The half-grown chrysanthemums staring up like accusers" (Roethke, page 81), "the walking sun/that poised an eye on me from its high floor" (Hall, page 81), "Time . . . the thief of youth" (Milton), and "Blow winds, and crack your cheeks! Blow! Rage!" (Shakespeare).

prose poem This form appears on the page in the sentences and paragraphs of prose yet its effect is achieved through rhythm, images, and patterns of sound associated with poetry.

quatrain Stanza of four lines. The quatrain is the most commonly used stanza form in English poetry. Quatrains may be rhymed, *abab, aabb, abba,* for example, or they may be unrhymed. The sonnets of Shakespeare (pages 82–83), the poem by Laurence Binyon (page 77), "Old Photograph of the Future" (page 79), and "The Sleeping Giant" (page 81) are also composed in quatrains.

rhyme In general, any repetition of identical or similar sounds among words that are close enough together to form an audible pattern. Rhyme is most evident when it occurs at the ends of lines of metrical verse. The *quatrains* of Shakespeare's Sonnet 55 (pages 83–84) have alternating rhyme as do those of Robert Penn Warren's poem "Old Photograph of the Future" (page 79).

rhyme scheme A regular pattern of end rhyme in a poem. The rhyme scheme in Shakespeare's sonnets, for example, is *abab/cdcd/efef/gg.*

satire A form or style that uses elements of irony, ridicule, exaggeration, understatement, sarcasm, humor, or absurdity to criticize human behavior or a society. All satire is *ironic* (see page 96) in that meaning or theme is conveyed in the discrepancy between what is said and what is meant, between what is and what should be, between what appears and what truly is. While satire is often entertaining, its purpose is serious and meant to provoke thought or judgment. The verse of Alexander Pope is often extended satire, and many poems by e. e. cummings are satiric.

simile An expression that is a direct comparison of two things. It uses such words as *like, as, as if, seems, appears.* For instance: "A line of elms plunging and tossing like horses" (Theodore Roethke); "Mind in its purest play is like some bat" (Richard Wilbur); "I wandered lonely as a cloud" (William Wordsworth).

soliloquy A form of monologue found most often in drama. It differs from a dramatic monologue in that the speaker is alone, revealing thoughts and feelings to or for oneself that are intentionally unheard by other characters. In Shakespeare's plays, for example, the principal characters' reflections on how to act or questions of conscience are revealed in their soliloquies. Hamlet's "To be, or not to be . . ." is probably the most famous dramatic soliloquy in English.

sonnet A poem of fourteen lines in *iambic pentameter* that may be composed of different patterns of stanzas and rhyme schemes. The most common forms are the English, or Shakespearean, sonnet, which consists of three quatrains and a closing couplet, and the Italian sonnet, which consists of an *octave* of eight lines and a *sestet* of six lines.

speaker The narrative voice in a poem. Also, the character who speaks in a *dramatic monologue.* The poems "The Sleeping Giant" and "Old Photograph of the Future" have distinctive speakers who are also the central characters in the dramatic experience of the poem.

stanza The grouping of lines within a poem. A stanza provides the basic organization and development of ideas, much as a paragraph does in an essay. Many stanza patterns have a fixed number of lines and a regular pattern of rhyme; the poems of Robert Penn Warren (page 79) and Donald Hall (page 81) are good examples. Poets, however, often create stanzas of varying length and form within a single poem. A stanza that ends with a period, completing an idea or image, is considered "closed," while a stanza that ends with a comma or with no punctuation, is called "open," indicating that there should be very little pause in the movement from one stanza to another. Roethke's poem "Child on Top of a Greenhouse" (page 81) is an example of a poem composed in a single stanza.

symbol Most generally, anything that stands for or suggests something else. Language itself is symbolic; sounds and abstract written forms may stand for almost any human thought or experience. Symbols are real objects and *concrete* images that lead us to think about what is suggested. Symbols organize a wide variety of ideas into single acts of understanding. They embody not single "meanings" but suggest whole areas of meaning.

tone The attitude or feeling of the speaker toward the subject. Tone may also refer to the dominant mood of a poem. (See discussion of *tone* on page 86.)

understatement Expression in which something is presented as less important or significant than it really is. The first and third stanzas of Stephen Crane's "Do Not Weep, Maiden" (page 88) ironically understate the horror of death in battle and the loss for those who mourn. Understatement is often used for humorous, *satiric,* or *ironic* effect. Much of the satire in *Huckleberry Finn* stems from Huck's naive and understated observations. One particular form of understatement, actually a double negative, includes such expressions as "I was not uninterested," which really means "I was interested," or "He was not without imagination," which really means "He had some imagination."

Chapter 6

WRITING ABOUT LITERATURE: A GENERAL REVIEW

For most students, writing papers and responding to essay questions on exams are the most challenging aspects of their course work. Writing requires that you articulate and focus your understanding of what you read. Like all good writing, writing about literature not only demonstrates to others what you understand and think but also obliges you to clarify *for yourself* what you truly know. That process is sometimes hard, but it is worthwhile. Writing is essential to developing your critical reading and thinking skills.

TOPICS FOR LITERARY ESSAYS

Much of your writing about literature is done in response to assignments and exam questions. Students are also urged to maintain notes and journals. For essays, instructors may assign very specific topics, or they may offer general subjects that require you to develop your own topic and controlling idea.

In your literature courses and exams you will find that the majority of the questions focus on **character**. Because essay topics may apply to many works of nonfiction you read—personal essay, memoir, and autobiography in particular—the term *character* should be understood to refer to any persons, not exclusively to those of fiction and drama.

As you think about characters in the literature you read, keep the following questions in mind: What are a character's values and motives? beliefs and principles? moral qualities? strengths and weaknesses? illusions or delusions? For what is a character searching? striving? devoting his or her life? What significant decisions and actions does a character take? What are the consequences of those decisions and actions? To what extent does a character "succeed" or "fail"? understand or fail to understand?

Literature also seeks to account for the forces outside individuals, that is, the external forces that influence the direction and outcome of their lives. These "forces" range from those of nature and history to the demands of family, community, and society. The response of individuals to inner and outer forces is what literature considers and dramatizes. (See Chapters 4 and 5 for discussions of reading literature and for glossaries of important terms and techniques.)

101

TOPIC AND FOCUS

As any essay must, your paper must have a clear purpose, a controlling idea; moreover, the development of the purpose must be convincing to the reader. *Focus* means in writing, as it does in a photograph, that the subject is clear! We can see it, even recognize it. And, if the photographer/writer has "framed" the material properly, we see the relationship of the background details to the principal subject. When you take a picture of your best friend at camp, or of the place you most want to remember from a vacation trip, you keep the lens of your camera directed at what is most important—not at the tree next to your friend, not at the bus that took you to Niagara Falls.

SELECTION OF SIGNIFICANT DETAILS

One of the most widely observed characteristics of short stories is that they are very selective in detail. The author of a short story includes only those elements of setting, character, and plot that reveal the significance of the central incident. In "The Lottery," for example, we do not know when the story takes place, we do not even know the name of the town or where it is located, and we know little about the lives of individual characters. Those details are not *significant*—they do not matter—to the story Shirley Jackson tells; comparable details *are* significant in "Haircut," and, therefore, Ring Lardner includes them.

To achieve focus in your essays about works of literature, you must exercise the same rigorous process of selection. However interesting you may find a particular incident or aspect of a character, do not include those details if they do not directly explain or clarify your topic.

DEVELOPING THE TOPIC

Many of the common methods of developing arguments are discussed in Chapter 4—Reading Prose. Here are some of those methods as they might be used to develop essays on works of literature:

Comparison/Contrast

Although *compare* means to identify similarities, and *contrast* means to identify differences, the term *comparison* is often used for a discussion that examines both similarities and differences among the items being compared. This is one of the most useful approaches, and one of the most commonly used, because the process of comparing helps sharpen thought. To compose a meaningful comparison, the writer must understand the objects of comparison in detail.

Any literary aspect found in two or more works may serve as a basis for comparison. For example, one could compare the effective use of first-person narration in *The Great Gatsby* and *Ethan Frome,* or in *The Catcher in the Rye* and *Huckleberry Finn.* Although the circumstances of their lives are vastly different, the fact that both Ethan Frome and Jay Gatsby fail to achieve what they most desire—a life with the women they love—offers a rich possibility for comparison and contrast. "Haircut" and "The Lottery" share common elements of setting and irony. *Othello* and *Romeo and Juliet* have a common theme—the tragic destruction of great love.

Comparison may, of course, focus on much narrower topics and be confined to a single work. The best way to develop notes for a comparison is first to list the aspects common to the items under comparison, then to list for each all the specific details that differentiate them. Finally, as you do in preparation for any essay, you select those that are most significant.

Analysis

Analysis requires detailed examination of a particular aspect of a literary work. The purpose of an analytic paper is to show the significance of that aspect to the meaning of the work as a whole. Examples of analytic topics include the use of time in Miller's *Death of a Salesman,* the imagery of light and dark in *Othello,* and the extended metaphor in Emily Dickinson's poem "I Taste a Liquor Never Brewed."

Classification

Classification organizes objects, people, and other living things into categories; it is a process of identifying and relating. In discussions of literature, classification may be an important part of an essay, or it may constitute a topic in its own right. An essay in which the writer shows how a particular work exemplifies a **genre** is considered classification: *The Scarlet Letter* as a **romance**; Shakespeare's *Macbeth* as Elizabethan **tragedy**; Dreiser's *Sister Carrie* as **naturalism**.

Cause and Effect

Many of the topics for writing and discussion of literature may be developed by showing how circumstances or actions have direct and observable consequences. Demonstrating actual cause and effect, however, requires careful thinking and attention to detail. Cause and effect are more easily demonstrated in logic and chemistry than in human experience.

Literary topics that focus on **plot** often lend themselves to cause and effect development because essentially any plot is built on cause and effect: specific circumstances, actions, or decisions lead to others and have consequences in the lives of the characters. Plot summary alone does *not* establish cause and effect; it simply relates "what happened." Cause-and-effect argument requires the writer to show how and why incidents are related.

Exemplification

Whenever you cite specific details to support a thesis, and when you choose the works you will use to answer the literature question in Part B of Session Two, you are using exemplification. *To exemplify* means to illustrate the meaning of a general concept through use of specific examples. This method is fundamental to the development of nearly any essay or literary topic.

LOOKING AT KEY TERMS IN LITERATURE QUESTIONS

identify   To name and also to characterize and to place in context; sometimes you may be required to state the significance of what you are identifying. Often identification includes linking characters to the theme or experience that serves as the topic.

describe   To give the essential characteristics of a person, object, or experience. If you are asked to describe, your choice of details or characteristics must reveal your understanding of a larger question. Why are these details relevant to the topic? Description alone will not be the focus of a literature topic.

explain/show/discuss   These terms indicate the most important parts of a question, which will be developed in the body of an essay. Once you have identified and described your subject, you must interpret and demonstrate the significance of your examples and details; you must offer evidence, using specific references, to support your argument.

USING FLUENT AND PRECISE LANGUAGE

Effective writing is characterized by interesting and vivid language, and "use of precise and engaging language" is among the criteria for evaluation of Regents essays. From the list of what writers *do*, here are some terms to help you articulate your observations about creation of plot:

> *convey, create, delineate, depict, describe, dramatize, foreshadow, illustrate, invent, portray, present, recreate, reveal, select, shock, show, symbolize*

The following terms offer precision and variety in discussing details of a plot:

> *affair, circumstance, climax, development, episode, event, experience, incident, instance, juncture, moment, occasion, occurrence, opportunity, scene, situation*

Terms useful in referring to *character* include:

> *disposition, identity, individuality, makeup, mettle, nature, persona, personality, self, spirit, temperament*

Finally, here is a list of adjectives collected by students to describe some of the many relationships and attitudes among characters in literature (and in our own lives!):

> *admiring, affectionate, bitter, cautious, compassionate, curious, deceitful, disapproving, disdainful, dishonest, distant, envious, false, fearful, generous, hostile, indifferent, loving, optimistic, reluctant, resentful, reserved, respectful, scornful, sincere, skeptical, stern, suspicious, sympathetic, treacherous, watchful*

(See also Using Synonymies to Enhance Your Writing in Chapter 7.)

CHOOSING YOUR OWN TOPIC: REPRESENTATIVE LITERARY SUBJECTS AND THEMES

In many high school and college literature courses, students must select their own topics for writing. The subjects of literature are as varied as human experience itself, and below are some of the many themes authors dramatize. You will encounter these as topics in class discussion and as topics for essays and examination questions. These topics may, of course, serve for discussion of more than one work in an essay.

Topics That Focus on Character

- In many works of literature, an important theme is an **individual's achievement of self-knowledge as a result of undergoing an ordeal**. This self-knowledge may be a recognition of the individual's own strengths, weaknesses, values, prejudices, aspirations, or fears. Identify the individual and the self-knowledge he or she achieves. Using specific references from the work, explain how the ordeal led the individual to the self-knowledge.
- **Nature** can have different effects on different people. It can defeat someone with its power; it can inspire someone with its beauty. Identify the character; using specific references, show how he or she was either defeated or inspired by nature.
- It has been said that to live with **fear** and not be overcome by it is the final **test of maturity**. Explain what fear a character lives with; show how the character "passes" or "fails" the test of maturity on the basis of his or her response to that fear.
- A commonly held belief is that **suffering strengthens an individual's character**. The suffering can be physical, mental, or emotional. Identify the individual; describe the nature of the suffering; explain how the suffering did or did not strengthen the individual's character.
- Sometimes a person **struggles to achieve a goal** only to discover that, once the goal is achieved, the results are not what was expected.
- In many works of literature there are characters who are **troubled by injustice** in society, such as poverty, discrimination, or lawlessness, and **who try to correct** the injustice. Identify the character and the injustice, explain what actions the character takes; discuss whether or not the efforts are successful.
- In many works, characters who love one another or share a special friendship often face **obstacles to their relationship**. Sometimes characters overcome the obstacle; sometimes they are defeated by it. Identify the characters and the obstacle; explain how the characters overcome or are defeated by the obstacle; discuss the effect this outcome (the success or failure, not the obstacle) has on the relationship.
- In many works of literature, **a character sacrifices something of value** in order to achieve something of greater value.
- Sometimes a character faces a **conflict between his or her conscience** and the standards of behavior expected by others. Identify the character; explain the specific nature of the conflict; discuss how the character was affected by this conflict.
- In many works of literature, a character reaches a **major turning point** in his or her life. From that point onward, the character undergoes a significant change.
- Characters in works of literature frequently **learn about life or themselves** by taking risks.

- The phrase **"rite of passage"** describes a situation in which a young person is faced with an experience that results in his or her becoming mature. Explain the experience; discuss how the young person matures as a result of the way in which he or she deals with the experience.
- In many works of literature, characters are **challenged by unfamiliar environments**. Show how the character was or was not successful in meeting the challenge.
- Some individuals in literature **try to do what they believe is right**, even though they face opposition.
- In some works of literature, an important character **makes a mistake that advances the reader's understanding of that individual**.
- Confusion, danger, or tragedy sometimes results when **one character misunderstands the words or actions of another character**.
- In many works of literature, a character **struggles against circumstances that seem to be beyond his or her control**. Sometimes the character is victorious, sometimes not.

Topics That Focus on Literary Elements and Techniques

While topics that focus on character may be the most common in literature courses or on exams, various literary elements also provide topics for essays. The AP literature exam, for example, often features a question based on a literary element or technique.

- Some authors are especially successful at creating **a memorable visual image** that contributes to the reader's understanding of a work. Identify the image and its importance; show how the image contributes to the meaning of the work.
- In many works of literature, the **setting** contributes to the reader's understanding of the central conflict in the plot. Describe the setting; show how it contributes to the reader's understanding of the conflict on which the plot hinges.
- Authors often create a **predominant mood** in a work of literature. Using specific references, discuss incidents that convey that mood and explain the importance of mood to the work.
- Authors sometimes use **foreshadowing** to help develop the plot of a work. Foreshadowing usually takes the form of incidents that seem to be unimportant at first, but take on added significance later. Discuss examples of foreshadowing and show how they contribute to the overall effect and meaning of the work.
- A work of literature may be defined as **a classic** because it promotes deep insight into human behavior, presents a universal theme, or uses

language in an exceptional way. Show how a particular work meets the above definition of the term *classic*.
- Through their work, some **authors reveal their acceptance or rejection of values** held by society. Identify the value; state whether the author accepts or rejects it; using specific references, show how the author reveals his or her attitude toward that value.
- In literature, **symbols** are used to reinforce the central idea or to represent characters. Using specific references, explain how the symbol in a particular work enriches the reader's understanding of either the central idea or a character.
- The **narrative point of view** is significant to the effect and meaning of a literary work. Illustrate the truth of this statement by specific references to a work of literature.

AUDIENCE AND LITERATURE ESSAYS

Most teachers mention audience in the assignments they give; if it is not clear for whom you are writing, it is a good idea to ask before you complete an assignment. For most outside examinations, including the Regents, assume that you are writing for a reader who is familiar with the works of literature but who has not considered the topic; background discussion and *detailed* explanation of plot are not needed.

A NOTE ON CONCLUSIONS

No essay, however brief, should simply stop. Even if you run out of time or things to say, try not to telegraph that information to the reader. A conclusion must come back to the topic, must complete the discussion, in a way that leaves the reader feeling convinced by what you have written. On examinations, most students close with a brief, summative conclusion that highlights the relationship of the literary work or works to the topic or restates the thesis of the essay. Even if the reader of a short essay does not really *need* the conclusion to appreciate your argument, the obligation to compose a conclusion keeps you focused on the topic.

Student writers are urged to avoid the following in their conclusions: the expression "what this paper has shown . . ." or "As you can see . . ."; a reminder that Shakespeare was a great playwright or that Mark Twain was an important figure in American literature; a confession that the reader *really* liked or did not like a particular work. Above all, the conclusion is not the place to introduce a new topic or tack on an idea that properly belongs in the body of the essay.

Chapter 7

WRITING ON DEMAND

Writing has always been an important part of a student's education as well as an essential skill for a successful professional life. The National Commission on Writing is only one of the more recent initiatives in American education to emphasize the importance of good writing among our students. American colleges and universities also seek independent assessment of students' writing skills as part of the admissions process. In this chapter you will find some guidelines for effective writing on demand.

WRITING TO INFORM OR PERSUADE

A General Review

Much of the work you do in high school or college requires writing to demonstrate your ability to understand, analyze, and organize information and ideas. On exams and essays for science and social studies courses, as well as in English and writing courses, you are expected to do many of the following:

- Tell your audience (readers) what they need to know
- Use specific, accurate, and relevant information
- Use a tone and level of language appropriate for the task and audience
- Organize your ideas in a logical and coherent manner
- Follow the conventions of standard written English

These guidelines are also reminders of what your teachers mean when they direct you to compose a "well-written essay" on a given topic.

Personal Narrative

Here is an example of an informal essay written in response to a specific task. It is a good example of what is meant by **tone and level of language** appropriate for the audience. The essay is also organized in a logical and coherent manner.

> **Task:** A representative of a middle school in your district has invited you to speak at the middle school graduation ceremonies on the topic "Getting Off to a Good Start in High School." Write a brief speech that you would give to the students, stating your recommendations for a successful start in high school. Use specific reasons, examples, or details to support your recommendations.

Sample Student Response

Not so long ago, I too was sitting where you are now, thinking and worrying about what my life in high school would be like. Will I stand out? Will I make friends? How should I approach people? Will my classes be too difficult? Will I be able to cope with the stress? These questions kept badgering me throughout the summer before ninth grade. I was especially nervous about starting school because I had just moved to a new neighborhood and did not know a single person.

By the end of the summer, the thought that especially frustrated me was that I would have no one to eat lunch with on the first day of school. This does not seem like such a big deal but it bothered me a lot. I knew that at the high school people went out to eat with a group of friends. I had no one to go out with. I told myself that I still had a week before school started and did not need to worry.

The first day of school finally arrived. As I neared the high school, I felt helpless and lonely. I wanted to plead with my mom to turn the car around and go back home. But I reluctantly got out of the car and slowly approached the front entrance of the school.

Luckily, I found my first class and quickly took a seat in the front. I felt as if all eyes were on me. The new kid. The freak. While everyone was talking and laughing about their summer, I sat in my seat trying to look as though I was busy fiddling with my notebook. I couldn't wait to get out of the classroom. I wanted to run home and hide, for this was one of the most difficult experiences of my life.

Things started to look better around fifth period. I got up the courage and started talking to people. I even went out to lunch with a few girls and had a comfortable time. I was not totally relaxed but knew that I would adapt and soon make more friends.

I have just finished my junior year in high school. I have many friends and am very happy in my school. I will be a senior this coming September and expect to experience new ideas and challenges. I am now starting to think about what I want to do with my life and what colleges I might want to attend. Soon I will be leaving high school and will again feel the nervousness and anxiety that all of you are going through in preparing for high school. I guess what we are experiencing is not trepidation but life, and what to expect in the future. You may be scared now, but be confident that you will overcome those fears and the experiences will only make you stronger.

Analysis

Although this speech is more a personal narrative than a list of recommendations, the writer/speaker clearly understands the purpose of the task and understands her audience:
"Not so long ago, I too was sitting where you are now. . . ." The diction is informal, the tone is conversational, and first-person narrative is highly appropriate for the occasion.

The theme is established in the opening sentence, but the speaker's main point is not stated until the very end: "You may be scared now, but . . . you will overcome those fears . . . and [be] stronger." She leads her audience to this conclusion by narrating her own feelings and experiences, starting with a series of "fears" she knows her listeners have. The narrative covers a period of many weeks, but it is made coherent by specific references to time: "throughout the summer . . . by the end of summer . . . on the first day of school . . . my first class . . . around fifth period . . . lunch." She also uses a reference to time to come back to the present and bring the speech to a close: "I have just finished my junior year. . . ."

The ideas are well expressed; and the paragraph in which the writer describes what it was like to sit in her first class—"The new kid." "The freak."—pretending to be busy with her notebook is especially vivid and convincing. We also trust the speaker when she tells us that she had "a comfortable time" at lunch but that she "was not totally relaxed" either. If she had claimed that after lunch all her fears had disappeared, we would not believe her. This is also a good example of what is meant by honesty in writing: it rings true in our ears. This piece would be even better if the writer had included more specific examples of how she overcame her fears.

Persuasive Writing

Here are two examples of what is called persuasive writing, pieces that develop and support an opinion on a particular topic. In contrast to the essay of argument in Part 2 of the Regents ELA exam, which must be based on evidence from given sources, these essays are developed with the writer's own reasoning and examples. Note what makes each a successful argument.

Task: The students in your science class have been invited to submit essays on topics of current interest or controversy for possible publication on the Op-Ed page of the school newspaper.

Sample Student Response

Using Animals for Scientific Research
The question of whether or not to use animals as subjects for scientific research is a difficult one. Those in opposition claim that using animals in research is inhumane, while those holding a diametrically opposing view maintain that it is a necessary evil whose long-term benefits far outweigh the sacrifice of a handful of animals. I am an ardent supporter of the latter view. I feel that the use of animals is justified by the benefits that are reaped by all of mankind, and that halting the use of animals as subjects would greatly impede advancements in the field of medicine.

One example of the tremendous benefits that animal research can bring about is the case of the discovery of insulin by Dr. William Banting and his assistant, Charles Best. Before this amazing discovery, diabetes mellitus was a devastating and inevitably fatal disease. The extent of treatment that doctors could offer afflicted patients was a starvation diet, which prolonged life only for a short time and caused the obviously detrimental and painful effects of virtual starvation.

When Dr. Banting came up with a unique idea that linked the cause of the disease to a hormonal secretion of the pancreas, a potential way to control this deadly disease arose. But the idea had to be tested and proven successful before it could be offered to human patients. Dr. Banting proceeded with his experiments, using fifteen dogs as his subjects. Although several of the dogs did die as a result of the experiment, the benefits that society gained because of the tests are infinitely greater. If those opposed to utilizing animals in testing had their way, the concept would have died prematurely because there would have been no

112

way to test the idea. Fortunately for the field of science and for the millions of diabetics that have lived in the past few decades, Dr. Banting was able to find this treatment.

As a diabetic, I am greatly indebted to the work of Dr. Banting and the studies he conducted using animals as subjects. Today, I am not only alive, but healthy and active. I cannot help but be a supporter of animal testing because I owe my life to it. I understand how one may object to senseless cruelty to animals and the wasting of their lives worthlessly. But using animals strictly for scientific use is not "senseless cruelty" and it is clearly justified.

Analysis

This is a good example of a short essay of opinion because the student has chosen a subject that he could develop with expertise and compelling personal experience; it also demonstrates his skill in organizing and presenting an argument.

One of the most effective ways to approach a controversial topic is to "acknowledge the opposition." Indicate that you recognize, and even respect, the opposing view. This writer agrees that the question "is a difficult one," but goes on to say he is "an ardent supporter" of animal testing. Note that he skillfully saves his personal reasons for the end, first developing a factual but dramatic example of the benefits of testing for millions of people. Introducing his personal reasons earlier would have made the argument less persuasive because he would have appeared less objective. The conclusion is emotionally effective when he says, "I cannot help but be a supporter of animal testing because I owe my life to it." More importantly, the writer demonstrates skillful argument when he says, "I understand how one may object. . ." and closes with a distinction between scientific experiment and "senseless cruelty." This essay would be a good contribution to an Op-Ed page.

Task: The editor of your local newspaper has proposed that businesses that hire high school graduates pay them salaries in proportion to their grades from the last two years of high school; that is, the higher a graduate's grades for the last two years of high school, the higher the salary. Write a letter to the editor in which you state your opinion of the proposal. Use specific reasons, examples, or details.

Sample Student Response

I vehemently oppose the proposal that graduates be paid salaries in proportion to their grades for the last two years of high school.

First, grades should not affect the equal opportunity of all workers to receive the same paycheck for the same work. It must be taken into account that there are many factors that influence a student's grades in high school. For example, one student may have a harder course load than another student with higher grades. It is unfair to compare grades from different level classes. Perhaps a student does not do well on tests, but is an excellent student in class. Participation and the ability to speak one's mind are very beneficial in a career, yet that is not reflected by grades. Furthermore, if a student has an inborn proficiency in a subject (and gets good grades), it is unfair to assume that that student works hard to achieve his or her scores. An average student works harder and may still not get the same scores. Hard work and dedication are important factors in choosing an employee, but these factors cannot always be relayed by a report card.

There are other factors besides grades that play a role in whether a student is right for a job. The applicant may have experience in the field of interest, but the proposed system would not take this into account. Perhaps a student has been a volunteer or has been active in clubs and organizations outside of school. By looking at his or her track record with reference to involvement in organizations, the student's ability to follow through would be noted. This is an important factor to take into account when hiring a worker.

Also, grades do not indicate strength of personal character, an important determinant in the selection of an employee. One must not make the generalization that a student with good grades is also a good person, and that a student with poor grades is not a good person. Only a personal interview can give the employer some sense of personal character of the worker. Positive interactions with other workers are vital to the success of a business.

Finally, by locking in different salaries and pay rates based on high school grades, the employer is creating unnecessary competition and tension in the workplace. A worker with a lower salary may not work as hard, as a result. The worker with the lower salary might be treated differently, or unfairly, by the employer by not being encouraged to work up to potential.

Thank you for your attention to this matter. Perhaps now an employee will be viewed as a person, and not as a report card. Everyone deserves a fair chance.

Analysis

This essay would receive a relatively good evaluation because it expresses a clear and thoughtful opinion, it is well organized, and it is excellent in its development; on the other hand, the essay is not always focused on the specific topic. The letter begins well, with a clear statement of position, and the first section makes several important points about the limited significance of grades. Note, however, that the argument shifts from a discussion of how workers should be paid to how they should be hired in the first place. The second section makes several good points, but it too refers to *hiring* workers. The writer comes back to the topic of differentiated pay only in the third full paragraph.

If the writer had followed her statement of opinion with a *because* statement and a summary of her main points, she could have established the focus needed. This writer clearly took time to gather good examples and reasons, but she did not always show how they related to the topic. The task directed the student to write a letter to an editor and to write *the body of the letter only*, but such letters are really essays of argument and must have focus and coherence to be effective. Composing "letters" of this kind is a very good way to practice writing persuasive essays.

WRITING FROM A PROMPT

On many examinations and in high school or college courses, you will encounter the term *prompt*. This term is used to refer in general to any set of directions for a writing task. In the theater, the prompter is the one who gives an actor or singer in danger of forgetting his or her lines the phrase that he or she needs to remember to continue the performance. In writing, a prompt serves to recall ideas or stimulate discussion. A prompt is also meant to inspire, or even provoke. A prompt may be in the form of a task and directions, as in the examples above, or it may be in the form of a quote or even a photograph—anything that offers the writer a subject and a reason to produce a piece of writing.

Here are two examples of persuasive writing where the prompt was in the form of a quote only; the writers had to establish controlling ideas and develop the examples on their own.

"All the World's a Stage"

William Shakespeare once wrote, "all the world's a stage and all the people players . . ." This well-known phrase has stuck in people's minds through time because theater is a prominent medium in society; whether it's an amphitheater in ancient Rome or Broadway in New York City, crowds of people are drawn to the theater every day.

The theater appeals to people for many different reasons. Some attend the theater to escape from the harsh realities of life for a little while. While sitting in a dark auditorium and watching trials and disputes played by live actors in front of you, it is very easy to forget your own problems. Other people find the theater simply entertaining. Plays and musicals involve audiences because they stimulate the senses and the mind. And some people go to the theater as a social event.

But theater is not only something to be watched. For many people, theater is their life. Every day, more and more people are becoming actors and actresses in hopes of becoming rich and famous. And for some people, that dream actually comes true. Many actors join the world of theater for their love of expressing themselves through their bodies, the tools of the trade. Nothing can compare to that adrenaline rush an actor gets just before he or she steps on stage in front of hundreds of people who all have their eyes focused on him or her, and the applause of an audience is all the gratitude some actors need to feel appreciated.

Many people don't realize that theater goes beyond the actors though, and that is where they are deceived. Sometimes the technical aspect of a production is more interesting than the acting is. A Broadway production can have a set with more complicated plans than a skyscraper building. Shows like "Phantom of the Opera" can have over twenty major trap doors and more than ninety minor ones. There are dozens of people in charge of sound, lighting, props, and costumes that no one ever sees or thinks about when sitting in the audience. There is just that wonderful feeling that these things just magically happen; no one seems to be responsible.

The theater is an art that will live on for a long time to come, as long as people take the time to support it. The magic of a show that enthralls most viewers, though, is a culmination of the hard work, time, and dedication of many people who never get credit for their actions. But Shakespeare was right because, for many people in the theater, all the world is a stage.

"All the World's a Stage"

All the world is indeed a stage. And we are the performers. Everything we do in life is a production, and we must constantly perform our best because, in life, there are no rehearsals. Each of us performs on a separate stage, some for a larger audience than others. But each performance, regardless of the size of the audience, is of equal importance, and each performer must meet the standard of life's most important critic—himself.

As a high school student, I often find that there exists much pressure to perform: pressure to perform academically, pressure to perform in sports, pressure to perform in social situations, and countless others. Furthermore, there are many individuals for whom I constantly must perform. At this juncture in life, parents, teachers, friends, and others comprise what I often perceive as an overwhelmingly large audience, which is sometimes overly critical.

As I grow older, I am learning to accept new responsibilities, and I find that my role in life is changing. Often in life, we cannot constantly adhere to a routine performance; sometimes we must improvise. The improvisation, or adjustment to new responsibility, is often difficult though of critical importance to a successful production. In life, I have come to expect the unexpected and have done my best to deal with new situations. As performers, we must not allow tragedy, depression, and self-doubt to unnerve us. Instead, we must cope, adjust, and continue to perform.

Throughout my performance I have received evaluation from many critics, some of which I have taken better than others. No matter how many critics we have, we should remind ourselves that we are our most important critics, for of life's performance we will make the ultimate evaluation. Even though all the world's a stage, each of us need be concerned with only one performance.

Analysis

The first essay stumbles at the beginning: The introduction has a central idea, but it is not well expressed and there is no coherence in the reference to ancient Rome. This essay reads like a first draft, and perhaps the writer was pressed for time. It would be improved not only in revision of the opening paragraph but also in the transitions. This writer begins too many sentences with *and* or *but*, and the language is not always fluent or precise. The writer, however, does establish organization and some unity in the opening of the second paragraph: "The theater appeals to people for many different reasons."

The writer also shows skill in development by moving from the role of theater for audiences to its importance for participants. The concluding sentence also works well because it relates the major part of the essay to a fresh meaning of the quote. In this case, a good conclusion rescues an essay with a weak introduction.

The second essay is effective because of the exceptional way in which the writer developed the topic as an extended metaphor. The essay is brief, but it is absolutely focused; every detail supports the central idea, the comparison of one's life to a dramatic performance. The writer has maintained a consistent point of view and has developed the topic in a creative way.

EVALUATING COMPOSITION

Every student has seen on a paper or an essay test the comment "develop this point more." The Regents rubric on page 229 is a reminder that one of the most important criteria in evaluating essays for class or for an exam is the extent to which <u>the topic has been developed</u> to achieve the writer's purpose. Simply to announce a subject and say that you have thoughts on that subject is not enough.

For any topic, the student must show skill in establishing a central idea and in creating an effective way to develop it. All compositions must be unified and expressed in fluent and precise language, and they must follow the conventions of standard written English. (See Guide to Standard Written English beginning on page 161.)

PREPARING FOR ESSAY EXAMS

Nearly all the writing you have done, both personal and for school, serves as preparation. Just as an athlete or musician practices regularly in order to have the skills to draw on in a performance, high school students are developing their skills whenever they compose written responses. Reflect on what you know your strengths and weaknesses are. To review, go over the essays and exams you have written in high school; note what is consistently strong and what needs revision; review carefully your teachers' comments.

Good writers are also readers. Read good writing, observe what makes it effective, emulate it, and imitate for practice what you admire. In serious magazines and in the editorial pages, letters to the editor, and Op-Ed sections of newspapers you can often find good essays of argument on current topics. (See also Recommended Reading on page 215 for suggested works and authors of nonfiction.)

To succeed in any assigned task, you need to know what is expected and how you will be evaluated. Review the Regents exam scoring guides, which describe the criteria for scoring the written responses.

WRITING ON TIMED EXAMINATIONS

If you are writing an essay for an examination, you do not have time for extensive preparation, but you can learn to condense the kind of thinking and notetaking you do for course assignments into a process for planning an examination response. How to begin?

Gather Your Ideas

First, be sure you understand the task or the meaning of the topic. One way to do that is to rephrase the question into a topic assertion. This may not be original, but if a restatement of the question serves as a topic sentence for your introduction and gets you started—use it! You may not use such statements in your final essay, but the fact that you can express them for yourself means you understand what the question expects or that you have something to say about the topic

If you are creating your own topic, be sure you know what you want to say about it. This may seem obvious, but only when you sketch or outline can you be sure you have sufficient material for an essay. Use the brainstorming techniques you have learned in class or workshops. For example, if you have practiced "freewriting" in the past or have written journal entries as a way of developing ideas, take a few minutes to address the topic in that way, without regard to organization or "getting it absolutely

119

right." Similarly, you can just note down in words or phrases everything the prompt brings to mind. It is better to note more ideas than you can use than to discover after twenty-five minutes that you have too few.

Organize

Second, take a few minutes to make a plan or outline. All essay writing requires this step. Do not leave it out, even on the SAT, in which you have only 25 minutes for the essay. The outline may consist of only phrases or a brief list to remind you of the points you want to make. Consider possible lines of argument. That is, answer for yourself the questions "How can I prove that? What information in the text (if given) can I quote or paraphrase as evidence? How can I show or persuade someone who is interested in what I have to say? What do I know or believe that will make my discussion convincing?" Finally, decide on the order that is best: chronological? sequence of cause and effect? order of importance or intensity? (Common methods of developing ideas in essays are reviewed, with examples, in Reading Nonfiction, Chapter 4.)

Compose

The essays you write for the Regents exam and for the SAT are, of course, "tests." You are not being asked to demonstrate acquired knowledge so much as you are to demonstrate how well you can communicate in standard written English what you understand about the given subjects and texts or what you think about a particular issue. What is being assessed is your ability to articulate a controlling idea and support it with reasons and appropriate examples. On the Regents exam, you must also be able to work from given texts and write for clearly defined purposes and audiences.

Concentrate on good development—not a finished product. An essay that reveals critical thinking and coherence and effectively develops several appropriate examples or reasons with command of sentence variety and language will receive a high score even if it remains somewhat unfinished or lacks a formal conclusion. Remember, on the SAT optional essay you are writing what will be evaluated as a first draft. Regents essays are viewed as somewhat more "finished," but those too are understood to have been written in only one sitting.

Edit as You Go

The time you take in planning is also well spent because on-demand writing requires you to edit and revise as you compose your response. If you still make spelling errors in commonly used words, make a deliberate effort to look for those errors and correct them on the exams. A few neatly corrected spelling or usage errors are not only acceptable, they reveal the writer's ability to edit his or her own work. (See Chapter 9 on Grammar and Usage and Chapter 10 on Punctuation.)

USING SYNONYMIES TO ENHANCE YOUR WRITING

Included in the expectations for any well-written essay is use of language that is vivid and appropriate; the rubrics for scoring Regents essays include "use of original, fluent, and precise language." The term *synonymy* refers to words that can be grouped according to general meaning; that is, they all denote or describe a specific instance of a general concept. Reviewing and creating synonymies will help you develop the vivid and precise language characteristic of good writing. Below are some examples of synonymies for commonly used but often vague or overused expressions.

to cause

bring about	generate	originate	raise
create	give rise to	persuade	spawn
effect	incite	produce	
engender	invent	promote	
excite	lead to	provoke	

to change

adapt	develop	grow	revise
adjust	deviate	mature	rework
alter	differ	metamorphose	transform
amend	digress	modify	turn (into)
become	diverge	modulate	vary
convert	diversify	mutate	
correct	edit	progress	
depart	evolve	remake	

to look upon someone/something

analyze	discern	judge	scrutinize
appraise	dismiss	observe	stereotype
censure	distinguish	perceive	summarize
classify	esteem	ponder	typecast
conclude	evaluate	reckon	value
condemn	honor	regard	view
consider	hypothesize	review	watch
deem	infer	ruminate	

121

to look down upon someone/something

belittle	diminish	frown upon	ridicule
censure	discredit	have disdain for	scorn
condescend	disfavor	hold inferior	shame
condemn	disgrace	humiliate	shun
degrade	disparage	ignore	taunt
demote	disregard	jeer	vilify
depreciate	show disrespect	mock	
deride	embarrass	rebuke	
devalue	find fault with	reject	

bad

abhorrent	detrimental	inequitable	scandalous
atrocious	devilish	infamous	scurrilous
awful	dirty	inferior	shameless
base	disquieting	loathsome	sinful
belittling	evil	malevolent	sinister
blemished	false	malign	slanderous
calumnious	fiendish	marred	sour
catastrophic	foul	mean	spiteful
contemptible	fraudulent	merciless	spoiled
corrupt	grotesque	monstrous	squalid
counterfeit	hateful	nefarious	tasteless
criminal	heinous	negative	terrible
cruel	hellish	notorious	unethical
damaged	hideous	odious	unscrupulous
deceptive	horrible	ominous	vile
defective	horrid	perverse	villainous
defiled	horrific	putrid	wicked
delinquent	immoral	rotten	
depraved	imperfect	ruthless	
despicable	impish	scabrous	

effective

capable	dazzling	forceful	persuasive
cogent	dramatic	impressive	potent
commanding	effectual	influential	powerful
compelling	efficacious	lively	strong
convincing	emotional	moving	telling

caring

affectionate	devoted	giving	selfless
benevolent	doting	goodhearted	sympathetic
bountiful	empathetic	humane	tender
compassionate	empathic	kind	thoughtful
concerned	fond	loving	warm
courteous	generous	philanthropic	warmhearted

due to

as a consequence of	because of	from	on account of
	by reason of	in light of	resulting from
as a result of	caused by	in view of	
because	following from	induced by	

hard/difficult

arduous	fatiguing	intricate	strong
bitter	galling	labyrinthine	tiresome
challenging	grievous	mighty	toilsome
complex	grim	oppressive	tough
daunting	harsh	relentless	unattainable
demanding	Herculean	resistant	unbending
enigmatic	impenetrable	rigorous	uncompromising
esoteric	impossible	serious	unyielding
exacting	impregnable	severe	wearisome
exhausting	inflexible	sharp	
exigent	insurmountable	strenuous	

sad/depressing (depressed)

abject	dejected	forsaken	somber
aching	desolate	gloomy	sorrowful
aggrieved	despairing	joyless	tormenting
bereaved	disconsolate	lugubrious	tragic
bereft	discontent	melancholy	unhappy
bleak	distraught	miserable	upset
blue	distressing	morose	wretched
cheerless	down	painful	
dark	forlorn	saddening	

same

akin	compatible	generic	parallel
alike	conformable	homogeneous	photocopy
allied	conforming	identical	related
analogous	congruent	imitation	replica
associated	consonant	indiscernible	same
clone	copy	inseparable	shared
cognate	correspondent	interchangeable	similar
collective	corresponding	joint	synonymous
common	duplicate	like	tantamount
comparable	equal	matching	twin
comparative	equivalent	mutual	

A GLOSSARY OF TERMS FOR WRITING*

anecdote   A brief story or account of a single experience, often biographical, which illustrates something typical or striking about a person. Anecdotes, like parables, are effective as vivid, specific examples of a general observation or quality.

argument   The development of reasons, examples to support a thesis; narrowly, to outline a position on an issue or problem with the intent to clarify or persuade. Argument is also used in a broad sense to refer to the way a writer develops any topic.

audience   For the writer this term refers to the intended reader. Awareness of an audience determines, for example, what the writer may assume a reader already knows, level of diction, and tone.

coherence   A piece of writing has coherence when the logical relationship of ideas is evident and convincing. In a coherent discussion, statements and sections follow one another in a natural, even inevitable way. A coherent discussion hangs together; an incoherent one is scattered and disorganized.

cohesion   This refers to the grammatical and usage aspects of writing. **Cohesive** writing means that the connection of ideas within each sentence and at the paragraph level is clear and that the writing follows the conventions of standard written English.

controlling idea   This refers to the writer's thesis or main idea. It asserts what the writer has to say <u>about</u> the topic or question.

conventions   These are the "rules" or common guidelines for punctuation, spelling, and usage.

description   The expression in words of what is experienced by the senses. Good description recreates what is felt, seen, heard—sensed in

---

*Many of the terms in this glossary are also discussed in Chapter 4, Reading Prose.

any way. We also use the term describe to mean *identify, classify, characterize,* even for abstract ideas. Description permits readers to recreate the subject in their own imaginations.

development   This refers to the choice and elaboration of examples, reasons, or other details that support an argument or illustrate a controlling idea. (See also the rubric for scoring Regents essays in Appendix D.)

diction   This refers to word choice. Diction may be formal or informal, complex or simple, elegant or modest, depending on the occasion and the audience. The language we use in casual conversation is different from the language we use in formal writing. The good writer uses language that is varied, precise, and vivid; the good writer has resources of language to suit a wide range of purposes.

exposition   The development of a topic through examples, reasons, details, which explain, clarify, show, instruct—the primary purpose of exposition is to convey information. Much of the writing assigned to students is referred to as expository writing: Through exposition you can demonstrate what you have learned, discovered, understood, appreciated.

focus   This refers to the way a writer contains and directs all the information, examples, ideas, reasons in an essay on the specific topic.

narrative   Because it tells a story, narrative has chronological order. Narrative method is commonly used in exposition when examples are offered in a chronological development.

position paper   A form of persuasive writing, a position paper is meant to generate support for an issue or cause; the essay is based on specific evidence that can be cited to support the writer's argument. A position paper may also evaluate solutions or suggest courses of action.

prompt   This refers to a set of directions for a writing task; may also be a quote or passage meant to stimulate a piece of writing.

tone   In writing, tone refers to the attitude of the writer toward the subject and/or toward the reader. Tone may range from *harsh and insistent* to *gentle and reflective.* There is as much variety of tone in writing as there is in human feeling. Some pieces, essays of opinion, for example, usually have a very distinct tone; other works, especially in fiction or personal expression, may have a more subtle and indirect tone. (See discussion of Tone on page 65 in Reading Prose and on page 86 in Reading Poetry.)

transition   Words or phrases used to link ideas and sections in a piece of writing. Common transitions include *first, second . . . in addition . . . finally; on the other hand, moreover, consequently, therefore.* Transitions make the development of an argument clear.

unity   In the narrowest sense, unity refers to focus: The ideas and examples are clearly related to the topic and to one another. In the largest sense, unity refers to a feature of our best writing: All elements—ideas, form, language, and tone—work together to achieve the effect of a complete and well-made piece.

Chapter 8

VOCABULARY

Formal vocabulary study may begin as early as kindergarten; associating meaning with different sounds begins virtually at birth. As all students have discovered, however, there always seem to be new words to learn. Every novel, essay, or newspaper article we read is likely to include some new expressions or unfamiliar words. Deliberately studying new words and preparing for tests on them is certainly one way to expand our vocabularies, and every serious student has developed a method for such study. But if you do not continue to use those new words—that is, read, speak, and write with them—they may be forgotten soon after the test.

The thousands of words you *know* were acquired through repeated use over time and through association with their contexts, that is, through reading and listening. As you study vocabulary words associated with a course in English, social studies, or science, you are learning them in a context, and you are also expanding your reading and writing vocabularies. Every word you study should create some kind of image for you: try to associate it with a phrase, an experience or feeling, an object or person, an action or incident. If you have no image, you do not truly know the word yet.

The vocabulary you are expected to know and use, and that will be assessed on the Regents ELA, the SAT, and the ACT exams, is the language of literary authors, essayists, historians, and scientists. On the Regents ELA exam, this means that your mastery of relevant vocabulary will be assessed through questions about the meanings of words within the extended reading comprehension passages. You will also be expected to understand how particular words or expressons establish tone and clarify an author's meaning in the texts for analysis. This shift in how vocabulary is assessed represents a shared goal of the Common Core aligned state exams (Regents, PARCC, SBAC) and the SAT and ACT. For high school students, this means less need to study exotic and unfamiliar vocabulary in isolation; rather, students will need to be able to understand—and use—what is called academic language.

In the next section, you will find examples of what is meant by academic language. At the end of the chapter, you will find three collections of words to review as well. The first represents words that have been tested on Regents exams over several years. The second is a list compiled by high school students from their reading of the Op-Ed pages of *The New York Times* and other sources. The third, from published book reviews, was also compiled by students. Each list offers the thoughtful reader and writer a rich source of vocabulary in current use.

ACADEMIC LANGUAGE

Academic language is the language you use to express understanding of texts in class discussion, lecture, and writing. It is the language of interpretation, analysis, evaluation, and explanation. This term also refers to the language of a particular subject or discipline: literature, history, biology, economics, art, and so on. Reviewing the glossaries of literary and poetic terms and the terms for writing is another way of strengthening your command of academic language.

Here is a list of **verbs**, followed by their noun and adjective forms, commonly used to express how nonfiction texts are written and how arguments are developed. You will recognize many of these terms from the list of What Writers Do at the beginning of Chapter 4.

allege	allegation	alleged, allegedly
analyze	analysis	analytic, analytically
apply	application	
argue	argument	argumentative
arrange	arrangement	
articulate		
assemble		
assert	assertion	assertive
assess	assessment	
associate	association	
assume	assumption	
categorize	category	categorical
cite	citation	
characterize	characterization	
claim	(a/the) claim	
clarify	clarification	
classify	classification	
compare	comparison	
compile	compilation	
complement	(a/the) complement	complementary
compose	composition	
comprehend	comprehension	comprehensive
conclude	conclusion	conclusive
construct	construct, construction	
contend	contention	contentious
contradict	contradiction	contradictory
contrast	contrast	contrasting
correlate	correlation	correlative
criticize	criticism	critical, critically
critique	(a/the) critique	

debate	(a/the) debate	debatable
deduce	deduction	deductive, deductively
defend	defense	defensive
define	definition	definitive
demonstrate	demonstration	demonstrative
derive	derivation	derivative
design	(a/the) design	
develop	development	
differentiate	differentiation	
discern	discernment	discerning
discover	discovery	
discuss	discussion	
distinguish	distinction	distinguished
elaborate	elaboration	elaborate, elaborately
emphasize	emphasis	
estimate	estimation	
evaluate	evaluation	
exaggerate	exaggeration	
examine	examination	
exclude	exclusion	
explain	explanation	
explore	exploration	exploratory
focus	(a/the) focus	
form	(a/the) form	formal, formally
formulate	formulation	
frame		
generalize	generalization	
highlight	highlight	
hypothesize	hypothesis	hyhpothetical
identify	identification	
illustrate	illustration	
imply	implication	
include	inclusion	inclusive
infer	inference	inferential, inferentially
influence	influence	influential
inquire	inquiry	
integrate	integration	
interpret	interpretation	interpretive
introduce	introduction	
investigate	investigation	
judge	judgment	judgmental, judgmentally
mean	meaning	meaningful
modify	modification	
observe	observation	
oppose	opposition	

organize	organization	
originate	origin	original
outline	(a/the) outline	
paraphrase	paraphrase	
persuade	persuasion	persuasive
predict	prediction	predictive
presume	presumption	presumptive
project	projection	
propose	proposition	
recall	recollection	
refer	reference	referential
report	report	
represent	representation	
respond	response	responsive
review	review	
select	(a/the) selection	selective, selectively
sequence	(a/the) sequence	sequential, sequentially
specify	specification	
speculate	speculation	speculative
state	statement	
structure	(a/the) structure	structural, structurally
suggest	suggestion	suggestive
summarize	summary	summarily
support	support	supportive
suppose	supposition	supposed, supposedly
symbolize	symbol	symbolic
synthesize	synthesis	
translate	translation	
utilize	utilization	
vary	variation	
verify	verification	

Note: The -ed (past participle) forms of all these verbs are also used as modifiers: *assembled, classified, identified*, and so on. The adjective/adverb forms listed previously are widely used as separate forms and some have differences in meaning from the verb and noun forms.

Here is a list of **nouns and adjectives** used to identify and describe rhetorical methods as well as a writer's tone and purpose:

abstraction	abstract
analogy	analogous
approach	
	appropriate
	approximate

argument	argumentative
aspect	
audience	
authenticity	authentic
background	
chronology	chronological
coherence	coherent
concision	concise
	concrete
consequence	consequentially
consistency	consistent, consistently
constancy	constant
context	contextually
credibility	credible
criterion/criteria	
detail	
diction	
dimension	
direction	direct
effect	effective
element	elemental
equivalence	equivalent
	essential
evidence	evident
example	
excerpt	
exercise	
expository	exposition
extract	extraction
fact	factual
factor	
feature	
	figurative, figuratively
fragment	
frequence	frequent
general	generally
graph	graphic
highlight	
image	
inclination	
indirection	indirect
intention	intentional
irony	ironic
irrelevance	irrelevant

131

literalness	literal, literally
logic	logical, logically
metaphor	metaphorical
method	*methodical
motivation	motivating
narration	narrative
narrator	
objectivity	objective
opinion	opinionated
order	ordered
origin	original
pattern	
perspective	
plagiarism	plagiarized
plan	
plausibility	plausible
point of view	
possibility	possible
primary	
priority	*prior
probability	probable
process	
profile	
prompt	
proposition	
purpose	purposeful
relevance	relevant
revision	revised
sequence	sequential
series	
signal	
significance	significant
source	
speaker	
specificity	specific
strategy	strategic
structure	
style	stylistic
subject	*subjective
subsequence	subsequent
substitution	substitute
succinctness	succinct
summary	
survey	

technique	technical
theme	
thesis	
tone	
topic	*topical
transition	
uniqueness	unique
validity	valid
variation, variety	varied
viewpoint	
voice	

*Note: As in the list of verbs, some nouns and adjectives with a common derivation may have differences in meaning.

Throughout *Let's Review*, you will find sources of what is meant by academic language, along with glossaries of terms for fiction, nonfiction, poetry, and writing. Your ability to recognize examples of various literary and rhetorical elements strengthens your comprehension; you will also be expected to use them appropriately when you write essays of argument and text analysis.

UNFAMILIAR AND ARCHAIC LANGUAGE

Here is some of the vocabulary you will encounter as you read and discuss what are considered authentic or historically significant texts. Some of the words are familiar in their current use; but, the meanings offered here are from texts as early as the 16th century, including works of Shakespeare, and are also found in 18th, 19th , and early 20th century writings in English.

Verbs

address	to consider, think about, speak to
apprise	to give verbal or written notice
behold	to observe with care, witness
breach	to break through
discover	to learn, to disclose
dispose	to be inclined
divine	to guess, figure out, foresee
endeavor	to try, attempt a task or challenge
fashion	to form or make something

forbear	to pause, delay, avoid voluntarily or decline to do something
have	to prefer, think, believe, consider, think about
peruse	to read or examine with care
relish	to enjoy, take delight in
smart	to cause pain
suffer	to put up with, tolerate
thirst	to have an intense desire for something
thwart	to oppose, frustrate or defeat
want	to fail, be deficient or lacking
witness	to see by personal presence, observe directly
wreak	to revenge, throw or dash with violence

Nouns

appendages	arms and legs
appetite	desire, interest
ardor	passion
aught, naught	anything, nothing
conveyance	vehicle
countenance	look, appearance
dominion	area of authority, knowledge or power
eloquence	artful, expressive speech
faculties	senses, aptitudes, abilities
fashion	a distinctive or habitual manner
forebearance	patience, tolerance
grievance	suffering, distress; grudge, resentment
humor	temperament
idleness	unimportance, uselessness, emptiness
infirmity	weakness, disorder; personal failing
justice	accuracy, wisdom
labors	efforts
nature	disposition, inherent quality
perusal	reading, consideration
petulance	irritability, contrariness
rapture	extreme joy or pleasure; passionate intensity
sensibility	acuteness of perception; capacity to feel or perceive
temper	disposition of mind
vanity	emptiness, untruth, unfruitful labor
virtue	strength of character, bravery, valor; moral excellence

Adjectives

base	corrupt, vile
bumptious	arrogant, brash
clever	intelligent, skilled
familiar	agreeable in conversation, not formal or distant
idle	unimportant, trivial
imbued	tinged, affected with
infirm	weak of mind, body, or will
petulant	pert, wanton, sour in temper
prevailing	having effect; persuading, succeeding
puerile	childish, trifling, weak
rough	coarse in manners, uncivil; terrible, dreadful
sensible	having perception by the mind or the senses
sober	serious, calm, subdued
stout	bold, intrepid, brave
sublime	high in excellence, lofty, grand
wholesome	contributing to health of mind, conducive to good

STUDYING NEW WORDS

Learning in Context

Even the most diligent student cannot reasonably expect simply to memorize—out of context—the hundreds, even thousands, of words on Regents and SAT lists. Recent studies also confirm that vocabulary study confined to lists of words without a context or pattern of association—as with a particular work of literature, for example—does not result in long-term retention. Moreover, the practice of recording dictionary definitions alone gives only general and sometimes misleading information about the meaning and correct use of words. Learning words means learning their precise meanings, connotations, and appropriate context.

Unless you are working with an unabridged dictionary, which often includes illustrative examples in sentences or phrases, you are likely to find in a desk dictionary only brief definitions, general in nature, and possibly a list of synonyms. This limited information is valuable as a *reference,* especially if you are reading a passage and need to know a word's meaning in order to understand the passage. Learning the full meaning of unfamiliar words, however, requires more active study. In the sections below you will find recommendations for ways to prepare and organize your vocabulary study.

ROOTS AND PREFIXES FROM LATIN AND GREEK

Although English is certainly not derived from Greek and Latin only, familiarity with the Greek or Latin forms in English words is often useful to students taking vocabulary tests. Recognition of root meanings in particular may help you determine the correct answer for a word you may not be sure of. Even more important, however, is the value of knowing the Latin and Greek origins of English when you are first studying new words. When you are aware of the meanings of the individual parts of a word you often can form an image for it. Think of the Latin root *spect*, for example. This root means *look into, observe, behold* and, with variations in spelling *spec* and *spic,* is the base of many English words: *inspect, introspect, expect, respect, speculate, spectacle, spectacular, conspicuous*—and many others. Even the word *spy* is related to this Latin root.

When you are looking up words in the dictionary, do not skip over the etymology—the section that shows you in abbreviated form the origin and history of a word. Grouping words by related origin can be a very useful way to organize when you are studying large groups of new words; by using their common origin, you will learn to associate a new word with others you already know. It is the process of forming associations in meaning, forming images, and knowing contexts that permits you to learn efficiently—and to remember—the words you study. (Familiarity with roots and prefixes is also very helpful in understanding spelling patterns, as you will see in Chapter 11.)

Listed below, with examples, are many of the Latin and Greek roots found in English. (As you review the meanings of these roots, provide additional examples from your own knowledge; you should also guess about possible examples—then look them up in a dictionary to confirm your guess.) This process is a demonstration of what is meant by *active* vocabulary study. It means you are thinking about a word and associating it with others you know.

As you examine the list of Greek and Latin roots common in English, you should be struck by how familiar many of these forms are. You should also note that all these roots denote specific actions or ideas. Knowing the meanings of these elements as you study new words, or review familiar ones, will give you specific images or experiences to associate with them. This in turn will make the meaning of many words more vivid and easier to remember than will an abstract definition or list of synonyms alone.

LATIN ROOTS

Forms	Meaning	Examples
alter	other	altercation, alternative
ami (amicus)	friend	amiable, amicable, amity
amor	love	amorous, enamored
anima	breath, mind, spirit	animation, unanimous, inanimate, animosity
bell (bellum)	war	bellicose, belligerent, antebellum
cad (cadere), cid	to fall	decay, decadence, deciduous
cap, cip	contain	captivate, capacity, capable
capit (caput)	head	capital, capitol, recapitulate
cede, ceed, cess (cedere)	to move, yield	proceed, accede, exceed, precede, excess, success, procession
cept (capere)	to take, seize, hold	intercept, reception, accept
cid, cis (caedere)	to cut, kill	precise, incisive, homicide
clam, claim (clamare)	to cry, call out	exclaim, proclaim, clamor
clud, clus (claudere)	to shut, close	include, exclusion, recluse
cred (credere)	to believe, loan, trust	creditable, incredible, credulous
culp (culpa)	fault, guilt	culpable, exculpate
cur, curs (currere)	to run	course, cursor, current, incur, precursor, recur
dict (dicere)	to say, tell	dictator, diction, edict, predict
doc (docere)	to teach	doctor, docile, indoctrinate
duc, duct (ducere)	to lead	deduce, induction, conduct
err (errare)	to go, lead astray	error, erroneous, erratum
err (errer)	to travel, wander	errand, arrant, erratic
fac, fact, fect, fic (facere)	to make, do	affect, defect, effect, facsimile, factor, artificial, deficit
fer (ferre)	to bear, carry	inference, offer, reference
fid (fidelitas)	faith, loyalty	infidel, perfidious, diffident
flect, flex (flectere)	to bend	reflex, reflection, flexibility
flu, fluct, flux (fluere)	to flow	affluent, fluctuation, fluent, influence, influx
fund (fundare) (fundus)	to base, bottom	(to) found, fundamental, profundity
fus (fundere)	pour	effusive, foundry, fusion
gen (genus) (genare)	kind, sort, birth, to beget	genre, heterogenous, genetic, generate, progenitor, genocide
grad, gress (gradus)	to walk, go, stage or step	digress, graduate, progress, grade, gradient, retrograde
greg (gregis)	flock, herd, group	egregious, gregarious, integrate
her, hes (haerere)	to cling, stick	adhesive, coherence, inherently
ject, jet (jacere)	to throw	inject, projection, jettison
jud, jur, jus (jus)	to judge; to swear just, right; law	abjure, adjudicate, prejudge, jury, justification, perjury
lat (latus)	borne, carried	correlative, related, superlative
leg (legis, lex)	law	legality, legislative
locus	place	location, locale, locomotive

137

locu, loqu (loqui)	to speak	eloquent, loquacious, soliloquy,
locutor	speaker	interlocutor, locution, obloquy
lude (ludere)	to play	interlude, ludicrous, prelude
mit, mitt, mis,	to dispatch, send,	emit, permit, remit, submissive,
miss (mittere)	to let go	commission, missile, permission
mob, mot (movere)	to move	demote, motivate, promote,
		commotion, mobility
mor, mort (mortis)	death	immortal, mortality, mortified
ped (pedis)	foot	expeditious, impede, pedestrian
pel, puls (pellere)	to drive, push	compel, dispel, impulse,
		repel, compulsive, repellent
pend, pens	to hang, weigh, pay	append, compensate, dependent,
(pendere)		impending, pension, pensive
ple, plet (plere)	to fill	complete, complement, deplete
plen (plenus)	full	plentiful, replete
pon, pos, posit	to place, put	component, depose, propose,
(ponere)		juxtapostion, impose, opponent
port (portare)	to carry	comport, deportment,
		purport, portable, portfolio
pot, poten,	to be able	impossibility, omnipotent,
poss (posse)		potential
rad (radius)	root, spoke (wheel)	eradicate, radical, radiation
rect, reg (regula)	right, straight	direction, rectified, regal
(regire)	to guide, rule	regimen, regime
rupt (rumpere)	to break, burst	disrupt, corrupt, interruption
sat (satis)	enough	dissatisfy, insatiable, saturated
sci (scire)	to know	conscience, omniscient,
		prescience, scientific
scrib, script (scribere)	to write	describe, inscription, scripture
sect (sectare)	to cut	dissect, intersection
secu, sequ (sequi)	to follow	consequence, obsequious,
		sectarian, sequel
sed, sid, sess	to sit	dissidence, possess, residual,
(sedere)		sedation, sedentary
sent, sens (sentire)	to feel	consensus, insensitive, sentient
son (sonus)	sound	consonant, dissonance, sonic,
		sonogram, sonority, unison
spec, spect, spic	to look at, observe	auspicious, conspicuous, expect,
(spectare)		inspect, respect, spectacular
spir, spirit	to breathe	inspiration, respiratory, spirit
sta, state, stit (stare)	to stand	constitute, instability, obstacle,
		stability, status
strict, string	to draw tight	constrict, restriction, stringent
(stringere)		
sume, sump	to take	assume, consume, presumption
(sumere)		
tact, tang, ting,	to touch	contact, contiguous, intangible,
tig (tangere)		tactile, tangential

ten, tain (tenere)	to hold, keep	abstain, pertain, restrain, tenacious, untenable
tend, tens (tendere)	to reach, stretch	contend, intensity, portent, pretentious, tendency
tort (torque)	to twist	contortion, extort, tortuous
tract (trahere)	to draw, pull	distract, intractible, protracted, retraction
ver (veritas)	truth	aver, veracity, verification
vers, vert (vertere)	to turn	adverse, aversion, diversity, inadvertent, reversion, subvert, version, versification
vid, vis (videre) (video)	to see	evident, improvident, supervise, revision, visage, visionary
vit, viv (vivere) (viva)	to live; life	revival, survive, vivacious, unviable
vinc, vict (vincere)	to conquer	conviction, eviction, invincible
voc, voke (vocare)	to call	advocate, equivocal, invocation, provocative, revoke, vocation
volv, volu (volvere)	to roll, turn	convoluted, evolution, revolving

GREEK ROOTS

Forms	Meaning	Examples
anthrop	man, humankind	anthropocentric, misanthropist, philanthropy
arch	rule, ruler	anarchy, patriarchal
astr, astron	star	astronomical, disastrous
bio	life, living things	biography, microbiology
chron	time	anachronistic, chronic
cosm (kosmos)	order, universe	cosmic, microcosm
demo	among the people	democratic, demography
gen	birth, race	genesis, progeny
gno, gnosis	know	agnostic, diagnosis, gnomic
gram, graph	write, writing	epigrammatic, biography
log, logue	word, reason	analogy, illogical, prologue
lect, lex	language, speak	dialect, lexical
lysis	dissolution, destruction	catalyst, paralysis
metr	measure	diametric, metrical
morph	form, shape	amorphous, metamorphose
mne, mnes	memory, remember	amnesty, mnemonic
onym	a name	eponymous, synonym
opti, optic	eye, sight	optical, synopsis
path (pathos)	feeling, suffering	apathy, empathetic, pathetic
ped	child	pediatrician, pedagogy, pedantic
phon	sound	euphony, phonetic, symphonic

Prefixes are units of one or two syllables that are not words in themselves but that have distinct meanings. The addition of a prefix to the beginning of an existing word (what is called a *stem* or *root)* creates a word with an additional meaning. The spelling variations for many of the prefixes listed below are reminders that in English the spelling of a prefix will be altered to match the root to which it is attached. For example, *ad,* which means *to* or *toward*, is attached to many words in English; the *d* often changes to the first letter of the word to which it is added, making the resulting new forms easier to pronounce. (See the examples below as well as those in Chapter 11—Spelling.)

LATIN PREFIXES

Forms	Meaning	Examples*
a, ab, abs	away, from	abdicate, absence, abstraction
a, ad (ac, af, al, etc.)	to, toward	absent, acclimate, adherent, alliteration, assign, attribution
ambi	both, around	ambiance, ambiguous, ambidextrous, ambivalent
ante	before	antebellum, antecedent
bene, ben	good, well	beneficial, beneficent, benign
circum	around	circumnavigate, circumstances, circumlocution
co (col, com, cor)	together	coincidence, collaboration, commiserate, correspondence
contra, contro, counter	against, opposite	contradiction, controversy, counterfeit, counteract
de	away, down, from	deduction, deterrence, deviate
dis (di, dif)	apart, away; not; separate	disavow, disdain, disappear, disregard, disperse, discern
en (var. of in)	make, put into	enable, enhance, encourage
equ, equi	equal, even	equable, equanimity, equivalence, equivocate
ex (e, ef)	away from, out	efface, effective, ejection, exodus, expiration
in (il, im, ir)	in, within	immersion, impending, innate
in (il, im, ir)	not, without	illegible, imprudent, incognito
inter	among, between	intercede, intermediary, interim
magn	great	magnificence, magnanimous
mal	bad, evil	malevolent, malice, malefactor, malign, malignant
ob (oc, of, op)	to, toward; against; over; totally	objection; obdurate, obnoxious; obfuscate; obsolete, obliterate
omni	all	omnipotent, omniscient
per	completely; through	perceive, perdurable, pervasive
post	after	posterity, posthumous

pre	before, in advance	pre-empt, preclude, premonition
pro	before, forward	proclivity, prodigy, profane
re	again	reiterate, reverberate, retort, revise, remember
retro	backward	retrogression, retroactive
se	apart, aside	secession, sedition, select
sub (suf, sup, sus)	from below, under	subsidize, substandard, suffuse, suppress, sustenance
super	above, over	supercilious, superfluous, supervise, supersede
tra, trans	across, beyond	transgression, transcend

GREEK PREFIXES

Forms	Meaning	Examples
a, an	not, without	agnostic, anarchy, apathetic
ana	back, backward according to; through	anagram, anachronistic, anapest analogy, analysis
ant, anti	against, opposite	antipathy, antithesis, antipodes
auto	self	autonomous, autocracy
cata	down	cataclysm, catalyst, catastrophe
dia	through, between	dialect, dialogue, diameter
dys	bad, ill, difficult	dysfunctional, dyspeptic
epi	upon	epicenter, epigram, epilogue
eu	good, well	euphemism, euphoria, eugenics
hetero	different	heterodox, heterogeneous
homo	alike, same	homogeneous, homonym
macro	large, long duration	macrocosm, macroscopic
meta, met	after, beyond; changed	metaphor, metaphysical, metamorphosis
micro	small	microscope, microbe
mon, mono	one, single	monotheism, monolith
pan	all, complete	panacea, pandemonium
pro	before; favorable	prophecy; propitiate
proto	first, primary	protagonist, prototype
sym, syn	together, with	symmetry, synergy, synopsis

* When you review the lists for study at the end of the chapter you will readily see how many words in English are formed with these prefixes. Use those lists to add to the examples offered here.

Here is the first group of vocabulary words from the Regents exams list on page 149. Note how many are formed from the Greek or Latin prefixes reviewed on the previous pages.

abdicate	**ad**monish	amorphous	**as**pire
aberrant	**ad**versity	**ana**chronistic	assay
abhorrent	**af**flict	**an**ecdotes	astute
abridgment	agrarian	animation	**a**sylum
absolve	**al**lot	**ap**pease	atrocious
acclaim	**al**lure	**ap**prehend	audacity
accost	**al**ly	arbitrator	**auto**nomous
accredit	**alter**cation	archaic	avarice
acme	amass	ardent	**a**verse
acquiesce	**ambi**ance	armistice	**a**version
acquittal	**ambi**dextrous	**ar**ray	avidly
adage	**ambi**guous	**ar**rogantly	azure
adhere	**ambi**valent	**as**cendancy	
adjunct	amnesty	ashen	

In many of these examples, the meaning of the original prefix has been absorbed into the meaning of the entire word, in **adage** and **allot**, for example. The highlighted prefixes illustrate, however, how extensively Greek and Latin forms are found in English.

A NOTE ON SYNONYMS AND USING A THESAURUS

As thoughtful students and careful writers know, synonyms are rarely equivalents. Synonyms are words closely related in meaning to a given word, but they should not be considered equally interchangeable with it.

Here is a list of synonyms for **acquiesce** that you might gather from a thesaurus:

accede	capitulate	concur	permit
accept	come to terms	conform	submit
agree to	with	consent	surrender
allow	comply with	give in	yield
assent	concede	grant	

This list is very helpful in enriching your understanding of the word, especially because it includes several terms that emphasize that there is a sense of giving in, of reluctance, in **acquiesce**. The closest synonyms in this list are *accede, come to terms with, conform, give in, yield. Capitulate, submit,* and *surrender* accurately reflect the connotation of the word, but they denote a more forceful sense of defeat than does *acquiesce*. The others, *accept, agree to, concur, consent, permit*, are less precise because they reflect only the general meaning and do not denote the sense of reluctance and the lack of enthusiasm inherent in **acquiesce**.

Learning to distinguish among variations in meaning and context is an important part of developing your vocabulary. It is also essential to the craft of good writing. In Chapter 6, Writing About Literature, and Chapter 7, Writing on Demand, you will find several *synonymies,* which are words grouped by general meaning or connotation. The purpose of the *synonymies* is to help you develop precision and variety in your own writing. You should review those as part of your vocabulary study as well.

ORGANIZING VOCABULARY STUDY

Another way to work with lists such as the ones at the end of this chapter is to *sort* them, much as you would sort playing cards. Depending on the card game you are playing, you might sort a hand by suit, by numerical sequence, or by kind. You can sort a group of words in various ways as well: by part of speech, by connotation, by human or abstract qualities, and so on. Many students create their own flash cards for the words they study, which makes sorting in various ways easy.

Here are some suggestions for how you might sort the first group of words from the Regents list (page 149). First, sort by part of speech. In the list below, the *verbs* are printed in bold type:

VERBS

abdicate	adversity	anecdote	asylum
aberrant	**afflict**	animation	atrocious
abhorrent	agrarian	**appease**	audacity
abridgment	**allot**	**apprehend**	autonomous
absolve	allure	arbitrator	avarice
acclaim	**ally**	archaic	averse
accost	altercation	ardent	aversion
accredit	**amass**	armistice	avidly
acme	ambiance	**array**	azure
acquiesce	ambidextrous	arrogantly	
acquittal	ambiguous	ascendancy	
adage	ambivalent	ashen	
adhere	amnesty	**aspire**	
adjunct	amorphous	**assay**	
admonish	anachronistic	astute	

143

Then classify the group of verbs further as either *transitive* or *intransitive;* that is, according to the nature of the action they denote and the nature of the objects, if any, they take. When you look up these words in a dictionary, they will be identified as *v.i.* or *v.t. Transitive verbs* (*v.t.*) take a direct object; the action is directed from the subject to an object. For example, "She *admonished* (scolded, warned) the unruly child" and "King Midas *amassed* (accumulated) a fortune in gold." *Direct objects,* of course, may be persons and living creatures, or they may be things, even abstractions: "She quickly *apprehended* the danger she was in."

Intransitive verbs (*v.i.*) denote actions that are contained within the subject or that signify what we call states of being: "He *adhered* strictly to his ethical principles." *Adhere* connotes a state of mind, an attitude.

The distinction between transitive and intransitive action is not always easily made, but one way to demonstrate the difference is to make an active statement passive. For example, we can reverse the statement "She admonished the child" and turn it into "The child was admonished by her." The statement above about King Midas can be expressed in the passive as "A fortune in gold was amassed by King Midas." Although transitive actions may be reversed in this way, intransitive actions do not reverse. For example, the sentence "The principles were adhered by him" has no meaning. Some verbs may function both as transitive and intransitive. A simple example is the verb *to sink*: "The small sailboat sank during the heavy storm" (*v.i.*), but "The submarine fired a torpedo that sank the enemy battleship." (*v.t.*).

Most verbs in this first group are transitive, so it would be useful to sort them by the kinds of objects they take; that is, whether they denote actions directed at persons or at things and abstractions. You would, of course, note this information as you look up each unfamiliar word in a dictionary. Here is the list of verbs further sorted:

ACTIONS DIRECTED AT PERSONS

to **absolve** (free from, relieve) someone of guilt or responsibility

to **acclaim** (praise, honor) a person's performance, action, or work

to **accost** (approach, confront) someone

to **admonish** (caution, scold) someone for misbehavior or inaction

to **afflict** (burden, attack) someone with suffering or illness

to **appease** (conciliate) a person, a nation, or a government

to **apprehend** (catch, capture) a suspect or a criminal

ACTIONS DIRECTED AT THINGS OR ABSTRACTIONS

to **abdicate** (relinquish, abandon) a throne, a responsibility

to **accredit** (certify, recognize) a school or university, the value of an idea

to **allot** (distribute, assign) funds, resources

to **amass** (gather, accumulate) a fortune, an army

to **append** (add, match) a section, passage, body of information

to **apprehend** (understand, comprehend, capture) an idea, a concept

to **articulate** (verbalize, clarify, explain) ideas, feelings, understanding

to **array** (arrange) a display, a number of objects

to **assay** (measure, evaluate) a task, a situation

to **assert** (declare, claim, affirm, profess) ideas, an opinion, a judgment

INTRANSITIVE ACTIONS

to **acquiesce** (give in to, agree reluctantly) in demands of others

to **adhere** (hold, cling to, comply) to demands or to principles

to **ally** (join, support) with another person, group, or nation

to **aspire** (strive, seek) to a goal, an achievement

For purposes of study, these verbs could be shuffled, and then resorted, by *connotation*. Which are generally positive in feeling and association, and which are negative? There are many words for which this is not a useful distinction, but appreciation of connotation is often essential to fully understanding the meaning of a word.

POSITIVE

absolve	accredit	ally
acclaim	adhere	aspire

NEGATIVE

abdicate	acquiesce	afflict
accost	admonish	appease

145

As you make your notes or compose your flash cards, be sure to include connotation if it is relevant. A dictionary usually does not define a word by its connotation; you must infer it from the meanings and examples offered.

NOUNS

The *nouns* are in bold type:

abdicate	**adversary**	anachronistic	aspire
aberrant	**adversity**	**anecdote**	**assay**
abhorrent	afflict	**animation**	assert
abridgment	affluent	appease	astute
absolve	agrarian	append	**asylum**
acclaim	allot	apprehend	atrocious
accost	**allure**	apprehensive	**audacity**
accredit	**ally**	**arbitrator**	autonomous
acme	**altercation**	archaic	**avarice**
acquiesce	amass	ardent	averse
acquittal	**ambiance**	**armistice**	**aversion**
adage	ambidextrous	**array**	avidly
adamant	ambiguous	arrogant	azure
adhere	ambivalent	articulate	
adjunct	**amnesty**	**ascendancy**	
admonish	amorphous	ashen	

As you look at a collection of nouns, try to group them in various ways based on the kinds of things or persons they name. Note that in this group only two, **adversary** and **arbitrator,** name persons. This list, however, includes several political or legal terms that would form a useful group for study:

acquittal
adversary (adversarial)
ally
amnesty

arbitrator (arbitration)
armistice
ascendancy
asylum

A small group of terms is related to literature:

abridgment   **adage**   **anecdote**

Other terms name attitudes or feelings. (Note the contrast in connotation here.)

POSITIVE

acclaim   **animation**

NEGATIVE

audacity   **aversion**   **avarice**

Finally, there are nouns that name forces, situations, conditions, and other concepts.

acme   **ambiance**   **allure**   **array**

ADJECTIVES

The *adjectives* are in bold type:

abdicate	adversary	**anachronistic**	aspire
aberrant	adversity	anecdote	assay
abhorrent	afflict	animation	assert
abridgment	**affluent**	appease	**astute**
absolve	**agrarian**	append	asylum
acclaim	allot	apprehend	**atrocious**
accost	allure	**apprehensive**	audacity
accredit	ally	arbitrator	autonomous
acme	altercation	**archaic**	avarice
acquiesce	amass	**ardent**	**averse**
acquittal	ambiance	armistice	aversion
adage	**ambidextrous**	array	avidly
adamant	**ambiguous**	**arrogant**	**azure**
adhere	**ambivalent**	articulate	
adjunct	amnesty	ascendancy	
admonish	**amorphous**	**ashen**	

Because adjectives modify—that is, qualify, limit, or describe—nouns, a useful way to group them is by the nature of what they describe. For example, some of the adjectives in the list above describe human behavior or *actions*:

aberrant   **abhorrent**   **atrocious**

(all strongly negative in connotation)

Several adjectives describe human *attitudes, feelings, aspects of character:*

NEGATIVE

adamant   ambivalent   arrogant

POSITIVE

ardent   astute   avid

Still others characterize *the way people appear or express themselves:*

ambiguous   ambivalent   apprehensive   averse

Language may be:

ambiguous   anachronistic   archaic

Two adjectives relate to color:

ashen   azure

One term, **ambidextrous,** describes a physical characteristic.

This particular group contains no adverb forms, but for many of the adjectives in the list, the adverb is formed by adding *-ly*. For example:

aberrantly	apprehensively	avidly
adamantly	astutely	
ambiguously	atrociously	

Reminder: If you prepare your own note cards for study, be sure to include all forms of the word. For example, your notes for **ambivalent** (adj.) would also include **ambivalence** (n.). This is how the lists of academic vocabulary on page 128 are organized.

These groups overlap and should be combined in different ways as you work through larger numbers of words. The process of sorting, or reshuffling, as new categories and associations occur to you is a very effective way to learn new words. Each time you sort, you are actively thinking about a word in a particular context and are associating it with other words; this process is essential to making a word a permanent part of your reading and writing vocabulary.

VOCABULARY FOR STUDY

Below are lists of words that have been collected from past Regents exams, Op-Ed pages, and book reviews. You will recognize many of them from the section on academic language.

Vocabulary from Regents Exams

abdicate	admonish	amorphous	aspire
aberrant	adversity	anachronistic	assay
abhorrent	afflict	anecdotes	astute
abridgment	agrarian	animation	asylum
absolve	allot	appease	atrocious
acclaim	allure	apprehend	audacity
accost	ally	arbitrator	autonomous
accredit	altercation	archaic	avarice
acme	amass	ardent	averse
acquiesce	ambiance	armistice	aversion
acquittal	ambidextrous	array	avid
adage	ambiguous	arrogantly	azure
adhere	ambivalent	ascendancy	
adjunct	amnesty	ashen	
badger	belied	blatant	breach
barrage	bemused	bleary	brevity
bask	benevolent	boisterous	
beguile	berate	brazen	
cache	charisma	commencement	converse
carnage	chasm	commiserate	convivial
celebrated	clandestine	conception	craven
chafe	clique	congeal	credence
chagrin	coalition	consecrate	crestfallen
charade	collate	constrict	cringe
dauntless	deified	desist	discreet
de facto	deluge	desolate	dissidence
debonair	delve	deter	dissuade
decrepit	demeaning	detest	divulge
deduce	denizen	diffuse	domain
deferred	depict	dilemma	dredge
deflect	deride	diminutive	dynamic
defunct	derogatory	discord	

eccentric
edify
eject
elicit
elude
elusive
embroil
eminence

encore
endorse
endow
enfeeble
enhance
ensnare
entail
entreaty

envoy
equanimity
equilibrium
equitable
equivocal
eradicate
erratic
escapade

euphoric
eviction
exemplary
exodus
exonerate
expedite
exploitation
exulted

facet
fallible
fanatic
fanfare
farcical

feasible
fiasco
fidelity
finesse
finite

flail
fleeting
forage
foreboding
formidable

fortitude
fortuitous
fracas
frugal
futility

garish
garrulous
gaudy
genial

genuine
geriatric
gesticulate
grapple

grate
gratuity
grievously
grisly

guise
guttural

hallowed
harangue

harrowing
heinous

heretical
hinder

homage
humid

idiosyncrasies
ignoble
illuminate
immutable
impartial
impending
imperative
imperceptible
imperiled
imperious

impertinent
imprudent
inadvertent
inaugural
incensed
incessant
incognito
incompetent
incorrigible
indignant

indisputably
induce
infernal
infringe
ingenuity
inherent
inimitable
innocuous
insatiable
insolent

insomnia
insubordinate
insurgent
inundated
invoked
irate
irksome
irrational
itinerant

jeer
jocular

jovial
juncture

jut

lacerated
lackluster
lament
languorously

latent
lateral
lavish
laxity

lesion
lineage
liquidate
loquacious

lucrative
lugubrious
lull

madcap	marauding	meticulous	mollify
maim	martial	militant	morose
malefactor	meager	misconstrue	mortify
malice	mediate	misgivings	mundane
malleable	melancholy	mitigate	muzzle
nefarious	niche	nostalgia	nuptial
negligible	nimble	notorious	nurture
nepotism	nonentity	nullification	
obliquely	omnipotent	optimum	override
obliterate	omniscient	oscillate	
obstinate	onslaught	oust	
oligarchy	opportune	ouster	
pacifism	perplexity	poise	profoundly
palatable	philanthropic	precariously	proponent
pandemonium	piety	precipice	protrude
parable	pinnacle	precludes	prowess
paraphrase	placid	prestige	proxy
penchant	plague	prevail	putrid
perjury	plausible	procrastinate	
perpetual	plight	prodigious	
qualms	quandary		
ramification	recalcitrant	reparation	revulsion
rampant	reciprocal	repercussion	roster
ramshackle	recoil	repress	rouse
rancid	recrimination	resolute	rue
rant	rectify	retort	ruinous
rapport	refute	revamped	russet
ravenous	reminiscent	reverberate	
sacrosanct	sheen	squalor	substantiate
salve	shortcomings	stalwart	subtlety
sanction	shrewd	stark	sullen
sanctity	singularly	stealthily	sumptuous
saunter	skeptical	strew	superfluous
scandalous	skulk	strut	suppress
scathing	sleek	subliminal	surcease
scrupulous	slipshod	submissive	surreptitious
scrutiny	smolder	subside	swagger
seedy	sporadic	subsidize	synopsis

tainted	throng	transient	trudge
tally	token	trauma	tumult
tawny	topple	traverse	
tenacity	transcend	trifling	

| unassuming | unnerve | unpalatable | utilitarian |
| uncanny | unobtrusive | unscrupulous | |

vanquish	verbatim	viable
variance	verbose	vigilance
vehement	veritable	virtually

waive	whack	wrangle
warily	wield	wrath
weather (vb.)	wily	writhe

yield

zenith

Vocabulary from Op-Ed Pages

a priori	ad hoc	amiss	arcane
abdicate	adamant	amorphous	archetype
aberration	addled	androgyny	archive
abrogation	aegis	annals	ardent
abysmal	affidavit	annotate	artifice
abyss	affront	anoint	ascribe
accede	aggrieved	antidote	assessment
acclimate	agnostics	antipathy	assimilate
accolade	albeit	apathy	assuage
accrue	alleviate	append	asylum
acrimonious	allude (to)	arbiter	au courant
actuary	amalgamation	arbitrage	audit
acumen	ambivalence	arbitrary	autonomous

barrage	berth	blighted	bureaucrats
beguile	besmirch	blunder	burgeoning
beleaguered	bias	brass (slang def.)	
benighted	bipartisan	brute (vb.)	
bereft	blatant	budgetary	

cacophony	civics	concubine	convocation
cajole	clandestine	condone	covet
callous	clerical	confrere	crafty
canard	coda	conspiratorial	craven
candor	coffer	constituent	credibility
canonical/canon	collusion	contemporaries	cul-de-sac
capitulate	compliant	contend	cupidity
cataclysmic	complicit	contender	curtail
caveat	compound (vb.)	contingent	cushy
censure	compulsion	conundrum	cynical
chasm	concede	convene	cynicism
chimera	conciliate	conversant	
circumspect	conciliatory	conversely	
daunting	demur	despot	dispirit
debase	demystify	deter	disposition
decadence	denounce	detract	disquieting
decibel	denuded	didactic	dissemble
decree	denunciation	disavow	disseminate
decry	deplorable	discernible	dissident
deferment	depredation	discourse	dissipate
defrocked	deprivation	discretion	diversity
defunct	derail	discretionary	don (vb.)
deluded	derangement	disenchantment	doting
demagogue	deregulation	disingenuous	Draconian
demise	deride	disjointed	
demonize	derisive	dispel	
earmark	enclave	equivocate	exorbitant
egregious	enfranchise	eradicate	expenditure
electorate	enmesh	erode	expostulate
elixir	ennobling	ethos	expunge
eminence	ennui	eugenics	exude
empathetic	envoy	eviscerate	
empathy	epitomize	exhort	
encapsulate	equanimity	exonerate	
fallacious	firebrand	forlorn	frothing
farcical	fiscal	formidable	furor
fedora	flounder (vb.)	formulate	fusillade (fig.)
feint	flummoxed	fray (n.)	futility
fiasco	fodder (fig.)*	frenetic	
finagle	folly	fritter (vb.)	

---

*In this case, consider the figurative meaning of the words.

gaffe	gaudy	gouging	gubernatorial
gag rule	gauge	grapple	guffaw
galvanize	gerrymander	grim	
garner	glut	grotesque	

habeus corpus	hapless	hectoring	hubris
hackneyed	harbor (vb.)	heresy	hyperbole
hamlet	heckle	hoosegow (slang)	

iconography	importune	indignity	insular
ideological	impunity	ineptitude	integrity
idiosyncratic	incendiary	infiltrate	interlocking
idyllic	incessant	infirmity	intransigence
ignominious	incipient	inflationary	inure
ilk	incite	infuse	invaluable
impede	incontrovertible	inherent	inviolate
imperil	incumbent	innuendo	irk
implement (vb.)	indefatigable	inquisitorial	irredentism
implicit	indigenous	insignia	

lacerate	largess	leery	lout
laconic	latent	leitmotif	lucid
lambaste	laureate	levitate	
languish	lebensraum	litany	

malady	maudlin	molder	mortar
malaise	megalomaniac	monolith	murky
malign	meritorious	morass	myopic
manifestation	meticulous	moratorium	
mantra	milieu	moribund	
martyr	mimesis	morose	

nadir	nexus	nuance
nascent	nomadic	

obfuscate	odious	oppression	overweening
obsolescence	ominous	outlay	
obstreperous	omnipresent	overhaul	
oddity	oncology	overt	

palliative
panacea
pandering
paradox
paramount
parochial
parsimonious
partisan (adj.)
passel
pathology
patrician
pedantic
peevish
pejorative
penchant

perennial
peripheral
pernicious
peroration
perpetuate
perquisite
perversion
pillage
pinnacle
pious
pique
placable/placate
plaudits
plight
plummet

plunder
pogrom
polarization
polemic
polyglot
portend
pragmatism
prattle
preeminent
preempt
preclude
presage
probity
profound
progeny

prohibitive
proliferate
proliferation
propensity
protocol
provocation
prurience
psyche
pugnacity
pundit
purport
purvey/purveyor
pusillanimous
pyrotechnics

quagmire
qualm

quaver
quibble

quintessential

rabid (fig.)
rakish
rancor
rapacious
rapprochement
raucous
realpolitik

recidivism
reconcile
rectitude
rejoinder
relegate
reparations
replete

resolute
resonance
restorative
retributive
reverberate
reverence
revile

rhetoric
rifle (vb.)
rogue
rudimentary
ruse

salve (vb.)
sartorial
sashay
scion
scoff
scourge
seamy
self-effacing
sham
shaman
shore up
shudder

siphon
snare
snide
sobriquet
sophomoric
sordid
sorghum
sovereignty
spate
speculative
staggering
stagnation

staid
stark
staunch
steely eyed
stint
stipend
strident
stringent
stymie
subsidize
substantive
subterfuge

sullen
summarily
sumptuary
sunder
supersede
supplant
surfeit
swindle
sword of
   Damocles
sycophant
synergy

temporal
temporize
tenacity
tendentious

throng
thwart
torpor
totter

tout
transgression
transitory
treacherous

troupe
tsunami
turbulent

undergird	unduly	unilateral	unrelenting
undermine	unencumbered	universality	unscrupulous
undiluted	unfettered	unprecedented	usurp

vagaries	vestige	vigilante	volatile
venality	vexing	vilify	voyeurs
veracity	viable	visceral	
verdant	victimize	vituperation	

waffling	welter	writ	
wallow	wheedling	writhe	
wastrels	winnow	wrongheaded	

xenophobia

| zeal | zeitgeist |

Vocabulary from Book Reviews

accolade	adumbrate	animus	arduous
accretion	adversity	annotate	arsenal
accrue	aesthetic	antipodes	ascetic
acerbic	albeit	aphrodisiac	asinine
acolyte	alluring	aplomb	aspire
acrimonious	amatory	apotheosis	attenuate
acumen	amiable	arbiter	austere
adage	amok	arbitrary	authorial
adduce	anapest	archaic	
adherent	ancillary	ardor	

banal	bemused	blight	boulevardier
barren	bestiality	blithe	bowdlerize
bathetic	bevy	bohemian	Byzantine
bedraggled	bifurcation	boorish	

cache	chic	compendium	credo
cadence	clandestine	complicity	cribbed
canny	cleric	congenial	crotchety
catharsis	cloying	consign	cupidity
caveat	coffer	contend	curmudgeon
chafe	cohere	contrivance	cursory
charisma	coherence	copious	
chastening	colloquial	counterpoise	
chastise	compendious	covert	

dash	demigod	dichotomy	divagation
daunting	denouement	didactic	divergence
debunk	deploy	discursive	droll
deft	despotic	dispense	duplicity
delineate	detritus	dispossess	dysfunctional
delude	devolve	dither	dystopia
eccentric	ensconce	esoteric	exigency
eclectic	entreaty	espouse	existential
edify	envisage	esthetic	expansive
egregious	epigraph	ethereal	expatriate
elegy	epitomize	ethos	expurgate
elocution	equanimity	evangelical	exultant
elucidate	eradicate	evocative	
enclave	Eros	exacerbate	
encomium	eschew	exhort	
fabulist	farce	foray	fruition
facsimile	fervid	forbearance	furtive
faction	florid	formulaic	
galvanize	gorgon	guile	
gamut	grapple	gustatory	
hackneyed	harrowing	hewn (details)	
hagiography	hedonism		
iconoclast	implacable	ineffable	intercede
iconography	impresario	ineffectual	intractable
idiosyncratic	incoherent	inept	inured
idyll/idyllic	incongruous	inextricably	invidious
ignite (fig.)	incur	insidious	irreverent
imminent	indelible	insinuation	itinerant
imperative	indeterminate	insouciance	
impetus	indigenous	intelligentsia	
jarring	jettison	jostle	Joycean
kamikaze			
lacuna	largess	loquacious	lyricism
lament	libertine	Lothario	
languish	lilting	lucid	
lapidary	litigious	lucrative	

macabre	mawkish	minutiae	mosaic
malaise	melodrama	misogyny	muddle
malevolent	mendacious	mogul	murky
malign	mercurial	moldering	musing
manifold (adj.)	mien	mordant	muster
matrix	milieu	moribund	myopia
naiveté	natter	nonpareil	nuance
narcissistic	nihilism	non sequitur	
nascent	nimble	noxious	
obfuscation	opprobrium	ostensible	ostracize
palatable	penumbra	portent	prevaricate
pantheon	perdurable	portentous	prodigious
paradigm	peregrination	practitioner	prosaic
pathos	perennial	pragmatic	protean
paucity	petulance	prattle	punitive
pedagogical	piety	precocious	purport
pelt (vb.)	placebo	premonition	
penchant	plodding	prescient	
querulous	quintessential	quotidian	
query	quixotic		
rancor	recalcitrant	reverence	riveting
rapacious	recapitulate	revile	rudimentary
rapture	relegate	rhetorical	ruminate
rancor	repatriation	ricochet	
raucous	replete	riff	
reap	repository	risible	
sagacity	sedentary	stanch	sunder
salacious	self-effacement	standoffish	supercilious
sally forth	sepulchral	staunch	surreptitious
sap (vb.)	shaman	stilted	surrogate
savor	shenanigans	stultifying	symbiosis
scatological	snippet	sublimate	symmetry
scourge	solicitous	sublime	synoptic
scuttlebutt	spurn	subterfuge	
searing	squander	succumb	

taut	titillating	transient	trenchant
teeter	torpid	transitory	trilogy
temporal	tortuous	transmogrify	truism
thrall	traffic (vb.)	travail	tweak
throng	transcendent	treatise	
unabashed	uncanny	unfathomable	unflinching
vacillate	venality	vignette	vitriol
valediction	verisimilitude	vindictiveness	voluminous
vapid	vernacular	virtuosity	vortex
venal	vicissitude	vis à vis	votary
waft	wend	withal	
welter	whimsy		

Chapter 9

GRAMMAR AND USAGE FOR THE CAREFUL WRITER: A GUIDE TO STANDARD WRITTEN ENGLISH

The grammar of a language is its logic. We observe the conventions of standard usage in order to write and speak clearly, in order to communicate precisely what we mean. This section reviews those aspects of grammar and usage you are expected to know and to apply.

On the Regents ELA exam, your command of the conventions—standard written English—is evaluated by how well you write the essay of argument and the text analysis. On the SAT, your command of the grammar and usage is assessed in the writing and language section and on the optional essay; the ACT exam includes a specific section on grammar and usage, sentence structure, and mechanics (see Chapter 10 for Punctuation Guidelines and Reminders).

None of these exams requires you to identify errors in usage by name, but a review of the essential terms and structures will help you to recognize errors and to understand how to correct them. What are the essentials?

REVIEWING THE FUNDAMENTALS

The Parts of Speech

Below are the parts of speech that you should review. These include the noun, pronoun, adjective, verb, and adverb, as well as conjunction, preposition, and interjection.

NOUN

Names or identifies persons, creatures, objects, ideas. The articles *the, a, an* usually precede and signal a noun. For example:

book	education	history
child	English	politics
climate	happiness	woman

PRONOUN

Replaces or "stands in for" nouns or other pronouns already stated; the noun or pronoun referred to (replaced) is the **antecedent**.

Subject Forms: I, you, he/she/it, we, you, they

Object Forms: me, you, him/her/it, us, you, them

Possessive Forms: mine, yours, his/hers/its, ours, yours, theirs

Relatives: that, which, who, whom, whose, whoever, whomever

ADJECTIVE

Modifies nouns, that is, it describes, limits, specifies, what a noun names. For instance:

tall woman	*young* child	*illustrated* book
temperate climate	*American* history	*public* education

VERB

Denotes any *action*: run, talk, think, intend, suggest, play, strike, have, do; or *state of being*: appear, seem, be, feel. The principal parts of a verb are as follows:

Infinitive: to run, to talk, to think, to intend, to appear, to seem

Simple past: ran, talked, thought, intended, appeared, seemed

Present participle: running, talking, thinking, intending, appearing, seeming

Past participle: (has) run, (has) talked, (has) thought, intended, appeared, seemed

ADVERB

Modifies verbs; it indicates the manner, quality, or degree of an *action*.

run *swiftly*   talk *loudly*   think *clearly*

play *well*   strike *suddenly*

Adverbs also function as *intensifiers*; that is, they indicate the degree or intensity of modifiers, both adjectives and adverbs.

rather tall woman   *very* young child

talk *too* loudly   *nearly* complete project

CONJUNCTION

A word that connects two or more words or groups of words.

Coordinating conjunctions: and, but, yet, so, for

Subordinating conjunctions: because, although, since, while, if, until, when, unless, before, after

There are a tall woman *and* a young child.

We will stay home *if* it rains.

Because he trains regularly, he plays well.

PREPOSITION

Expresses relationships of time, space, or position.

above	behind	in	under
across	beside	into	within
after	between	on	without
at	except	over	
before	for	to	

INTERJECTION

An expression that begins or interrupts a sentence to express a particular feeling.

Ouch!, that hurts.   *Oh,* how interesting!   *Bravo!*

Phrases, Clauses, and Sentences

While we may express feelings and give commands with single words, our most useful expression is in words grouped in phrases, clauses, and sentences.

PHRASE

A meaningful group of words. There are many kinds of phrases in English. Here are some common examples:

A noun and its modifiers:

the large brick building   the tall young woman

A verb and its auxiliaries (to show different tenses):

has run   will arrive
should have been done

A preposition and its object:

across the room   in the final chapter
down the hill   on the roof

A participle and its object or modifiers:

opening the door carefully   sensing danger
returning after many years*   walking slowly

CLAUSE

A meaningful group of words that contains a verb and its subject.
Clauses are *dependent* when they form only part of a complex sentence of more than one clause:

Because he was late, . . .   If it rains tomorrow, . . .

. . . when the plane arrives   . . . that you requested

Each of these expressions contains a verb and *its* subject, but you can see that the sentence will not be complete—that is, the assertion will not be fully expressed or understood—until at least one additional clause is added.

---

* Note that prepositional phrases, which are modifiers because they function as adjectives and adverbs do, may be part of a larger participial phrase.

In these examples, one *independent* clause has been added to form a *complete sentence:*

[Because he was late], his appointment was canceled.

I will call you [when the plane arrives].

The book [that you requested] is now available.

A *sentence,* then, may be made up of a few words—a subject, and a predicate verb that establishes the action or state of being of the subject, and modifiers:

She ran.

The dog barked.

He was late.

The crowd cheered enthusiastically.

Or a sentence may be made up of more than one clause and contain several phrases as modifiers.

Because he was late, his appointment was canceled and had to be rescheduled for the following week.

The large crowd in the bleachers cheered enthusiastically as the home team took the field in the last inning.

Tests of standard usage are tests of how well you understand and can compose the many relationships of words, phrases, clauses, and sentences that make up standard written English.

Most of the problems in grammar and usage you are expected to recognize and be able to correct are considered "errors" because they result in a lack of clarity, even confusion, in the writer's expression.

Although writing that contains minor errors in standard usage may still be understood, careful writers seek expression that is precise and clear—even elegant—and that demonstrates their ability to use variety in language and structure. It is only through mastery of a wide range of expression that students may fully reveal their ideas, insights, and feelings.

AVOIDING COMMON ERRORS IN WRITING

When we refer to errors in writing, we are referring to expressions that are illogical, inconsistent, vague, or imprecise. The elements of usage reviewed here are those that high school students should be able to recognize.

Agreement of Subject and Verb

Agreement is a form of consistency and is one of the most basic elements of grammar. When you learn to conjugate verbs, for example, you are applying the concept of agreement. Singular subjects take singular verbs; plural subjects take plural verbs.

He speaks/they speak; One is/many are

Errors in agreement commonly occur in sentences where the subject follows the verb:

On the desk *are* my notebook, a few pencils, and the assignments for tomorrow.

"Desk" is not the subject of the verb; "notebook, pencils, assignments" is the subject, *they* are on the desk. In such inverted word order, the writer must hear and think ahead to choose the correct form of the verb. Similarly:

There *seems* to be only *one answer*.

There *seem* to be *several ideas* worth considering.

Here *are* the *pieces* you have been looking for.

Agreement errors may also occur when a subject followed by a phrase precedes the verb:

New York with its many historical sites and tourist attractions *is* a fascinating city to visit.

His *many talents* in sports, academics, and student leadership *make* him a popular candidate.

Subjects may be expanded by such prepositional phrases as *along with, in addition to, as well as, together with*. These phrases, however, do not form part of the *grammatical* subject; they modify the subject:

English, as well as math, science, and social studies, *is* a required subject for most high school students.

Evan, along with several of his friends, *is* planning to visit colleges in the fall.

In some sentences, the subject may be modified by one or more clauses before the predicate verb is stated. In such sentences the writer must "remember" the actual subject before composing the correct form of the verb:

The *fact* that Americans must now compete in a global economy and must recognize the necessity for higher standards in our schools *has led* to educational reform in many states.

Many common pronouns are singular and must take a singular verb:

Each one of these books *is* worth reading.

Every one of us *is* prepared to contribute.

None of these solutions *is* acceptable. (No *one* is)

Note how agreement with correlatives *either/or, neither/nor* is achieved:

Either Susan or her brother *is* home now.

(Either Susan is . . . or her brother is)

Neither rain, nor sleet, nor snow *deters* us . . . .

When the correlative contains both a singular and plural expression, the verb agrees with the one closest:

Neither Susan nor her sisters *are* at home.

Either the members of the legislature or the governor *is* authorized to submit a budget.

Do not be confused when the predicate is completed with a plural expression:

His most reliable *source* of encouragement *is* friends and family.

To avoid the correct but awkward-sounding expression above, rewrite as follows:

His *friends and family are* his most reliable source of encouragement.

Collective nouns take singular verbs because all the "members" are understood to act as a single unit:

The *jury was* unanimous in its decision to acquit.

A school *board has* extensive responsibilities.

Our *family has agreed* on plans for the vacation.

The *team practices* for two hours every day.

When there is not such unity of action, you may use a plural verb:

The *jury are* not in unanimous agreement.

The *family are* expected to arrive at different times.

It is better, however, to avoid such awkward-sounding expressions by rewriting to make the plural idea clear:

The members of the jury are not in agreement.

Players on the team are required to keep their uniforms and equipment in good order.

Family members are expected to arrive at different times.

Agreement of Pronoun and Antecedent

Because pronouns replace nouns or other pronouns, they must agree with their singular or plural antecedents.

Evelyn is very grateful to *her parents* for *their* constant support and encouragement.

Most pronoun/antecedent errors arise when we use the indefinite pronouns *anyone, anybody, everyone, everybody, someone, somebody, no one,* and so on. These pronouns are singular because they refer to *individuals:*

Everybody is responsible for *his* own work.

Someone has left *her* books on the floor.

If *anyone* calls while I am out, please tell *him* or *her* I will call back after lunch.

The common practice of replacing *him/her* with *them,* or *her/his* with *their,* solves the problem of choosing gender, but it is ungrammatical and illogical. The careful writer (and speaker) avoids these errors or rewrites:

Please tell *anyone who calls* that I will return at noon.

Someone's books have been left on the floor.

Everyone has individual responsibility for the assignments.

Form of Pronouns

Use the subject forms when pronouns are *subjects* of verbs or identify the subject after a linking verb:

He and I received the information we needed.

She is the favorite candidate of the party.

He is the head baseball coach.

The head baseball coach is *he*.

(Think of the verb *is* as an = sign.)

It is easy to avoid the awkward sound of the last sentence by choosing the preceding expression, which uses the pronoun first.

Pronouns as *objects* of verbs or prepositions must be in the object form:

Please give *him* the information.

Give the information to *them*.

Whom did you see yesterday?

Errors often occur when we have pronouns preceded by a noun; the writer no longer "hears" the preposition and is reluctant to use the object form. But,

Please give the information to Ellen and *him*. (to Ellen . . . to him)

The host was very gracious to Ellen and *me*.
(to Ellen . . . to me; *not* to Ellen and I)

Just between you and me, this is simple.

We also use the object form with infinitives:

We understand *her to be* the favorite candidate.

We understand the favorite candidate *to be her*.

Remember to use the possessive form with *gerunds* ("-ing" verb forms that function as nouns):

I do not approve of *your staying* out so late.
(of your "late hours")

She was concerned about *his working* too hard.
(about his excessive work)

169

Note the following:

> Mark's mother saw *him* [*running* after the bus].
>
> Mark's mother encouraged [*his running* on the cross-country team].

In the first example, *running* is a participle describing *him,* which is the object of the verb *saw.* In the second example, *running* is a noun; it is the object of the verb *encouraged.*

Parallelism

Parallelism is used for consistency and clarity. Parallel ideas and expressions in a series should be composed in the same form:

> He wants to spend the summer *reading, sleeping, and traveling.*
>
> He plans *to read, to sleep, and to travel.*

Use parallel phrases and clauses:

> She is known *for* her talent and *for* her generosity.
>
> We expect our presidents to be skilled *not only in* domestic affairs *but also in* foreign policy.
>
> Our state senator was reelected *because* she is honest, *because* she works hard for the district, *and because* she has an important leadership position in the senate.

Use parallel construction when you use correlatives: *either, or; not only, but also:*

> *Either* you will complete the work now, *or* he will complete it in the morning.
>
> We will *either take* a train this afternoon *or take* a plane this evening.

Consistency of active and passive voice is also a form of parallelism:

> The research team *formulated* its ideas and *developed* its proposal.
>
> Ideas *were formulated* and a proposal *was developed* by the research team.

Verbs: Using the Correct Tense

Use the simple past tense for actions completed in the past:

> The train *arrived* at 6:30.
>
> He *retired* in 1993.
>
> The Nobel prizes *were announced* in January.

Use the present perfect tense to establish facts, to assert that something *has occurred, has happened, has been done*, without reference to a specific time.

> *Have you done* your homework yet?
>
> The renovation of our house *has been completed.*
>
> I *have read Macbeth* several times.

Note the correct *sequence of tenses* in the following:

> The novelist *completed* the book in 1993, two years after he *had begun* it.
>
> She *recorded* the names of everyone who *had called* the day before.

> In the Middle Ages, most people *believed* that the earth *is* round.
>
> Copernicus *demonstrated* that the earth *orbits* the sun.

> If I *were* you, I *would accept* the offer.
>
> If the congressman *were indicted,* he *would* lose the support of many constituents.

> If we *had taken* more time to plan, our trip *would have been* more pleasant.
>
> If you *had trained* harder, you *would have* made the team.

If you would have called earlier is sometimes heard but this is not an acceptable construction in standard English.

Finally, you are generally expected to write about works of literature in the *present tense*.

> Macbeth *is driven* by ambition.
>
> Jay Gatsby *believes* he can recreate the past.
>
> Willy Loman *dies* believing his son will achieve great success.

Aspects of character, themes, plot, and setting remain constant—they *are* what they are—regardless of how the plot concludes or when we finish reading the work.

Logical Comparisons

My sister is *taller* than I [am].

She is *more* clever than he [is].

Josh is the *tallest* member of the team.

Among all of Miller's plays, *Death of a Salesman* is the *best* known.

Avoid incomplete comparisons in your writing:

Dreiser's novels are *more* popular now [than they were when they were first published].

Shakespeare's plays are *harder* to read [than modern works are].

The passages in brackets should be fully stated.
In informal speech we may use *so* as an intensifier:

I was *so* tired. He was *so* angry.

In writing, however, be sure every *so* is followed by a *that,* every *more* by a *than.*
Comparisons must be parallel and logical:

The paintings of Monet are more popular than Goya **should read**:

The paintings of Monet are more popular than *the paintings* of Goya.

You must compare paintings to paintings, not inadvertently compare paintings to a man.
And,

Anne is a better player than anyone on her team. **should read**:

Anne is a *better* player *than any other* [player] on her team.

or,

Anne is the *best player* on the team.

It is illogical to suggest Anne is better than she herself is.

Clear and Logical Modification

The careful writer must also be aware of errors in modification and in the logical relationships of ideas. Many such errors are corrected simply, with commas; others may require revision or reorganization of sentences.

Introductory subordinate (dependent) clauses must be set off by a comma:

> *After the lights had come back on,* the children were no longer frightened by the thunderstorm.
>
> *When it rains,* cats and dogs prefer not to go outside.

Without the comma, such sentences would be ambiguous.

Nonrestrictive (nonessential) phrases and clauses are set off by commas:

> My aunt, *who lives in Milwaukee,* will be flying in for a weekend visit to New York.
>
> Several stranded passengers, *feeling restless and impatient,* demanded flights on another airline.

When such phrases or clauses are restrictive* (essential to the meaning of the sentence), do not set them off with commas:

> Passengers *traveling with small children* will be permitted to board the plane first.
>
> My cousin *who lives in Milwaukee* will have to fly, but the cousins *who live in the New York area* will be able to drive to my brother's wedding.

A common error occurs when we begin a sentence with a participial phrase:

> Feeling restless and impatient, seats were demanded on other airlines' flights [by many travelers].
> (The seats are not restless . . .)
>
> *Barking loudly,* we were afraid the dog would wake our neighbors.
> (We are not barking, the dog is . . .)
>
> *Tired and hungry,* even cold leftovers looked good to us.
> (The leftovers are not hungry, we are . . .)

---

*For additional examples, see *which/that/who* on page 181.

The *subject* of the participle must also be stated as the subject of the clause that follows:

> *Feeling restless and impatient, many stranded travelers* sought seats on other airlines' flights.
>
> *Barking loudly, the dog* wakened our neighbors.
>
> *Tired and hungry, we* were satisfied with the cold leftovers.

You may also recompose sentences to make the modification clear:

> We were afraid our dog, *barking loudly,* would wake the neighbors.
>
> *Because we were tired and hungry,* even cold leftovers looked good to us.

EXPRESSIONS OFTEN CONFUSED, MISUSED, AND OVERUSED*

accept/except

To **accept** is to receive, take willingly, agree to:

> I **accept** your offer, apology, invitation

To **except** is to exclude, to separate out:

> I will **except** you from the requirement.

Except is also a preposition:

> Everyone **except** him will be leaving on Tuesday.

affect/effect

To **affect** (vb.) means to move, influence, or change. It also means to put on an artificial quality of personality or character; such an exaggerated or artificial person may be called **affected**.

An **effect** (n.) is a consequence or result.

To **effect** (vb.) means to put into action, to complete—a plan or a change, for example.

---

*See also Words Commonly Confused/Misspelled in Chapter 11, Spelling.

aggravate

To **aggravate** means to make worse. Do not use it when you really mean to irritate or annoy.

allusion/illusion

An **allusion** is a reference (see Glossary of Poetic Terms and Techniques, Chapter 5); an **illusion** is a false or deceptive idea or vision.

among/between

Use **between** for two, **among** for three or more:

between you and me

among all the members of the family

amount/number

One has an **amount** of something (the quantity as a whole) and a **number** of things (that can be counted):

an **amount** of time/a **number** of hours, days

a large **amount** of work/a **number** of tasks

See also **fewer/less** for the same distinction.

as far as . . . is/are concerned

The expression **as far as** used by itself creates an incomplete and illogical statement; it must be completed with **is/are concerned.** The expression as **far as . . . goes/go** is also widely used and correct as completed.

Faulty: **As far as** plans for school construction in the future, we expect the legislature to take action in the next session.

As far as the weather, it will be sunny and pleasant tomorrow.

Correct: **As far as** plans for school construction in the future are concerned, we expect the legislature to take action in the next session

As far as the weather goes, it will be sunny and pleasant.

bad/badly, good/well

Use **bad** and **good** (adjectives) to describe how one feels; use **badly** and **well** (adverbs) to describe how one does something.

He felt **bad** (sorry, regretful) because he caused the team to lose.

175

The team lost the game because he played so **badly**.

She feels **good** (in good spirits, positive) when her work is going **well**.

She is feeling **well** (no longer ill) now after a long bout with the flu.

The team lost because he did not play **well**.

being as, being that

These expressions are not standard speech. Use *because* or *since* instead.

compare to, compare with

Use **compare to** when you are expressing an analogy or similarity; use **compare with** when you are showing similarities and differences between two things.

He compared his small room **to** a closet.

The critics compared the movie **with** the book.

could of/ should of

Do not make this unfortunate confusion in the way words sound! You mean **could have/should have**.

different from (not **than**)

You should use the preposition **from** with **different** because you are making a distinction, a separation. Use **than** for comparisons, to show degrees of the same quality:

She is only slightly older **than** her sister, but her personality is very different **from** her sister's.

due to

This expression is popularly used for almost any cause and effect relationship. Avoid its overuse in your writing:

Absence **due to** illness is excused.

Delays **due to** bad weather are common in winter.

It is more precise to say:

The road was closed **because of** an accident.

The defendant was acquitted **by reason of** insanity.

There were many landslides **caused by** the heavy rains.

everybody, somebody, someone, nobody

These are *singular* forms; they may refer to many people, but they refer to *each one individually*. Singular antecedents take singular pronouns:

Everybody has *his/her* books, lunch, opinions.

Someone, a person has *his/her* opinions.

farther/further

In general, you may use **farther** or **further** for actual or figurative distance:

The nearest town is ten miles **farther** from here.

The latest agreements move us **further** toward a full peace.

Use **further** when you mean more:

We have nothing **further** to discuss.

A final agreement requires **further** negotiations.

fewer/less

One has **fewer** things and **less** something.

fewer hours/**less** time

fewer dollars/**less** money

fewer ideas/**less** content

first, second, . . .

To show transition and to enumerate examples, use these terms instead of *firstly, secondly*, . . .

hang/hanged/hung

When we use this verb in the past tense to denote an execution, we use **hanged**; for such things as clothes and pictures, we use **hung**.

The condemned man was **hanged** at dawn.

We **hung** our winter coats in the hall closet.

hopefully

This expression is popularly used to mean we hope, it is hoped, and so on. The careful writer should use it only as an adverb:

The cat looked **hopefully** at the leftover chicken.

177

But:

We **hope** the situation will improve.

It is hoped that research will lead to a cure.

however

Along with its cousins *therefore, moreover,* and *consequently,* **however** should be placed *within the sentence,* close to the verb it modifies; think of it as a conjunction, not as a transition at the beginning of a sentence.

if/whether

Use **if** to introduce conditional expressions; use **whether** (or not) for choices, decisions, questions:

If it rains, our game will be postponed.

If you work hard, you will succeed.

I do not know **whether** we will play or not.

infer/imply

To **infer** is to conclude, to draw an inference from evidence; to **imply** is to suggest or hint.

We can **infer** from his comments that he is pleased.

She **implied** in her speech that she is planning to run for public office.

its/it's

it's = a contraction* for it is.

its = a possessive form; do not add an apostrophe.

if ... were/if ... was

Use the **if ... were** construction for *hypothetical* conditions and situations:

If you were president, what would you do?

If I were you, I would accept the offer.

---

*Contractions should be avoided in formal writing, unless you are quoting someone. Contractions are features of spoken language.

Use **if . . . was** for situations that *were possible*:

> **If** that really **was** Linda who called yesterday, she should have left a message.

incredible/incredulous

Incredible means unbelievable, beyond belief or understanding. In formal writing, avoid using it as *hyperbole*. Use instead such terms as *astonishing* or *extraordinary*.

A person is **incredulous** when he/she utterly cannot believe what is being said.

kind of/sort of/type of

Avoid using *a* or *an* with these expressions:

> **That type of** character is popular in children's books.
>
> **Those types of** characters are . . .
>
> **This kind of** fabric is best for the new sofa.

Also avoid using **kind of** or **sort of** when you mean *a little, rather, somewhat*.

lie/lay

These verbs are often confused. Note their principal parts and distinctions in meaning: to **lie (down)** means to recline, be situated, rest:

> You **lie** on your bed to take a nap.
>
> The mail **has lain** on your desk since yesterday.
>
> Last winter the snow **lay** on the ground for weeks.

Note that to **lay** means to put or place something. (It is a transitive verb and always takes a direct object.):

> You can **lay** your hat and gloves on the hall table.
>
> Masons **lay bricks** and hens **lay eggs**.
>
> He cannot remember where he **laid** his car keys.

like/as/as if

Use **like** as a preposition, use **as** and **as if** as conjunctions:

> He looks just **like** his father.
>
> A talent **like** hers is rare.

It looks **as if** it will rain this afternoon.

You should do the assignments **as** you were instructed to.

"Do **as** I say, not **as** I do!"

only/just

These modifiers should be placed as close as possible to the expressions they actually limit:

I have **only** two dollars for lunch.

He has time for **only** a brief conversation.

I have **just** one thing to say.

presently

This should be used to denote the immediate future; it means right *away* or in *a little while:*

I will answer your question **presently**.

He is expected to arrive **presently**.

The meeting will begin **presently**.

For current time, use **at present** or **currently**:

He is **currently** a junior at North High.

At present, she is working on her master's degree.

purposely/purposefully

Use **purposely** to mean intentionally, knowingly, deliberately, that is, to describe an action done "on purpose" and not by accident.

purposefully is best used to mean decisively, firmly, resolutely, with determination, and with a specific purpose or goal in mind.

so

Try to avoid the casual use of "so" just to introduce an idea or an explanation. You will hear "so" widely used in informal speech to begin the answer to almost any question, but that should be avoided in your formal writing. Use *so* as a conjunction to show a consequence:

We were hungry, **so** we went to lunch early.

Our plane was delayed, **so** we spent several hours waiting at the airport.

toward/towards

Either is acceptable; **toward** is more formal.

when/where

These are terms of time and place; do not use them to introduce definitions.

which/that/who

These relative *pronouns* introduce *clauses* that describe or define. Use **that** for clauses that are *restrictive* (defining, limiting):

The books **that** you ordered will arrive tomorrow; the ones **that** Sam ordered will come next week. (those particular books . . .)

He likes the car **that** he bought last year better than any other he has owned. (that particular car)

Basketball is the game **that** he plays best.

Use **which** for clauses that are *nonrestrictive* (descriptive):

The house on the corner, **which** was built in the 1880s, will be restored to its original design.

Shakespeare's plays, **which** were written nearly 400 years ago, remain popular in theaters and movies as well as in English courses.

Use **who** for people. (**That** is sometimes used when the identification is distant or impersonal.) Do not use **which** for people:

Lady Macbeth is a character **that** (**who**) remains fascinating to many students.

Use **whom** when the pronoun is an object:

To **whom** should I give the information? (obj. of prep.)

Whom did you ask? (obj. of verb)

who/whom/whoever/whomever

When these *pronouns* introduce *clauses,* their form is determined *solely* by their function in the clause:

The new coach, **who** led the team to a county title, gave all the credit to her players.
(**Who** is the subject of the verb *led;* therefore, it is in the subject form.)

Please give the information to (**whoever** needs it.)

181

(**Whoever** is the subject in the clause; the *entire* clause is the object of *give to*.)

Please give the award to (**whomever** you choose.)
(**Whomever** is the object of the verb *choose;* the *entire* clause is the object of *give to*.)

Careful attention to the conventions of usage and style outlined in this chapter will enhance your ability to express ideas and discuss information clearly and persuasively. When you have command of the language you use, you have command of the relationship between thought and expression.

Chapter 10

PUNCTUATION: GUIDELINES AND REMINDERS

When is the semicolon or colon used? Are there any rules for commas? Do I underline titles of books and poems or put them in quotation marks? Where do I put the period when a sentence ends with quotation marks? Even experienced writers need to consult a usage handbook for the answers to some of these questions.

In conversation we use pauses, stresses, and tone of voice to make our meaning clear. The printed page, however, does not readily show what voice and gesture can reveal, so the writer uses punctuation to achieve absolute clarity. Below, you will find a review of the elements of punctuation high school students should know and use in their own writing. Featured are answers to those questions most often raised about how to punctuate. (Many of the examples from the writing of specific authors come from the passages reprinted elsewhere in the book.)

END PUNCTUATION

The period, exclamation mark, and question mark bring statements and expressions to a close; they signal a full stop.

The Period

Use a **period** to indicate the end of a sentence or of a group of words having the emphasis of a sentence.

Declarative sentences (make a statement):

Good writers are also good readers.

"The guns squatted in a row like savage chiefs." (Stephen Crane, *The Red Badge of Courage*)

183

Imperative sentences (give an order or direction):

Be sure to proofread.

Come to practice on time or leave the team.

Tell me how much I owe you.

Fragments for emphasis:

"No doubt my younger brother and sister were in the house and warm. *Eating cookies.*" (William Kittredge)

"Much of their [whales'] behavior seems to be recreational: they sing, they play. *And so on.*" (Robert Finch)

The Exclamation Mark

Use an **exclamation mark** to show intensity and emphasis in sentences or fragments.

Come to practice!

Be sure to proofread!

Look out!

Congratulations!

CAUTION: *Do not overuse the **exclamation mark** in expository writing; use effective language and sentence structure to achieve emphasis.*

The Question Mark

Use a **question mark** to signal interrogative forms in complete sentences, fragments, or series.

Can you explain how to do this?

Do you understand what he said?

Can you recommend a good restaurant in the theater district?

What was that all about? a joke? a mistake?

Where should we meet? at home? at school?

Ask questions as you read an essay: What is the author's purpose? tone? conclusion? Do you agree? disagree? feel convinced?

Question marks may also be used with single words or phrases as needed:

When?

Leave the team?

You did?

What homework?

SPECIAL CONSIDERATIONS

Periods are used in many abbreviations. For example:

U.S. government	Dipl. B.A. M.A. Ph.D.
U.N. Security Council	D.D.S. M.D. Esq.
N.Y.S. Board of Regents	A.M. P.M.

Some abbreviations take no periods:

CIA	mph
MTV	rpm
WCBS	

A sentence may end with more than one kind of punctuation. If it ends with an abbreviation using a period, do not add a second period.

Please report to my office promptly at 10:00 A.M.

In order to apply for a teaching position, you must have completed your M.A.

If it ends with a quotation or expression in quotation marks, place the final period *inside* the quotation marks.

Most high school students have read Poe's short story "The Cask of Amontillado."

When told his wife is dead, Macbeth remarks, "She should have died hereafter."

If the **entire sentence** requires a question mark, place it outside the quotation marks:

Have you read Poe's story "The Cask of Amontillado"?

Why does Macbeth say, "She should have died hereafter"?

If the quotation at the end of a sentence requires a question mark, keep it within the quotes. (Do not add an additional period.)

> The title of a recent editorial in *The New York Times* was "Where do we go from here?"

If a statement within the quotes is a question, the question mark within the quote is sufficient.

> Did you read the editorial entitled "Where do we go from here?"

Similarly, if an exclamation point is part of a quoted expression, place it within the quote. An additional period is not required.

> One of my favorite pieces by James Thurber is called "Excelsior!"

To make the above into a question, however:

> Have you read Thurber's story "Excelsior!"?

If a sentence ends with a passage in parentheses, put the period outside the closing parenthesis:

> We did not leave on time because Sally was late (as usual).

Even if the expression is a complete sentence, do not punctuate within the parentheses:

> We did not leave on time because Sally was late (she always is).

If, however, the expression within the parentheses requires quotation marks, a question mark, or an exclamation point, include them:

> We did not leave on time because Sally was late (isn't she always?).

In such cases, a better solution would be to separate the parenthetical statement:

> We did not leave because Sally was late. (Isn't she always?)

What is the logic to all this? When sentences or passages are made up of a variety of elements, punctuation should make the structure of each element clear. If the end of a sentence becomes cluttered by the need to bring several individual pieces to a close at the same time, punctuate from the inside out—smaller pieces first, then larger. But do not double the end punctuation unless it is required for accuracy. If you have a question within a question, one question mark will do. If a closing quotation ends with a "strong" piece of punctuation, don't add a modest and redundant period to the whole sentence. Close with the strength of the quote.

INTERNAL PUNCTUATION

Internal punctuation includes the comma, the semicolon, the colon, and the dash. The single purpose of internal punctuation is to prevent confusion, to achieve clarity. The comma indicates brief pauses between separate elements in a sentence; the semicolon establishes a direct connection between two independent statements to form a single sentence; the colon serves to introduce things; and the dash permits you to digress or emphasize.

The Comma

Use the comma in compound sentences with coordinating conjunctions *and, but, yet, so, or, for*. A compound sentence joins two or more independent clauses that could be expressed separately as simple sentences. *Note that the comma precedes the conjunction:*

> "I walked slowly, *for* the detail on the beach was infinite." (Ernie Pyle)

> "The luncheon hour was long past; *and* the two had their end of the vast terrace to themselves." (Edith Wharton, "Roman Fever")

> "I was not going to talk about Whitewater today, *but* then I thought that if I didn't you'd think I know something about it, *and* the only way for me to prove that I don't is to talk about it at length, *so* I will." (Garrison Keillor)

In sentences where the clauses are short and the meaning is clear, you may omit a comma:

> The team tied the score in the last seconds of the game and the crowd cheered wildly.

If there is any possibility of misreading, you must use a comma:

> I went to the movies with Roger and Sally stayed home.

> I went to the movies with Roger, and Sally stayed home.

What Is a Comma Splice?

One of the most common errors in writing is the use of a comma alone to join independent clauses. This is the error familiar to students as the "run-on" sentence.

Run on: The crowd cheered wildly, the game was tied in the last few seconds.

I went to the movies with Roger, Sally stayed home.

The novel was riveting, I did not want it to end.

Correct: The crowd cheered wildly when the game was tied in the final seconds.

I went to the movies with Roger, and Sally stayed home.

The novel was riveting, so I did not want it to end.

Do I Use a Comma Before the Last Item in a Series?

Some editors and instructors insist that all items in a series be set off by a comma; others prefer that you omit the last one, especially in a series of single words:

You can find models of style in books, newspapers, and magazines.

You can find models of style in books, newspapers and magazines.

SUGGESTION: *For sentences like the one above, the second comma needlessly slows down the sentence and makes no contribution to clarity. In a series of longer expressions, however, or in a series without a conjunction, set off each with a comma.*

For class you are expected to bring a notebook, a pen or pencil, and the text we are reading.

"He was white-headed as a mountain, bowed in the shoulders, and faded in general aspect." (Thomas Hardy)

Writing has many purposes: personal expression, persuasion, literary effect, information.

USE A COMMA AFTER INTRODUCTORY CLAUSES

As the crowd cheered them on, the home team scored the winning touchdown.

If you are hungry, please help yourself to a sandwich.

"As the bell sounded the hour, there came a knocking at the street door." (Edgar Allan Poe)

Do not use a comma if the main clause is followed by a dependent clause:

Please help yourself to a sandwich whenever you get hungry.

The home team scored the winning touchdown as the crowd cheered them on.

USE A COMMA AFTER AN INTRODUCTORY PHRASE ONLY WHEN NEEDED

At last, the rain began to ease, and the sun came through breaks in the clouds.

The son of a tanner, Grant was everything Lee was not.

After the Labor Day recess, Congress will reconvene.

Feeling ill and confused, he left the dinner table without speaking.

These sentences require no comma:

On the desk you will find your final check and a letter of recommendation.

"For a long time they continued to sit side by side without speaking." (Edith Wharton)

USE COMMAS TO SET OFF DESCRIPTIVE AND NONESSENTIAL CLAUSES OR PHRASES WITHIN SENTENCES

"They were two strong men, these oddly different generals, and they represented the strengths of two conflicting currents that, through them, had come into final collision." (Bruce Catton)

The house on the corner, which was built in the 1880s, will be restored to its original design.

Shakespeare's plays, written nearly four hundred years ago, remain popular in theaters and movies as well as in English courses.

Use Commas with Some Single Words and Expressions

"Well, Jim's habits and his jokes didn't appeal to Julie . . ." (Ring Lardner, "Haircut")

"Now, I'll read the names—heads of families first." (Shirley Jackson, "The Lottery")

Use Commas with Parenthetic and Transitional Expressions

Use commas to set off such expressions as *however, moreover, therefore, nevertheless, after all, by the way, of course, on the other hand, I think.*

"Yet it was not all contrast, after all . . . Furthermore, their fighting qualities were really very much alike." (Bruce Catton)

After all, what you learn is what really matters.

You must, of course, always proofread a paper before handing it in.

Commas in Dates

For expressions of day, month, and year:

July 4, 1776, marks the beginning of the American Revolution.

Registration will take place on September 9, 1994, for the fall semester and on January 12, 1995, for the spring semester.

Do not use commas for expressions of month and year only.

Joan completed graduate school in June 1987, began her legal work in September 1987, and joined our firm in January 1993.

Commas with Adjectives in a Series

Use a comma when it means *and:*

The little room in Appomattox was "the scene of one of the poignant, dramatic contrasts in American history." (Bruce Catton)

The Regents examinations require you to write thoughtful, well-organized essays.

190

Do not use a comma if the adjective is part of the meaning of the noun:

She greeted her guests in the large sitting room.

USE COMMAS TO SET OFF QUOTES

"I always used to think," Mrs. Slade continued, "that our mothers had a much more difficult job than our grandmothers." (Edith Wharton, "Roman Fever")

"It isn't fair, it isn't right," Mrs. Hutchinson screamed, and then they were upon her. (Shirley Jackson, "The Lottery")

ADDITIONAL ILLUSTRATIONS OF COMMA USE

If you must sing, sing quietly.
These incidents took place a long, long time ago.

That's not what you meant, is it?
You have everything you need, don't you?

First come, first served.
Now you see it, now you don't.

Shakespeare's tragedy, *Macbeth*, is one of his best-known plays.
Verdi's only comic opera, *Falstaff,* is the last work he composed.

My sister Anne lives in Seattle; my sister Julia lives in New York.
My only sister, Anne, lives in Seattle.

COMMON ERRORS IN COMMA USE

Do not separate compound elements or isolate essential elements with commas.

Correct: "They greeted one another and exchanged bits of gossip
               as they went to join their husbands." (Shirley Jackson,
               "The Lottery")
Faulty: They greeted one another, and exchanged bits of gossip as
               they went to join their husbands.

Alternative:	*They greeted* one another, and *they exchanged* bits of gossip as they went to join their husbands.
Correct:	"Whales possess a highly complex language and have developed sophisticated communications systems that transmit over long distances." (Robert Finch)
Faulty:	Whales possess a highly complex language, and have developed sophisticated communications systems, that transmit over long distances.
Alternative:	*Whales possess* a highly complex language, *and they have developed* sophisticated communications systems that transmit over long distances.

In the faulty examples, the first comma may *look* necessary, but it improperly separates the subject from the second verb; the final clause in each case is essential description and should not be separated from the rest of the sentence. The alternative versions are accurately punctuated and show how the original, correct sentences could be revised into compound sentences.

SUGGESTION: In all the examples and explanations above, the commas serve one purpose: to make the expression clear on first reading. Insert commas in your own writing as you compose, as you hear the need for them. When you revise, do not be tempted to add commas simply because they look right—chances are, they do not belong.

The Semicolon

A comma indicates a brief pause between separate elements in a sentence, whereas a semicolon indicates a longer pause between independent statements that form a single sentence. The semicolon may replace *and* or *but* in compound sentences. Here are some of the examples used earlier now revised with semicolons.

I walked slowly; the detail on the beach was infinite.

The luncheon hour was long past; the two had their end of the vast terrace to themselves.

I was not going to talk about Whitewater today; then I thought that if I didn't, you'd think I know something about it; the only way for me to prove that I don't is to talk about it at length; so I will.

In each of these revisions, you can see that the effect of the semicolon is to indicate a cause and effect relationship or to show consequence without stating it directly. This results in forceful and emphatic sentences. The semicolon also has a formal quality; it creates a feeling of balance and equivalence among statements.

> ". . . with a semicolon . . . you get a pleasant little feeling of expectancy; there is more to come; read on; it will get clearer." (Lewis Thomas)

The Colon

Use the colon to introduce something: a list, the body of a letter, a quotation, or an explanation.

> "Political courage stems from a number of sources: anger, pain, love, hate." (Madeleine Kunin)
>
> "Mrs. Slade began again: 'I suppose I did it as a sort of joke' — " (Edith Wharton)
>
> "The purpose of life is to be useful. It is, above all, to *matter:* to have it make some difference that you lived at all." (Leo Rosten)

The Dash

The dash permits you to pause without notice and insert an idea too interesting to delay and too important to put in parentheses — but don't overdo it!

> "At some gut level, the art of politics — combative, competitive, self-asserting — is sometimes difficult to integrate with our feminine selves." (Madeleine Kunin)
>
> "Different as they were — in background, in personality, in underlying aspiration — these two great soldiers had much in common." (Bruce Catton)
>
> "The wonder of ourselves, of each other, and of life — this is the true subject matter of all novels." (Sandy Asher)

The Ellipsis

The ellipsis is used in quoted passages to show that something has been omitted.

> "The purpose of life is to be useful . . . above all, to *matter*." (Rosten)

When an ellipsis comes at the end of a sentence, the final period must be retained; that is, you will use four periods, not three. The following example shows the use of three ellipses: one in the middle of a sentence and two, each with a fourth period added, at the ends of sentences:

> Mark Van Doren asserts that "Iago's cynicism consists of believing that . . . the passions of men are toys for him to play with . . . . He likes nothing better than to make plans which other men's emotions will execute . . . ."

The Bracket

Brackets indicate where the writer has added a word or phrase to a quoted passage. Such additions are sometimes necessary to make connections in extended quotes where you have used ellipsis.

> "The persons of the tale were long since types [to Hawthorne], as were their souls' predicaments. The broken law, the hidden guilt, the hunger for confession, the studious, cold heart that watches and does not feel . . ." (Mark Van Doren)

> Men's passions should lead them to "more and better feeling . . . ," but Iago's knowledge of men's hearts transforms those passions into destructive forces, into "toys . . . tools to use." Iago contrives malign "plans which other men's [benign] emotions will execute."

The Apostrophe

The apostrophe has many important uses: to form contractions, to show possession, and to form the plural of numbers, symbols, and letters. Apostrophes are also easily misused. Below are examples of the most common uses.

CONTRACTIONS

The apostrophe takes the place of a missing letter or letters in a contraction:

> It's very warm today. = It is very warm today.

> You don't have to return the book right now. = You do not . . .

Remember that contractions are characteristic of spoken language and are not generally used in formal writing.

The apostrophe is also used to abbreviate dates:

June '82

The Class of '98

POSSESSIVE FORMS OF NOUNS AND PROPER NAMES

You form the possessive of a singular noun or name by adding an apostrophe and an *s*:

The novel's major themes (= The major themes of the novel)

My neighbor's house

Charles's notebook

Dickens's novels

In general, you form the possessive of a plural noun by adding the apostrophe alone:

My neighbors' yards

the jurors' verdict

the witnesses' statements

The Smiths' house

the Davises' horse

NOTE: Be sure to avoid the common error of confusing the possessive form with the plural.

Mark Twain wrote several novels; he did not write "novel's."

The local nursery sells plants; it does not sell "plant's."

SOME PLURALS

Use the apostrophe to form the plurals of letters and some abbreviations:

There were sixteen A's on the last exam.

"Dot your *i*'s and cross your *t*'s."

Mark has earned two Ph.D.'s, each in a different discipline.

TITLES OF WORKS OF LITERATURE

Titles of books and other full-length, separately published works should be set in italics. If you are composing on a typewriter or writing by hand, *underline* such titles. Movies and plays are also set in italics.

The Great Gatsby	*Death of a Salesman*
Huckleberry Finn	*The Glass Menagerie*
To Kill a Mockingbird	*Macbeth*

The names of newspapers and magazines should also be in italics.

The New York Times	*Harper's*	*Newsweek*

Titles of poems, essays, and short stories are set off in quotes.

"The Tell-Tale Heart"	"The Sleeping Giant"
"Roman Fever"	"The Road Not Taken"
"The Lottery"	"Old Photograph of the Future"

A title should not be underlined *and* set in quotes; this is redundant and confusing.

Your own title for an essay or paper should not be underlined; use quotes only for names or phrases actually quoted within the title.

A FINAL NOTE ON PUNCTUATION

The topics reviewed here are meant to offer fundamental guidelines and to illustrate how accurate punctuation helps make writing clear. Review some of the prose passages in other parts of the book for vivid examples of how different authors use punctuation to make their meaning and tone clear.

Chapter 11

SPELLING

We know how to spell many words because we recognize them from our reading and because we have, from childhood or as English language learners, developed awareness of the conventions of English spelling. Even though English spelling may seem confusing at times, most of the troublesome sounds or patterns reflect the history of English pronunciation and the fact that the English language developed after the forces of William the Conqueror, a Frenchman from Normandy, had invaded and settled in what is now the island of Great Britain. The resulting language is a fusion of Anglo-Saxon, French, and Latin.

SPELLING ON WRITING EXAMS

Does spelling count? The rubrics for the essays on the English Regents ELA exam include the "conventions" as a quality to be assessed. These are defined as ". . . conventional spelling, punctuation, paragraphing, capitalization, grammar and usage"; and on the SAT essay, frequent errors in grammar, usage, and mechanics are considered significant weaknesses in a student's writing.

If you know you have difficulties in spelling, use this chapter to review the common patterns of English spelling and to study the list of words commonly misspelled.

A word misspelled is a word misused, and egregious spelling errors may affect the scoring of your essay. You would also be expected to observe conventional spelling in preparing a college essay, a resume, or cover letter, and would avoid the spelling "shortcuts" we sometimes find useful in composing e-mail or text messages.

SPELLING RULES AND PATTERNS

As you review spelling rules and patterns, you need to be familiar with the following terms:

vowels The letters *a, e, i o, u,* and occasionally *y* signal the vowel, or sustained, sounds in English. The variations in these vowel sounds are spelled as combinations of more than one letter or as combinations with consonants.

consonants In English, the consonant letters and sounds are composed by the following: *b, c, d, f, g, h, j, k, l, m, n, p, q, r, s, t, v, w, x.* In contrast to vowels, consonant sounds do not sustain.

syllable A vowel sound or a combination of a vowel and consonant sounds that makes up a single impulse, or "beat," in a word. Words of one syllable: *think, read, act.* Words of two syllables: *reflect, insist, review.* We regularly use words of six or more syllables: *unintentionally, coincidentally.*

endings Single letters or syllables that indicate grammatical forms, such as noun plurals or verb conjugations. English, in contrast to other languages high school students may study, has relatively few "endings." Among them are *-s* or *-es* to form plural nouns or to indicate third-person *singular* verb forms, and the verb endings *-ing* and *-ed.*

suffixes Endings used to form new words and different parts of speech: *love, lovely, loveliness; occur, occurrence.* The addition of endings and suffixes to words often alters their spelling. (See next page.)

prefixes Units of one or two syllables that, like suffixes, are not "words" in themselves but have distinct meanings. They are placed at the beginning of existing words, or of what are called *stems* or *roots.* (See the section "Roots and Prefixes from Latin and Greek," Chapter 8, for many examples in English of Latin and Greek roots.) Words formed in this way are spelled to show their meanings: *illogical, overreact, misspell.*

Although most spelling "rules" have exceptions, there are many common patterns for spelling in English. The first group (pages 198–202) involves adding endings or suffixes.

Words That End in Silent *e*

➤ Drop the *e* before adding a suffix or ending that begins with a vowel:

dare + -ing	➤	= daring	➤	+ -ed = dared
hope + -ing	➤	= hoping	➤	+ -ed = hoped
amuse + -ing	➤	= amusing	➤	+ -ed = amused
revise + -ion	➤	= revision	➤	+ -ed = revised
advise + -able	➤	= advisable,	➤	+ -ed = advised
reverse + -ible	➤	= reversible	➤	+ -ed = reversed

➤ When adding *s* or a suffix that begins with a consonant, retain the *e*:

amuse	➤	amuses	➤	amusement
arrange	➤	arranges	➤	arrangement
hope	➤	hopes	➤	hopeless
huge	➤	hugeness	➤	hugely
place	➤	places	➤	placement
spite	➤	spiteful		
sure	➤	surely		

➤ When the word ends in *ce* or in *ge,* retain the *e* when adding *able* or *ous:*

change	➙	changeable
peace	➙	peaceable
service	➙	serviceable
advantage	➙	advantageous
courage	➙	courageous
outrage	➙	outrageous

➤ But drop the silent *e* before adding *ing:*

change	➙	changing
rage	➙	raging
service	➙	servicing
trace	➙	tracing

➤ Note the following **exceptions:**

argue	➙	argument
true	➙	truly
judge	➙	judgment
nine	➙	ninety
whole	➙	wholly

Words That End in y

➤ For words preceded by a consonant, change the *y* to an *i* before adding a suffix:

accompany	➙	accompaniment		
busy	➙	business	➙	busily
easy	➙	easily		
funny	➙	funnier	➙	funniest
happy	➙	happiness	➙	happily
lonely	➙	loneliness		
silly	➙	silliness	➙	sillier	➙	silliest

➤ The same pattern applies when we add *s* to form plural nouns or third-person-singular verb forms:

army	➙	armies
baby	➙	babies
city	➙	cities
marry	➙	marries
try	➙	tries
worry	➙	worries

➤ But retain the *y* before adding *ing, ism, ish*:

baby	➤	babyish	➤	babying
copy	➤	copying		
crony	➤	cronyism		
marry	➤	marrying		
try	➤	trying		
worry	➤	worrying		

➤ For words that end in *y* preceded by a vowel, retain *y:*

annoy	➤	annoys	➤	annoyance	➤	annoyed	➤	annoying
boy	➤	boys	➤	boyish				
day	➤	days						
destroy	➤	destroys	➤	destroyed	➤	destroying		
monkey	➤	monkeys						
play	➤	plays	➤	played	➤	playing	➤	player ➤
playful								
valley	➤	valleys						

➤ However:

say	➤	says	➤	**said**
pay	➤	pays	➤	**paid**

Double Letters

In writing, we must often stop to think whether to double letters in adding suffixes to words. Here are guidelines to follow.

➤ For one-syllable words that end in a single consonant preceded by a single vowel, *double* the final consonant before a suffix beginning with a vowel:

bat	➤	batter	➤	batting	
big	➤	bigger	➤	biggest	
fit	➤	fitted	➤	fitting	➤ fittest
sit	➤	sitter	➤	sitting	
spot	➤	spotty	➤	spotted	

As you look at the examples, you will see that the effect of the double consonant is to retain the pronunciation of the base word.

➤ Words formed by adding prefixes to one-syllable words follow the same pattern:

outfit	➤	outfitted	➤	outfitter
unwrap	➤	unwrapped		

➤ For one-syllable words that have double vowels or that end in more than one consonant, do *not* double the final consonant:

beat	➤	beating		
neat	➤	neatest		
mail	➤	mailing	➤	mailed
read	➤	reading	➤	reader
fail	➤	failure		
list	➤	listed		
faint	➤	fainted		

➤ However:

quit	➤	quitting

Because *u* must follow the *q*, *-ui* is considered a single vowel.

➤ Do not double the final consonant for words ending in *w, x,* or *y:*

draw	➤	drawing		
mix	➤	mixing		
play	➤	playing	➤	player

It is when we add endings to words of more than one syllable that spelling errors commonly occur.

➤ For words of more than one syllable ending in one vowel and one consonant, double the final consonant before an ending that begins with a vowel *if the last syllable of the base word is accented*:

confer	➤	conferred
infer	➤	inferred
refer	➤	referred
begin	➤	beginning
deter	➤	deterrence
omit	➤	omitted
commit	➤	committed
occur	➤	occurrence
equip	➤	equipped

➤ If the accent is *not* on the syllable to which the ending is added, *do not* double the final consonant:

benefit	➤	benefited	
credit	➤	credited	
open	➤	opening	
happen	➤	happening	
develop	➤	developing ➤	developed
deliver	➤	delivered ➤	delivering

➤ Note how the shift in accent determines spelling:

confer	➤	conference
infer	➤	inference
prefer	➤	preference
refer	➤	reference

Note the following exceptions:

➤ The following words double the final consonant:

program	➤	programmed ➤	programmer
question	➤	questionnaire	
excel	➤	excellence ➤	excellent

➤ Either form is considered acceptable for the following, but the first form, with a single -*l*, is preferred:

canceled	➤	cancelled
traveled	➤	travelled
traveling	➤	travelling

Adding Prefixes and Suffixes

With the exception of the patterns reviewed on the previous pages, which reflect how we pronounce the words, most words formed by adding prefixes and suffixes retain the spelling of each separate part. As a result, the full meaning of the word is reflected in its spelling:

mis + spell + ed	➤	= misspelled (both *s*'s are required)
mis + understand + ing	➤	= misunderstanding
dis + agree + able	➤	= disagreeable
dis + taste + ful	➤	= distasteful
dis + appear + ance	➤	= disappearance
dis + satisfaction	➤	= dissatisfaction

un + necessary	➤	= unnecessary
un + ending	➤	= unending
cool + ly	➤	= coolly
moral + ly	➤	= morally
co + operate	➤	= cooperate
de + emphasize	➤	= de-emphasize
re + entry	➤	= reentry
mean + ness	➤	= meanness
amuse + ment	➤	= amusement

➤ Note that words ending in *c* add a *k* as follows:

panic, panics	➤	panicky, panicked, panicking
mimic, mimics	➤	mimicked, mimicking
picnic, picnics	➤	picnicking, picnickers

Words That Include *ie* or *ei*

➤ Is it *i* before *e* or *e* before *i*? This is the spelling pattern everyone remembers.

i before *e*:

| chief | thief | relief | yield |

➤ Except after *c*:

| receive | ceiling | conceit |

➤ Or, when *ei* sounds long *a*:

| sleigh | neighbor | weigh | veil |

There are, however, several **exceptions** to this pattern. They must be memorized:

caffeine	foreign	plebeian	sovereign
counterfeit	forfeit	protein	surfeit
either	leisure	seize	weird
financier	neither	sheik	

Noun Plurals

➤ Noun *plurals* are generally formed by adding *s*:

cat   ➤   cats
house   ➤   houses
delay   ➤   delays
piano   ➤   pianos

➤ Nouns ending in *s, sh, ch, x,* and *z,* add *es* to form the plural:

watch   ➤   watches
brush   ➤   brushes
waltz   ➤   waltzes

➤ Nouns ending in the consonant *y*: drop the *y* and add *ies*:

spy   ➤   spies
lady   ➤   ladies
quantity   ➤   quantities

➤ However, do *not* alter the spelling of proper names:

There are two "Sallys" in the junior class.

Shakespeare wrote plays about the "Henrys" of England.

➤ Some words ending in *o* add *es* to form the plural:

echo   ➤   echoes
tomato   ➤   tomatoes
potato   ➤   potatoes
hero   ➤   heroes
veto   ➤   vetoes

➤ Some nouns ending in *f* or *fe* form the plural with *ves*:

calf   ➤   calves
elf   ➤   elves
knife   ➤   knives
life   ➤   lives
self   ➤   selves
thief   ➤   thieves
wife   ➤   wives

➤ Other nouns change their form internally:

man	➤	men
woman	➤	women
child	➤	children
mouse	➤	mice

➤ In compound expressions, the principal noun is made plural:

sisters-in-law

passers-by

spoonsful

Homophones

Many spelling problems occur because words have syllables whose sounds are alike but could be spelled in more than one way: for example, *cede, ceed, sede*. These are called homophones.

➤ The most common form is *cede:*

precede	antecede
concede	intercede

➤ A few forms are spelled *ceed:*

exceed	proceed	succeed

➤ Only one form is spelled *sede:*

supersede

➤ For *able, ible,* the more common form is *able:*

curable	lovable	peaceable
imaginable	movable	

➤ Though fewer in number, there are many common words ending in *ible*:

admissible	horrible	possible
compatible	intelligible	visible
credible	legible	
eligible	perceptible	

➤ There are also words ending in *ance, ant,* or *ence, ent:*

assistant	extravagant	ignorance
attendant	fragrant	relevance
dominant	hesitance	resistance

➤ Note, however:

adolescent	current	permanence
competent	frequent	vehemence
correspondent	negligence	

➤ Many nouns end in *-er*:

consumer	interpreter	philosopher
defender	organizer	

➤ Note, however:

actor	counselor	professor
creator	governor	tailor

NOTE: *The careful writer must memorize the most common spellings. We cannot always use a dictionary or a spellcheck program!*

On the following pages you will find a list of words often confused and an extensive list of words commonly misspelled.

WORDS COMMONLY CONFUSED

Many words in English sound or look very similar to one another. Such words are often "misspelled" as a result of the writer's confusion about them. Here are some of the most commonly confused words; *all are correctly spelled.* Be sure you know their respective meanings.

accept/except	breath/breathe
access/excess	choose/chose/chosen
adapt/adopt	cite/sight/site
advice/advise	cloths/clothes
affect/effect	coarse/course
allusion/illusion	complement/compliment
already/all ready	desert/dessert
altogether/all together	device/devise

discreet/discrete
dyeing/dying
elicit/illicit
elude/allude
envelop/envelope
formally/formerly
fourth/forth
hear/here
holy/wholly
hoping/hopping
idle/idol
imminent/eminent/emanate
its/it's
loath/loathe
local/locale
loose/lose
medal/meddle/metal/mettle
moral/morale
night/knight

principal/principle
quite/quiet
rain/reign/rein
right/rite
shone/shown
sight/site
stationary/stationery
than/then
their/there/they're
thorough/through
though/thought
threw/through
throne/thrown
to/too/two
vain/vane/vein
weather/whether
which/witch
who's/whose
your/you're

WORDS COMMONLY MISSPELLED

You will recognize the most familiar and the most notorious spelling demons in this list.

absence	acquire	against	analysis
absolutely	across	aggravate	analyze
academic	actually	aggravation	ancient
accept	address	aggressive	angrily
acceptance	adequately	alleviate	announcement
accessory	adherence	alliance	annually
accidentally	adjournment	ally	antagonist
accommodate	adjustment	almanac	antibiotic
accompanying	admittance	already	anticipation
accomplish	adolescent	altitude	antique
accuracy	advantage	amateur	anxious
achievement	advantageous	ambassador	apologetically
acknowledge	advertisement	amendment	apologies
acquaintance	advising	among	apologize

apology	argument	assumption	authority
apostrophe	arising	assurance	auxiliary
apparently	arrangement	atheist	availability
appreciate	article	athlete	avalanche
appropriate	artistically	athletic	average
approximate	ascend	attempt	awfully
aptitude	ascent	attendance	awkward
architecture	assassin	attractive	
Arctic	assent	audience	
argue	assistance	authoritative	
bachelor	before	boring	bruise
baggage	beginning	boundary	budget
banana	belief	breakfast	buoy
bankruptcy	believing	breath	buoyant
bargain	beneficial	breathe	bureau
barrel	benefit	bribery	burglar
basement	benefited	brief	burglarize
basically	bibliography	brilliant	business
beautify	bicycle	Britain	businesslike
becoming	biscuit	brittle	busy
cafeteria	cemetery	client	compatible
caffeine	censor	closet	compel
calculator	censure	clustered	compelled
calendar	century	coalition	competitive
calorie	certainly	coherence	competitor
campaign	challenge	collar	comprehensible
candidate	changeable	college	conceivable
cannibal	changing	colonel	conceive
canoe	channel	column	concentrate
capable	characterize	combustible	conception
capacity	chauffeur	comfortable	condemn
captain	chief	coming	condescend
career	chimney	commencement	conference
carrying	chivalry	commercial	conferred
cashier	chloride	commission	confidence
catastrophe	cholera	commit	confidential
category	choose	committee	connotation
caucus	choosing	communal	connote
carefully	choral	community	conqueror
cease	chose	companies	conscience
ceiling	chuckle	comparative	conscious
cellar	cite	comparison	consequence

consequently
considerable
considerably
consistency
consistent
conspicuous
contemporary
contempt
contemptible
contemptuous
continual
continuous
contribution

controlled
controlling
controversial
convenience
convenient
convertible
convocation
cool
coolly
cooperate
corollary
corps
correlate

corrode
corrupt
counterfeit
courteous
courtesy
cousin
credible
creditor
credulous
crisis
critical
criticism
criticize

cruel
cruelly
cupola
curiosity
curious
current
curriculum
curtain
customary
customer
cyclical
cylinder

dangerous
debris
debt
debtor
deceit
deceitful
deceived
decency
decent
deception
decide
decision
default
defendant
defense
defer
deference
deferred
define
definitely
definition
deity
delegate

deliberately
deodorant
dependable
dependent
depth
deputy
descend
descendant
descent
desert
desirable
despair
despite
dessert
destroy
detriment
devastate
developed
development
deviate
device
devise
dexterity

diameter
different
difficult
dilemma
diligent
dining
disappearance
disappointment
disapprove
disaster
disastrous
discern
disciple
disciplinary
discipline
discomfort
discriminate
discriminatory
disease
disillusion
dispatch
disposal
disregard

dissatisfied
dissent
dissimilar
dissipate
divinity
divisible
division
doesn't
dominant
dominate
dormitory
dough
dramatize
drunkenness
due
dully
duly
during
dye
dyeing
dying

earnest
easily
economically
economy
ecstasy
edge

edgy
edition
editor
effect
efficiency
efficient

eight
eighth
eighty
electoral
elicit
eligible

eliminate
eloquent
elude
emanate
embarrass
embassy

emigrant	entirely	evidently	existence
emigrate	envelop	exaggerate	expedite
emphasis	envelope	exaggeration	expedition
emphasize	environment	exceed	experience
emphatic	equality	excellence	experiment
empirical	equally	exceptional	explanation
employee	equipment	excessive	explanatory
encouragement	equipped	excitable	exploit
encouraging	equivalent	excitement	explore
endeavor	erroneous	exclusive	extension
enough	escapade	exclusively	extraordinary
entangle	especially	excursion	extravagant
enterprise	essential	exhibit	extremely
entertain	everything	exhibition	
facility	feminine	forbidden	frequently
fallacious	feminist	forehead	fried
fallacy	feud	foreign	friendless
familiar	fictitious	forewarn	friendliness
fantasy	fidelity	forgetting	friendly
fascinate	fiend	formally	friendship
fashion	fiery	formerly	fulfill
fatality	filial	forth	fulfillment
faulty	finally	forty	fundamental
favorable	financial	fourth	furious
favorite	financier	fraternity	furthermore
February	flair	freight	
felicity	fluent	frequency	
gaiety	genetics	governor	grievous
gallant	genius	gradually	grocery
gardener	genuine	grammar	guarantee
gaseous	global	grandeur	guidance
gasoline	glorious	graphics	guilt
generally	glossary	grief	gymnasium
generation	goddess	grievance	
generic	government	grieve	
hammer	headache	hereditary	hopeful
handkerchief	heard	heroes	hopeless
handsome	heathen	heroic	hoping
happiness	heavily	heroine	hopping
harassment	height	hindrance	humidity
harpoon	heir	honorable	humor

humorous	hybrid	hypnotize	hysteria
hundredth	hygiene	hypocrisy	
hungrily	hypnosis	hypocrite	
hurrying	hypnotism	hypothesis	
icicle	incidentally	infancy	interaction
ignorant	incompetent	inferiority	intercede
illegal	inconvenience	infinite	interrelated
illicit	incredible	ingenious	interrupt
illusion	indebted	ingenuity	intimate
illusory	indecisive	ingenuous	introduce
imaginary	indefinite	inhabitant	invisible
imagine	independence	initiative	ironic
immaculate	indispensable	innocence	irony
immediately	indivisible	inquiry	irrelevant
immense	indulge	insistent	irresistible
immigrant	interference	inspiration	irritable
immoderate	inertia	intelligence	island
impressionable	inevitable	intentionally	isle
jealousy	journey	junction	
jewelry	judge	justifiable	
journal	judgment	justify	
kerosene	knight	kowtow	
kindergarten	knowledge		
laboratory	leisure	limb	losing
laborer	leisurely	literary	lottery
launch	lenient	literature	lovable
lawyer	library	liveliness	loveless
league	license	loathe	luncheon
legacy	lighten	loneliness	luscious
legible	lightning	lonely	luxurious
legislator	likelihood	loose	lying
legitimate	likely	lose	
macaroni	management	meanness	memorable
machinery	managing	medical	merchandise
magazine	maneuver	medicinal	merchant
magnificent	marriage	medicine	merger
maintenance	massacre	medieval	meteor
malaria	mathematics	medley	mettle
manageable	maximum	melancholy	miniature

minimum
minister
miracle
mirror
mischief
mischievous

misdemeanor
misfit
missile
missionary
misspell
monarch

monogram
monopoly
moral
morale
mortgage
mortified

mosquitoes
mountain
movable
muffle
muscle
mysterious

naturally
necessary
necessity
negligent

neighborly
nickel
niece
ninety

ninth
noticeable
notorious
nuclear

nuisance

obedience
oblige
obnoxious
obscure
observant
obstacle
obtuse

occasionally
occur
occurred
occurrence
official
omission
omitted

opinion
opportunity
opposite
optimism
orchard
ordinarily
organize

originally
outrageous
overrated
owing

package
pageant
paid
pamphlet
parachute
paradox
paradoxical
paragraph
parallel
paralysis
parcel
parenthesis
parliament
partial
particle
particularly
pastime
patient
patriotic
patriotism
patron
peaceable
peasant
peculiar

pennant
perceive
percentage
perception
perilous
permanence
permanent
permissible
perplex
persistence
persistent
personally
personnel
persuade
persuasion
persuasive
pertinent
philosophy
physical
physician
pianos
picnic
picnicking
piece

pierce
pigeon
pillar
planned
plausible
playwright
pleasant
pledge
plentiful
politeness
politician
popularity
portable
possess
possession
possibility
possibly
potatoes
practicality
prairie
prayer
precede
precedent
precious

predominant
preference
preferred
prejudice
preoccupied
preparation
presence
presidency
prestige
prevail
prevalence
priest
primitive
principal
principles
priority
privilege
probability
probable
procedural
procedure
proceed
professional
professor

prohibitive
prologue
promenade
prominent
promising
pronunciation

propel
propeller
prophecy
proprietor
psychiatrist
psychoanalysis

psychologist
psychosomatic
publicity
punctuation
purchase
purchasing

purgatory
purity
pursue
pursuit

qualified
qualitative

quandary
quantity

query
questionable

quiet
quite

radiant
ratify
realize
really
recede
receipt
receive
recessive
recognizable
recollect
recommend

recruit
recur
reference
referred
reign
rein
reliable
relieve
reluctance
remembrance
reminisce

repetitious
requirement
requisition
residence
resistance
resolving
resourceful
responsible
restaurant
reveille
rewrite

rhapsody
rhetoric
rheumatism
rhyme
rhythm
ridiculous
rigidity
routine

sacrifice
safety
salary
satellite
satisfactory
savage
scandal
scarcely
scary
scenery
scent
schedule
schism
scissors
scold
sculptor
secede
secrecy
secretary
seize
seniority
senseless

sensible
sensitive
separate
sergeant
several
shadowy
shady
shepherd
sheriff
shield
shining
shoulder
siege
sieve
significant
simile
simultaneous
sincerely
singular
siphon
skillful
society

solemn
solicit
soliloquy
solos
sophomore
source
sovereign
spaghetti
specimen
spectacles
spectacular
spirited
sponsor
squirrel
statue
stifle
stomach
straight
strategy
strength
strenuous
stressful

studying
submission
subsidy
substantial
substitute
subtle
succeed
successful
successive
sufficient
suffix
summary
superb
surgeon
surprise
susceptible
suspense
suspicion
suspicious
sustained
syllable
syllabus

symbol	sympathize	symptom	
symmetrical	symphonic	synonym	
tableau	thematic	traction	treachery
tailor	theoretical	traffic	treason
technique	therefore	trafficked	treasury
temperament	thorough	tragedy	truant
temperature	tireless	tragic	truly
temporary	tobacco	transfer	turmoil
tendency	tolerance	transferred	twelfth
terrific	tomato	transistor	twilight
terrifying	tomatoes	transitive	typical
territory	tomorrow	transparent	tyranny
testimony	tournament	traveler	tyrant
umbrella	unison	urban	utterance
unanimous	unnecessary	urgent	
unconscious	unprecedented	usually	
undoubtedly	unveil	utensil	
vacuum	varying	vicinity	vinegar
valleys	vegetable	victim	volcano
valuable	vehicle	village	volunteer
variety	vengeance	villain	
various	vengeful	villainous	
warrant	weird	wholly	writing
warrior	whereabouts	woolen	written
wary	whimsical	wrangle	
weapon	whistle	wrestle	
weather	wholesome	write	
yacht	yield		

RECOMMENDED READING

The titles listed below, readily available in paperback, represent many of the classic and contemporary works most widely read and studied in comprehensive high school English courses; the emphasis is on works written in English, primarily by American writers. These titles are recommended to the student seeking to supplement regular course assignments or to prepare independently for the Regents exam. All would be suitable choices for an essay on the AP English Literature and Composition exam. These works also represent valuable additions to a student's personal library.

NOVELS

1984	George Orwell
A Death in the Family	James Agee
A Farewell to Arms	Ernest Hemingway
A Separate Peace	John Knowles
A Star Called Henry	Roddy Doyle
A Tale of Two Cities	Charles Dickens
All the King's Men	Robert Penn Warren
Americanah	Chimamanda Ngozi Adichie
Arrowsmith	Sinclair Lewis
Babbitt	Sinclair Lewis
Beloved	Toni Morrison
Billy Budd	Herman Melville
Brave New World	Aldous Huxley
Catch-22	Joseph Heller
Catcher in the Rye	J. D. Salinger
Cold Mountain	Charles Frazier
Daisy Miller	Henry James
Deliverance	James Dickey
Ethan Frome	Edith Wharton
Farenheit 451	Ray Bradbury
Felicia's Journey	William Trevor
Great Expectations	Charles Dickens
Huckleberry Finn	Mark Twain
Invisible Man	Ralph Ellison
Light in August	William Faulkner
Lord of the Flies	William Golding
Main Street	Sinclair Lewis

Native Son	Richard Wright
Netherland	Joseph O'Neill
Oliver Twist	Charles Dickens
One Hundred Years of Solitude	Gabriel Garcia Marquez
Ordinary People	Judith Guest
Rabbit, Run	John Updike
Ragtime	E. L. Doctorow
Rebecca	Daphne DuMaurier
Red Badge of Courage	Stephen Crane
Rumors of Peace	Ella Leffland
Sister Carrie	Theodore Dreiser
Slaughterhouse Five	Kurt Vonnegut
So Long, See You Tomorrow	William Maxwell
Summer	Edith Wharton
That Night	Alice McDermott
The Age of Innocence	Edith Wharton
The Assistant	Bernard Malamud
The Awakening	Kate Chopin
The Bean Trees	Barbara Kingsolver
The Bonfire of the Vanities	Tom Wolfe
The Caine Mutiny	Herman Wouk
The Centaur	John Updike
The Color Purple	Alice Walker
The Crying of Lot 49	Thomas Pynchon
The Grapes of Wrath	John Steinbeck
The Great Fire	Shirley Hazzard
The Great Gatsby	F. Scott Fitzgerald
The Heart Is a Lonely Hunter	Carson McCullers
The Human Stain	Philip Roth
The Joy Luck Club	Amy Tan
The Known World	Edward P. Jones
The Natural	Bernard Malamud
The Old Man and the Sea	Ernest Hemingway
The Secret Agent	Joseph Conrad
The Scarlet Letter	Nathaniel Hawthorne
The Time Machine	H. G. Wells
Things Fall Apart	Chinua Achebe
Things Invisible to See	Nancy Willard
To Kill a Mockingbird	Harper Lee
Underworld	Don DeLillo
Washington Square	Henry James
White Teeth	Zadie Smith
Wolf Hall	Hilary Mantel
World's Fair	E. L. Doctorow

AUTOBIOGRAPHY, ESSAYS, AND OTHER NONFICTION

A Civil Action	Jonathan Harr
A Hole in the Sky	Robert Finch
An American Childhood	Annie Dillard
Angela's Ashes	Frank McCourt
Black Boy	Richard Wright
Blood Dark Track	Joseph O'Neill
Cities on a Hill	Francis Fitzgerald
Dreams from My Father	Barack Obama
Growing Up	Russell Baker
Hiroshima	John Hersey
Hunger of Memory	Richard Rodriguez
I Know Why the Caged Bird Sings	Maya Angelou
Into Thin Air	Jon Krakauer
Iron and Silk	Mark Salzman
King of the World	David Remnick
Late Innings	Roger Angell
Nickel and Dimed	Barbara Ehrenreich
Night	Elie Wiesel
Notes of a Native Son	James Baldwin
Out of Africa	Isak Dinesen
Pilgrim at Tinker Creek	Annie Dillard
Stop-Time	Frank Conroy
Such, Such Were the Joys	George Orwell
The Art of Fiction	David Lodge
The Color of Water	James McBride
The Courage of Turtles	Edward Hoagland
The Crack-Up	F. Scott Fitzgerald
The Devils of Loudon	Aldous Huxley
The Duke of Deception	Geoffrey Wolff
The Last Cowboy	Jane Kramer
The Lives of a Cell	Lewis Thomas
The Mismeasure of Man	Stephen Jay Gould
The Solace of Open Spaces	Gretel Ehrlich
The Way to Rainy Mountain	N. Scott Momaday
The Warmth of Other Suns	Isabel Wilkerson
The White Album	Joan Didion
This Boy's Life	Tobias Wolff
This House of Sky	Ivan Doig
Travels with Charley	John Steinbeck
Up from Slavery	Booker T. Washington
Walden	Henry David Thoreau

There are many excellent collections of essays and literary nonfiction available. Here are some recommended classic and contemporary authors whose works are available in paperback editions:

Roger Angell	Stephen Jay Gould	Cynthia Ozick
Joan Didion	Garrison Keillor	David Remnick
Ralph Waldo	Tracy Kidder	Richard Rodriguez
Emerson	Verlyn Klinkenborg	Roger Rosenblatt
M. F. K. Fisher	Jane Kramer	Gore Vidal
Ian Frazier	Peter Mathiesson	Eudora Welty
Atul Gawande	Jane Mayer	E. B. White
Malcolm Gladwell	John McPhee	
Adam Gopnik	H. L. Mencken	

Recommended anthologies include:

The Art of the Personal Essay, by Philip Lopate; Anchor Books
The Best American Essays of the Century, Joyce Carol Oates, ed.; Houghton Mifflin Co.
The Best American Essays, compiled from essays written for magazines and journals and published annually by Houghton Mifflin Co.

Other volumes in the Best American Series, also published annually, include:

The Best American Sports Writing
The Best American Travel Writing
The Best American Science and Nature Writing
The Best American Nonrequired Reading

POETRY

Readers are urged to seek out collections of work by poets whom they encounter in class readings and whom they especially admire. *Dover Publications* offers nicely produced and very inexpensive paperback collections of poetry, including works of Shakespeare and other major British poets, as well as major American poets of the nineteenth and twentieth centuries. They are available from Dover online and in bookstores. Among the many poets introduced to high school students and whose work is widely available in paperback collections are the following:

W. H. Auden	Donald Hall	Adrienne Rich
Elizabeth Bishop	Langston Hughes	Theodore Roethke
Louise Bogan	Denise Levertov	Carl Sandburg
Gwendolyn Brooks	W. S. Merwin	Vijay Seshadri
Billy Collins	Edna St. Vincent	Charles Simic
e. e. cummings	Millay	*May Swenson
Emily Dickinson	Marianne Moore	William Stafford
*Rita Dove	Howard Nemerov	Richard Wilbur
T. S. Eliot	*Sharon Olds	Nancy Willard
Carolyn Forché	*Marge Piercy	William Carlos
Robert Frost	Robert Pinsky	Williams
Louise Glück	Sylvia Plath	

* denotes a poet whose work has appeared on a New York State English Regents exam

Some currently available paperback anthologies of poetry include:

Poetry 180, An Anthology of Contemporary Poems, Billy Collins, ed.; Random House
Good Poems, selected and introduced by Garrison Keillor; Penguin Books
Poetry Daily, 366 Poems, selected from the Poetry Daily website; Sourcebooks Inc.
The Best American Poetry, annual series, David Lehman, ed.; Scribner
Contemporary American Poetry, Donald Hall, ed.; Viking
The Mentor Book of Major American Poets, Oscar Williams and Edwin Honig, eds.; New American Library
The Vintage Book of Contemporary American Poetry, J. D. McClatchy, ed.

Websites for the interested reader:

Poetry Daily: *www.poems.com*
Poetry Foundation: *www.poetryfoundation.org*
Academy of American Poets: *www.poets.org*
Poet's House: *www.poetshouse.org*
www.poemhunter.com

SHORT STORIES

Some recommended authors whose stories are available in paperback:

Sherwood Anderson	Nathaniel Hawthorne	Edgar Allan Poe
John Barth	Ernest Hemingway	Isaac Bashevis Singer
Ambrose Bierce	Bernard Malamud	William Trevor
Willa Cather	Bharati Mukherjee	John Updike
Isak Dinesen	Alice Munro	Kurt Vonnegut
William Faulkner	Joyce Carol Oates	Edith Wharton
F. Scott Fitzgerald	Tim O'Brien	Eudora Welty
Mavis Gallant	Flannery O'Connor	John Edgar Wideman

Collections available in paperback include:

Annual publications:
The O. Henry Prize Stories
The Best American Short Stories
The Pushcart Prize: Best of the Small Presses

Anthologies:
American Short Story Masterpieces, Raymond Carver and Tom Jenks, eds.
The Norton Anthology of Short Fiction, R. V. Cassill, ed.
The Oxford Book of American Short Stories, Joyce Carol Oates, ed.
The Oxford Book of Short Stories, V. S. Pritchett, ed.
    (includes British and American writers)
The Vintage Book of Contemporary American Short Stories, Tobias Wolff, ed.

PLAYS

Shakespeare	*Macbeth, Julius Caesar, Othello, As You Like It, Hamlet, King Lear, Much Ado About Nothing, The Tempest, Henry V*
Paddy Chayevsky	*Marty*
Anton Chekov	*Three Sisters, The Cherry Orchard, Uncle Vanya*
Henrik Ibsen	*A Doll's House, The Master Builder*
Edward Albee	*Who's Afraid of Virginia Woolf?, Zoo Story*
David Auburn	*Proof*
Samuel Beckett	*Waiting for Godot*
Robert Bolt	*A Man for All Seasons*
Noel Coward	*Blithe Spirit, Private Lives*
Mart Crowley	*The Boys in the Band*

Horton Foote	*Dividing the Estate, The Trip to Bountiful, The Young Man from Atlanta*
William Gibson	*The Miracle Worker*
Susan Glaspell	*Trifles*
John Guare	*Six Degrees of Separation*
A. R. Gurney	*The Dining Room*
Lorraine Hansberry	*A Raisin in the Sun*
Lillian Hellman	*The Little Foxes*
Beth Henley	*Crimes of the Heart*
William Inge	*Come Back, Little Sheba; Picnic; Bus Stop*
Eugene Ionesco	*The Lesson, The Bald Soprano, Rhinoceros*
George S. Kaufman/Moss Hart	*You Can't Take It With You, The Man Who Came to Dinner*
Jerome Lawrence/ Robert Lee	*Inherit the Wind*
Terrence McNally	*Master Class*
Arthur Miller	*All My Sons, Death of a Salesman, The Crucible, The Price, A View From the Bridge*
Clifford Odets	*Waiting for Lefty, The Country Girl*
Eugene O'Neill	*Long Day's Journey into Night*
Harold Pinter	*The Caretaker*
Terrence Rattigan	*The Winslow Boy, The Browning Version*
Yasmina Reza	*Art*
Rod Serling	*Requiem for a Heavyweight*
Peter Shaffer	*Equus, Black Comedy, The Royal Hunt of the Sun, Amadeus*
George Bernard Shaw	*Pygmalion*
Neil Simon	*The Odd Couple, Brighton Beach Memoirs*
Tom Stoppard	*Rosenkrantz and Guildenstern Are Dead, Arcadia, The Real Thing, Jumpers, The Coast of Utopia*
Alfred Uhry	*Driving Miss Daisy*
Wendy Wasserstein	*The Heidi Chronicles*
Oscar Wilde	*The Importance of Being Earnest*
Thornton Wilder	*Our Town, The Matchmaker, The Skin of Our Teeth*
Tennessee Williams	*The Glass Menagerie, A Streetcar Named Desire, Cat on a Hot Tin Roof, Sweet Bird of Youth*
August Wilson	*Fences, The Piano Lesson, Ma Rainey's Black Bottom, Jitney, Joe Turner's Come and Gone*

Appendices

The New York State Common Core Learning Standards for English Language Arts

The following 11/12 grade-specific standards define end-of-year expectations and a cumulative progression designed to enable students to meet college and career readiness (CCR) expectations no later than the end of high school. The new ELA/Common Core Regents Exam is designed to assess many (but not all) of the standards in each of the categories: Reading Literature, Reading Informational Texts, Writing, and Language.

READING STANDARDS FOR LITERATURE GRADES 11/12 (RL)

1. Cite strong and thorough textual evidence to support analysis of what the text says explicitly as well as inferences drawn from the text, including determining where the text leaves matters uncertain.

2. Determine two or more themes or central ideas of a text and analyze their development over the course of the text, including how they interact and build on one another to produce a complex account; provide an objective summary of the text.

3. Analyze the impact of the author's choices regarding how to develop and relate elements of a story or drama (e.g., where a story is set, how the action is ordered, how the characters are introduced and developed).

4. Determine the meaning of words and phrases as they are used in the text, including figurative and connotative meanings; analyze the impact of specific word choices on meaning and tone, including words with

---

multiple meanings or language that is particularly fresh, engaging, or beautiful. (Include Shakespeare as well as other authors.)

5. Analyze how an author's choices concerning how to structure specific parts of a text (e.g., the choice of where to begin or end a story, the choice to provide a comedic or tragic resolution) contribute to its overall structure and meaning as well as its aesthetic impact.

6. Analyze a case in which grasping a point of view requires distinguishing what is directly stated in a text from what is really meant (e.g., satire, sarcasm, irony, or understatement).

7. Analyze multiple interpretations of a story, drama, or poem (e.g., recorded or live production of a play or recorded novel or poetry), evaluating how each version interprets the source text. (Include at least one play by Shakespeare and one play by an American dramatist.)

*8. Delineate and evaluate the argument and specific claims in a text, including the validity of the reasoning as well as the relevance and sufficiency of the evidence.

9. Demonstrate knowledge of eighteenth-, nineteenth-, and early-twentieth-century foundational works of American literature, including how two or more texts from the same period treat similar themes or topics.

10. By the end of grade 11, read and comprehend literature, including stories, dramas, and poems, in the grades 11–CCR text complexity band proficiently, with scaffolding as needed at the high end of the range.

11. By the end of grade 12, read and comprehend literature, including stories, dramas, and poems, at the high end of the grades 11–CCR text complexity band independently and proficiently.

*This anchor standard does not apply to literature.

READING STANDARDS FOR
INFORMATIONAL TEXT GRADES 11/12   (RI)

1. Cite strong and thorough textual evidence to support analysis of what the text says explicitly as well as inferences drawn from the text, including determining where the text leaves matters uncertain.

2. Determine two or more central ideas of a text and analyze their development over the course of the text, including how they interact and build on one another to provide a complex analysis; provide an objective summary of the text.

3. Analyze a complex set of ideas or sequence of events and explain how specific individuals, ideas, or events interact and develop over the course of the text.

4. Determine the meaning of words and phrases as they are used in a text, including figurative, connotative, and technical meanings; analyze how an author uses and refines the meaning of a key term or terms over the course of a text.

5. Analyze and evaluate the effectiveness of the structure an author uses in his or her exposition or argument, including whether the structure makes points clear, convincing, and engaging.

6. Determine an author's point of view or purpose in a text in which the rhetoric is particularly effective, analyzing how style and content contribute to the power, persuasiveness, or beauty of the text.

7. Integrate and evaluate multiple sources of information presented in different media or formats (e.g., visually, quantitatively) as well as in words in order to address a question or solve a problem.

8. Delineate and evaluate the reasoning in seminal U.S. texts, including the application of constitutional principles and use of legal reasoning (e.g., in U.S. Supreme Court majority opinions and dissents) and the premises, purposes, and arguments in works of public advocacy (e.g., The Federalist, presidential addresses).

9. Analyze seventeenth-, eighteenth-, and nineteenth-century foundational U.S. documents of historical and literary significance (including The Declaration of Independence, the Preamble to the Constitution, the Bill of Rights, and Lincoln's Second Inaugural Address) for their themes, purposes, and rhetorical features.

10. By the end of grade 11, read and comprehend literary nonfiction in the grade 11–CCR text complexity band proficiently, with scaffolding as needed at the high end of the range. By the end of grade 12, read and comprehend literary nonfiction at the high end of the grade 11–CCR text complexity band independently and proficiently.

WRITING STANDARDS
GRADES 11/12   (W)

1. Write arguments to support claims in an analysis of substantive topics or texts, using valid reasoning and relevant and sufficient evidence.

2. Write informative/explanatory texts to examine and convey complex ideas and information clearly and accurately through the effective selection, organization, and analysis of content.

3. Write narratives to develop real or imagined experiences or events using effective technique, well-chosen details, and well-structured event sequences.

4. Produce clear and coherent writing in which the development, organization, and style are appropriate to task, purpose, and audience.

5. Develop and strengthen writing as needed by planning, revising, editing, rewriting, or trying a new approach.

6. Use technology, including the Internet, to produce and publish writing and to interact and collaborate with others.

7. Conduct short as well as more sustained research projects based on focused questions, demonstrating understanding of the subject under investigation.

8. Gather relevant information from multiple print and digital sources, assess the credibility and accuracy of each source, and integrate the information while avoiding plagiarism.

9. Draw evidence from literary or informational texts to support analysis, reflection, and research.

10. Write routinely over extended time frames (time for research, reflection, and revision) and shorter time frames (a single sitting or a day or two) for a range of tasks, purposes, and audiences.

11. Develop personal, cultural, textual, and thematic connections within and across genres as they respond to texts through written, digital, and oral presentations, employing a variety of media and genres.

LANGUAGE STANDARDS
GRADES 11/12   (L)

Conventions of Standard English

1. Demonstrate command of the conventions of standard English grammar and usage when writing or speaking.

2. Demonstrate command of the conventions of standard English capitalization, punctuation, and spelling when writing.

Knowledge of Language

3. Apply knowledge of language to understand how language functions in different contexts, to make effective choices for meaning or style, and to comprehend more fully when reading or listening.

Vocabulary Acquisition and Use

4. Determine or clarify the meaning of unknown and multiple meaning words and phrases by using context clues, analyzing meaningful word parts, and consulting general and specialized reference materials, as appropriate.

5. Demonstrate understanding of figurative language, word relationships, and nuances in word meanings.

6. Acquire and use accurately a range of general academic and domain-specific words and phrases sufficient for reading, writing, speaking, and listening at the college and career readiness level; demonstrate independence in gathering vocabulary knowledge when considering a word or phrase important to comprehension or expression.

HOW IS THE REGENTS ELA
(COMMON CORE) EXAM SCORED?

WEIGHTING OF PARTS

Each of the three parts of the Regents Examination in English Language Arts (Common Core) has a number of raw score credits associated with the questions/tasks within that part. In order to ensure an appropriate distribution of credits across the test, each part is weighted.

For Part 1, each multiple-choice question is worth one point. The Part 2 essay is scored on a 6-point rubric and then weighted $\times$ 4. The Part 3 Text Analysis is scored on a 4-point rubric and then weighted $\times$ 2.

227

As you can see, the Part 2 Argument Essay is the most heavily weighted section.

The table below shows the raw score credits, weighting factor, and weighted score credits for each part of the test. This information will be used to determine each student's scale score (final exam score) through the use of a conversion chart provided by NYSED.

Part	Maximum Raw Score Credits	Weighting Factor	Maximum Weighted Score Credits
Part 1	24	1	24
Part 2	6	4	24
Part 3	4	2	8
			Total 56

The conversion table is determined independently for each administration of the exam. You can find the conversion tables for both forms of the Regents English Exams at *http://www.nysedregents.org*.

SCORING RUBRICS FOR THE REGENTS ELA (COMMON CORE) EXAM

Parts 2 and 3 of the Regents Examination in English Language Arts (Common Core) will be scored using new holistic rubrics. Part 2 will be scored using a 6-credit rubric, and Part 3 will be scored using a 4-credit rubric. Both rubrics reflect the new demands called for by the Common Core Learning Standards for English Language Arts and Literacy through the end of Grade 11.

New York State Regents Examination in English Language Arts (Common Core)
Part 2 Rubric
Writing from Sources: Argument

Criteria	6 Essays at this Level	5 Essays at this Level	4 Essays at this Level	3 Essays at this Level	2 Essays at this Level	1 Essays at this Level
Content and Analysis: the extent to which the essay conveys complex ideas and information clearly and accurately in order to support claims in an analysis of the texts	-introduce a precise and insightful claim, as directed by the task -demonstrate in-depth and insightful analysis of the texts, as necessary to support the claim and to distinguish the claim from alternate or opposing claims	-introduce a precise and thoughtful claim, as directed by the task -demonstrate thorough analysis of the texts, as necessary to support the claim and to distinguish the claim from alternate or opposing claims	-introduce a precise claim, as directed by the task -demonstrate appropriate and accurate analysis of the texts, as necessary to support the claim and to distinguish the claim from alternate or opposing claims	-introduce a reasonable claim, as directed by the task -demonstrate some analysis of the texts, but insufficiently distinguish the claim from alternate or opposing claims	-introduce a claim -demonstrate confused or unclear analysis of the texts, failing to distinguish the claim from alternate or opposing claims	-do not introduce a claim -do not demonstrate analysis of the texts
Command of Evidence: the extent to which the essay presents evidence from the provided texts to support analysis	-present ideas fully and thoughtfully, making highly effective use of a wide range of specific and relevant evidence to support analysis -demonstrate proper citation of sources to avoid plagiarism when dealing with direct quotes and paraphrased material	-present ideas clearly and accurately, making effective use of specific and relevant evidence to support analysis -demonstrate proper citation of sources to avoid plagiarism when dealing with direct quotes and paraphrased material	-present ideas sufficiently, making adequate use of specific and relevant evidence to support analysis -demonstrate proper citation of sources to avoid plagiarism when dealing with direct quotes and paraphrased material	-present ideas briefly, making use of some specific and relevant evidence to support analysis -demonstrate inconsistent citation of sources to avoid plagiarism when dealing with direct quotes and paraphrased material	-present ideas inconsistently and/or inaccurately, in an attempt to support analysis, making use of some evidence that may be irrelevant -demonstrate little use of citations to avoid plagiarism when dealing with direct quotes and paraphrased material	-present little or no evidence from the texts -do not make use of citations

Coherence, Organization, and Style: the extent to which the essay logically organizes complex ideas, concepts, and information using formal style and precise language	-exhibit skillful organization of ideas and information to create a cohesive and coherent essay -establish and maintain a formal style, using sophisticated language and structure	-exhibit logical organization of ideas and information to create a cohesive and coherent essay -establish and maintain a formal style, using fluent and precise language and sound structure	-exhibit acceptable organization of ideas and information to create a coherent essay -establish and maintain a formal style, using precise and appropriate language and structure	-exhibit some organization of ideas and information to create a mostly coherent essay -establish but fail to maintain a formal style, using primarily basic language and structure	-exhibit inconsistent organization of ideas and information, failing to create a coherent essay -lack a formal style, using some language that is inappropriate or imprecise	-exhibit little organization of ideas and information -are minimal, making assessment unreliable -use language that is predominantly incoherent, inappropriate, or copied directly from the task or texts
Control of Conventions: the extent to which the essay demonstrates command of conventions of standard English grammar, usage, capitalization, punctuation, and spelling	-demonstrate control of conventions with essentially no errors, even with sophisticated language	-demonstrate control of the conventions, exhibiting occasional errors only when using sophisticated language	-demonstrate partial control, exhibiting occasional errors that do not hinder comprehension	-demonstrate emerging control, exhibiting occasional errors that hinder comprehension	-demonstrate a lack of control, exhibiting frequent errors that make comprehension difficult	-are minimal, making assessment of conventions unreliable

- An essay that addresses fewer texts than required by the task can be scored no higher than a 3.
- An essay that is a personal response and makes little or no reference to the task or texts can be scored no higher than a 1.
- An essay that is totally copied from the task and/or texts with no original student writing must be scored a 0.
- An essay that is totally unrelated to the task, illegible, incoherent, blank, or unrecognizable as English must be scored as a 0.

New York State Regents Examination in English Language Arts (Common Core)
Part 3 Rubric
Text Analysis: Exposition

Criteria	4 Responses at this Level	3 Responses at this Level	2 Responses at this Level	1 Responses at this Level
Content and Analysis: the extent to which the response conveys complex ideas and information clearly and accurately in order to respond to the task and support an analysis of the text	-introduce a well-reasoned central idea and a writing strategy that clearly establish the criteria for analysis -demonstrate a thoughtful analysis of the author's use of the writing strategy to develop the central idea	-introduce a clear central idea and a writing strategy that establish the criteria for analysis -demonstrate an appropriate analysis of the author's use of the writing strategy to develop the central idea	-introduce a central idea and/or a writing strategy -demonstrate a superficial analysis of the author's use of the writing strategy to develop the central idea	-introduce a confused or incomplete central idea or writing strategy and/or -demonstrate a minimal analysis of the author's use of the writing strategy to develop the central idea
Command of Evidence: the extent to which the response presents evidence from the provided text to support analysis	-present ideas clearly and consistently, making effective use of specific and relevant evidence to support analysis	-present ideas sufficiently, making adequate use of relevant evidence to support analysis	-present ideas inconsistently, inadequately, and/or inaccurately in an attempt to support analysis, making use of some evidence that may be irrelevant	-present little or no evidence from the text
Coherence, Organization, and Style: the extent to which the response logically organizes complex ideas, concepts, and information using formal style and precise language	-exhibit logical organization of ideas and information to create a cohesive and coherent response -establish and maintain a formal style, using precise language and sound structure	-exhibit acceptable organization of ideas and information to create a coherent response -establish and maintain a formal style, using appropriate language and structure	-exhibit inconsistent organization of ideas and information, failing to create a coherent response -lack a formal style, using language that is basic, inappropriate, or imprecise	-exhibit little organization of ideas and information -use language that is predominantly incoherent, inappropriate, or copied directly from the task or text -are minimal, making assessment unreliable

| Control of Conventions: the extent to which the response demonstrates command of conventions of standard English grammar, usage, capitalization, punctuation, and spelling | -demonstrate control of the conventions with infrequent errors | -demonstrate partial control of conventions with occasional errors that do not hinder comprehension | -demonstrate emerging control of conventions with some errors that hinder comprehension | -demonstrate a lack of control of conventions with frequent errors that make comprehension difficult
-are minimal, making assessment of conventions unreliable |

- A response that is a personal response and makes little or no reference to the task or text can be scored no higher than a 1.
- A response that is totally copied from the text with no original writing must be given a 0.
- A response that is totally unrelated to the task, Illegible, incoherent, blank, or unrecognizable as English must be scored as a 0.

Regents ELA (Common Core) Examination June 2015

English Language Arts

PART 1—Reading Comprehension

Directions (1–24): Closely read each of the three passages below. After each passage, there are several multiple-choice questions. Select the best suggested answer to each question and write its number in the space provided. You may use the margins to take notes as you read.

Reading Comprehension Passage A

Newland Archer is reacquainted with Ellen Mingott (now Countess Olenska) while attending a party with some of 1870s' New York aristocracy.

It was generally agreed in New York that the Countess Olenska had "lost her looks."

She had appeared there first, in Newland Archer's boyhood, as a brilliantly pretty little girl of nine or ten, of whom people said that she
(5) "ought to be painted." Her parents had been continental wanderers, and after a roaming babyhood she had lost them both, and been taken in charge by her aunt, Medora Manson, also a wanderer, who was herself returning to New York to "settle down." ...

Every one was disposed to be kind to little Ellen Mingott, though
(10) her dusky red cheeks and tight curls gave her an air of gaiety that seemed unsuitable in a child who should still have been in black for her parents. It was one of the misguided Medora's many peculiarities to flout the unalter-

able rules that regulated American mourning, and when she stepped from
the steamer her family were scandalised to see that the crape veil she wore
(15) for her own brother was seven inches shorter than those of her sisters-
in-law, while little Ellen was in crimson merino and amber beads, like a
gipsy foundling.[1]

But New York had so long resigned itself to Medora that only a few
old ladies shook their heads over Ellen's gaudy clothes, while her other
(20) relations fell under the charm of her high colour and high spirits. She
was a fearless and familiar little thing, who asked disconcerting questions, made precocious comments, and possessed outlandish arts, such
as dancing a Spanish shawl dance and singing Neapolitan love-songs
to a guitar. Under the direction of her aunt (whose real name was Mrs.
(25) Thorley Chivers, but who, having received a Papal title,[2] had resumed her
first husband's patronymic,[3] and called herself the Marchioness Manson,
because in Italy she could turn it into Manzoni) the little girl received an
expensive but incoherent education, which included "drawing from the
model," a thing never dreamed of before, and playing the piano in quin-
(30) tets with professional musicians. ...

These things passed through Newland Archer's mind a week later as he
watched the Countess Olenska enter the van der Luyden drawing-room on
the evening of the momentous dinner. The occasion was a solemn one, and
he wondered a little nervously how she would carry it off. She came rather
(35) late, one hand still ungloved, and fastening a bracelet about her wrist;
yet she entered without any appearance of haste or embarrassment the
drawing-room in which New York's most chosen company was somewhat
awfully assembled.

In the middle of the room she paused, looking about her with a grave
(40) mouth and smiling eyes; and in that instant Newland Archer rejected the
general verdict on her looks. It was true that her early radiance was gone.
The red cheeks had paled; she was thin, worn, a little older-looking than
her age, which must have been nearly thirty. But there was about her the
mysterious authority of beauty, a sureness in the carriage of the head, the
(45) movement of the eyes, which, without being in the least theatrical, struck
him as highly trained and full of a conscious power. At the same time she
was simpler in manner than most of the ladies present, and many people
(as he heard afterward from Janey)[4] were disappointed that her appearance was not more "stylish"—for stylishness was what New York most

---

[1]foundling—an abandoned child
[2]Papal title—a title given by the Pope
[3]patronymic—male family name
[4]Janey—Newland Archer's sister

(50) valued. It was, perhaps, Archer reflected, because her early vivacity[5] had disappeared; because she was so quiet—quiet in her movements, her voice, and the tones of her low-pitched voice. New York had expected something a good deal more resonant in a young woman with such a history.

The dinner was a somewhat formidable business. Dining with the van
(55) der Luydens was at best no light matter, and dining there with a Duke who was their cousin was almost a religious solemnity. It pleased Archer to think that only an old New Yorker could perceive the shade of difference (to New York) between being merely a Duke and being the van der Luydens' Duke. New York took stray noblemen calmly, and even (except
(60) in the Struthers set) with a certain distrustful *hauteur*;[6] but when they presented such credentials as these they were received with an old-fashioned cordiality that they would have been greatly mistaken in ascribing solely to their standing in Debrett.[7] It was for just such distinctions that the young man cherished his old New York even while he smiled at it. ...

(65) The Countess Olenska was the only young woman at the dinner; yet, as Archer scanned the smooth plump elderly faces between their diamond necklaces and towering ostrich feathers, they struck him as curiously immature compared with hers. It frightened him to think what must have gone to the making of her eyes.

(70) The Duke of St. Austrey, who sat at his hostess's right, was naturally the chief figure of the evening. But if the Countess Olenska was less conspicuous than had been hoped, the Duke was almost invisible. Being a well-bred man he had not (like another recent ducal[8] visitor) come to the dinner in a shooting-jacket; but his evening clothes were so shabby and
(75) baggy, and he wore them with such an air of their being homespun, that (with his stooping way of sitting, and the vast beard spreading over his shirt-front) he hardly gave the appearance of being in dinner attire. He was short, round-shouldered, sunburnt, with a thick nose, small eyes and a sociable smile; but he seldom spoke, and when he did it was in such low
(80) tones that, despite the frequent silences of expectation about the table, his remarks were lost to all but his neighbours.

When the men joined the ladies after dinner the Duke went straight up to the Countess Olenska, and they sat down in a corner and plunged into animated talk. Neither seemed aware that the Duke should first have
(85) paid his respects to Mrs. Lovell Mingott and Mrs. Headly Chivers, and the Countess have conversed with that amiable hypochondriac, Mr. Urban

---

[5]vivacity—liveliness
[6]hauteur—display of arrogance
[7]Debrett—British aristocracy reference book
[8]ducal—relating to a duke

Dagonet of Washington Square, who, in order to have the pleasure of meeting her, had broken through his fixed rule of not dining out between January and April. The two chatted together for nearly twenty minutes;
(90)   then the Countess rose and, walking alone across the wide drawing-room, sat down at Newland Archer's side.

It was not the custom in New York drawing-rooms for a lady to get up and walk away from one gentleman in order to seek the company of another. Etiquette required that she should wait, immovable as an idol,
(95)   while the men who wished to converse with her succeeded each other at her side. But the Countess was apparently unaware of having broken any rule; she sat at perfect ease in a corner of the sofa beside Archer, and looked at him with the kindest eyes. ...

—Edith Wharton
excerpted from *The Age of Innocence*, 1920
Windsor Editions, by arrangement with D. Appleton and Company

1 In the context of the entire passage, the tone established by line 1 can best be described as

   (1) indifferent   (3) compassionate

   (2) judgmental   (4) admiring   1_____

2 The use of flashback in lines 3 through 30 serves to

   (1)   relate Countess Olenska's history

   (2)   describe Newland Archer's ancestry

   (3)   explain Medora Manson's talents

   (4)   identify Thorley Chivers's perspective   2_____

3 The meaning of "flout" as used in line 12 is clarified by the word

   (1)   "wanderer" (line 7)

   (2)   "dusky" (line 10)

   (3)   "scandalised" (line 14)

   (4)   "relations" (line 20)   3_____

4 The description of Ellen in lines 18 through 30 conveys that people viewed her as

   (1) unique   (3) fashionable

   (2) simple   (4) unhealthy   4_____

5 The words "disconcerting" (line 21) and "precocious" (line 22) imply that, as a child, the Countess Olenska was

   (1) impatient   (3) timid

   (2) untamed   (4) hesitant   5_____

6 Medora Manson, as described in the passage, can best be characterized as

   (1) cautious   (3) intellectual

   (2) overprotective   (4) unconventional   6_____

7 Based on the text, the reader can infer that Newland Archer is

   (1) oblivious to the party's guests
   (2) intimidated by the Duke's presence
   (3) intrigued by the Countess Olenska
   (4) resentful toward the wealthy class   7____

8 The Duke and the Countess Olenska are similar in that they are both

   (1) ignored by almost everyone at dinner
   (2) interested in marriage opportunities
   (3) unconcerned with social expectations
   (4) considered to be of lesser nobility   8____

9 What effect is created by viewing the Countess at the party through Archer's eyes?

   (1) It emphasizes a distinction between the Countess and the guests.
   (2) It reveals a conflict between the Countess and Medora.
   (3) It clarifies a growing relationship between the Countess and the Duke.
   (4) It enhances the differences between the Countess and Archer.   9____

10 The fact that the Countess leaves one gentleman to speak with another (lines 89 through 91) shows that she

   (1) has an unnatural need for the Duke's attention
   (2) is concerned about her reputation at the party
   (3) is actively avoiding Newland Archer's conversation
   (4) has little regard for customs associated with gender   10____

Reading Comprehension Passage B

Machines

I hear them grinding, grinding, through the night,
The gaunt machines with arteries of fire,
Muscled with iron, boweled with smoldering light;
I watch them pulsing, swinging, climbing higher,
(5)   Derrick[1] on derrick, wheel on rhythmic wheel,
Swift band on whirring band, lever on lever,
Shouting their songs in raucous notes of steel,
Blinding a village with light, damming a river.
I hear them grinding, grinding, hour on hour,
(10) Cleaving the night in twain,[2] shattering the dark
With all the rasping torrents of their power,
Groaning and belching spark on crimson spark.
I cannot hear my voice above their cry
Shaking the earth and thundering to the sky.

(15) Slowly the dawn comes up. No motors stir
The brightening hilltops as the sunrise flows
In yellow tides where daybreak's lavender
Clings to a waiting valley. No derrick throws
The sun into the heavens and no pulley
(20) Unfolds the wildflowers thirsting for the day;
No wheel unravels ferns deep in a gulley; No
engine starts the brook upon its way.
The butterflies drift idly, wing to wing,
Knowing no measured rhythm they must follow;
(25) No turbine drives the white clouds as they swing
Across the cool blue meadows of the swallow.
With all the feathered silence of a swan
They whirr and beat—the engines of the dawn.

—Daniel Whitehead Hicky
from *Bright Harbor*, 1932
Henry Holt and Company

---

[1]derrick—a large machine used for lifting
[2]twain—two

11 The use of figurative language in lines 2 and 3 contributes to the poem's meaning by

   (1) expressing a frustration with the loss of nature
   (2) establishing a parallel between man and machine
   (3) affirming the essential human need for machines
   (4) illustrating the struggle for society's survival   11____

12 The description of the machines' songs as "raucous" (line 7) conveys that the songs are

   (1) extremely harsh
   (2) largely misunderstood
   (3) deeply inspirational
   (4) highly engaging   12____

13 The poet's use of "groaning and belching" (line 12) is used to convey

   (1) his affection for most machines
   (2) the importance of inventions
   (3) his desire for progress
   (4) the difficult work of machines   13____

14 A central idea that is reinforced by lines 27 and 28 is that nature

   (1) contributes to its own destruction
   (2) accomplishes its tasks with ease
   (3) endorses the notion of progress
   (4) reveals the mysteries of life   14____

Reading Comprehension Passage C

Speech of Patrick Henry, delivered in the House of Delegates of Virginia, in support of his motion to put the colony in a state of defense against the encroachments[1] of Great Britain, March, 1775.

...Mr. President, it is natural to man to indulge in the illusions of hope. We [American colonists] are apt to shut our eyes against a painful truth, and listen to the song of that syren [siren], till she seduces our judgments. Is it the part of wise men, engaged in a great and arduous struggle for liberty?
(5)   Are we disposed to be of the number of those, who having eyes, see not, and having ears, hear not the things which so nearly concern our temporal salvation? For my part, whatever anguish of spirit it might cost, I am willing to know the whole truth; to know the worst, and to provide for it. I have but one lamp by which my feet are guided, and that is the lamp of experience. I
(10)   know of no way of judging of the future, but by the past; and, judging by the past, I wish to know what there has been in the conduct of the British ministry for the last ten years, to justify those hopes with which gentlemen have been pleased to solace themselves and the house? Is it that insidious[2] smile with which our petition has been lately received? Trust it not, sir, it
(15)   will prove a snare to your feet. Suffer not yourselves to be betrayed with a kiss. Ask yourselves how this gracious reception of our petition, comports[3] with those warlike preparations which cover our waters and darken our land? Are fleets and armies necessary to a work of love and reconciliation? Have we shown ourselves so unwilling to be reconciled, that force must be
(20)   called in to win back our love? Let us not deceive ourselves, sir. These are the implements of war and subjugation[4]—the last arguments to which kings resort. I ask gentlemen, sir, what means this martial array, if its purpose be not to force us to submission? Can gentlemen assign any other possible motive for it? Has Great Britain any enemy in this quarter of the world, to
(25)   call for all this accumulation of navies and armies? No, sir, she has none: they are meant for us: they can be meant for no other purpose—they are sent over to bind and rivet upon us those chains, which the British ministry have been so long forging. And what have we to oppose to them? Shall we try argument? Sir, we have been trying that for the last ten years. Have
(30)   we any thing new to offer upon the subject? Nothing. We have held the subject up in every light of which it is capable; but it has been all in vain.

---

[1]encroachments—aggressions
[2]insidious—slyly deceitful
[3]comports—agrees
[4]subjugation—oppression

Shall we resort to entreaty and humble supplication?[5] What terms shall we find, which have not been already exhausted? Let us not, I beseech you, sir, deceive ourselves longer. Sir, we have done every thing that could be done,

(35) to avert the storm which is now coming on. We have petitioned—we have remonstrated[6] we have supplicated—we have prostrated[7] ourselves before the throne, and have implored its interposition to arrest the tyrannical hands of the ministry and parliament. Our petitions have been slighted; our remonstrances have produced additional violence and insult; our sup-

(40) plications have been disregarded; and we have been spurned, with contempt, from the foot of the throne.

In vain, after these things, may we indulge the fond hope of peace and reconciliation. *There is no longer any room for hope*. If we wish to be free—if we mean to preserve inviolate those inestimable privileges for which we

(45) have been so long contending—if we mean not basely to abandon the noble struggle in which we have been so long engaged, and which we have pledged ourselves never to abandon, until the glorious object of our contest shall be obtained—we must fight!—I repeat it, sir, we must fight—An appeal to arms and to the God of Hosts, is all that is left us!

(50) They tell us, sir, that we are weak—unable to cope with so formidable an adversary. But when shall we be stronger? Will it be the next week, or the next year? Will it be when we are totally disarmed; and when a British guard shall be stationed in our House? Shall we gather strength by irreso- lution and inaction? Shall we acquire the means of effectual resistance, by

(55) lying supinely on our backs, and hugging the delusive phantom of hope, until our enemies shall have bound us, hand and foot? Sir, we are not weak, if we make a proper use of those means which the God of nature hath placed in our power—three millions of people, armed in the holy cause of Liberty, and in such a country as that which we possess; are invincible by any force

(60) which our enemy can send against us.

Sir, we shall not fight our battles alone. There is a just God, who presides over the destinies of nations, and will raise up friends to fight our battles for us. The battle, sir, is not to the strong alone; it is to the vigilant, the active, the brave. Besides, sir, we have now no election. If we were base enough to

(65) desire it, it is now too late to retire from the contest. There is no retreat, but in submission and slavery. Our chains are forged:—their clanking may be heard on the plains of Boston! The war is inevitable—and let it come!! I repeat it, sir, let it come!!!

---

[5]supplication—begging
[6]remonstrated—pleaded in protest
[7]prostrated—laid down in a humble manner

It is in vain, sir, to extenuate the matter. Gentlemen may cry, peace,
(70) peace—but there is no peace! The war is actually begun! The next gale that
sweeps from the north, will bring to our ears the clash of resounding arms!
Our brethren are already in the field! Why stand we here idle? What is it that
gentlemen wish? What would they have? Is life so dear, or peace so sweet,
as to be purchased at the price of chains, and slavery? Forbid it, Almighty
(75) God!—I know not what course others may take; but as for me, GIVE ME
LIBERTY, OR GIVE ME DEATH!

—Patrick Henry
excerpted and adapted from *The Mental Guide, Being a Compend of
the First Principles of Metaphysics, and a System of Attaining an
Easy and Correct Mode of Thought and Style in Composition by
Transcription; Predicated on the Analysis of the Human Mind*, 1828
Marsh & Capen, and Richardson & Lord

15 Lines 1 through 3 help to frame the speaker's argument by

    (1)   addressing human frailties
    (2)   exposing outside criticisms
    (3)   explaining common misconceptions
    (4)   proposing certain compromises   15_____

16 Lines 7 and 8 help to express the speaker's desire to

    (1)   locate the necessary resources
    (2)   rely on outside assistance
    (3)   insist on short-term solutions
  *(4)   confront the unpleasant reality   16_____

17 The major effect of the figurative language used in
lines 26 and 28 ("they are sent … so long forging") is
to emphasize the

    (1)   loyalty of subjects
    (2)   respect for authority
    (3)   penalty for treason
    (4)   loss of freedom   17_____

18 The overall purpose of the first paragraph (lines 1
through 41) is to

    (1)   explain the role of government
    (2)   question the importance of reason
    (3)   analyze the existing situation
    (4)   expose the failings of law   18_____

19 In the context of the speech, the purpose of the
statement, "They tell us, sir, that we are weak—
unable to cope with so formidable an adversary"
(lines 50 and 51) is to

    (1)   introduce a counterclaim
    (2)   address a financial crisis
    (3)   explain a confusing concept
    (4)   defend a known fact   19_____

20 Which phrase clarifies the speaker's view of Britain's intentions for the colonies?

  (1) "gracious reception" (line 16)
  (2) "war and subjugation" (line 21)
  (3) "inestimable privileges" (line 44)
  (4) "irresolution and inaction" (lines 53–54)   20_____

21 The purpose of the rhetorical questions in lines 43 through 47 is to emphasize the consequence of

  (1) selfishness   (3) greed
  (2) arrogance   (4) indecision   21_____

22 What is the main message delivered by the speaker to his audience in lines 42 through 49?

  (1) If we fight together we will win.
  (2) The state will supply us with arms.
  (3) The enemy is weaker than first thought.
  (4) We must outlaw slavery forever.   22_____

23 As used in line 64 the word "election" most nearly means

  (1) support   (3) enemies
  (2) choice   (4) politics   23_____

24 The speaker's overall tone may best be described as

  (1) contented   (3) passionate
  (2) frightened   (4) satirical   24_____

PART 2—Argument Response

Directions: Closely read each of the *four* texts on pages 248 through 256 and write a source-based argument on the topic below. You may use the margins to take notes as you read and scrap paper to plan your response. Write your argument on a separate sheet of paper.

Topic: Should college athletes be paid?

Your Task: Carefully read each of the *four* texts provided. Then, using evidence from at least *three* of the texts, write a well-developed argument regarding whether or not college athletes should be paid. Clearly establish your claim, distinguish your claim from alternate or opposing claims, and use specific, relevant, and sufficient evidence from at least *three* of the texts to develop your argument. Do *not* simply summarize each text.

Guidelines:

Be sure to

- Establish your claim regarding whether or not college athletes should be paid.
- Distinguish your claim from alternate or opposing claims.
- Use specific, relevant, and sufficient evidence from at least *three* of the texts to develop your argument.
- Identify each source that you reference by text number and line number(s) or graphic (for example: Text 1, line 4 or Text 2, graphic).
- Organize your ideas in a cohesive and coherent manner.
- Maintain a formal style of writing.
- Follow the conventions of standard written English.

Texts:

Text 1—The Case for Paying College Athletes

Text 2—It's Time to Pay College Athletes

Text 3—Sorry Time Magazine: Colleges Have No Reason to Pay Athletes

Text 4—There's No Crying in College: The Case Against Paying College Athletes

Text 1

The Case for Paying College Athletes

The college sports industry generates $11 billion in annual revenues. Fifty colleges report annual revenues that exceed $50 million. Meanwhile, five colleges report annual revenues that exceed $100 million. These revenues come from numerous sources, including ticket sales, sponsorship

(5) rights, and the sale of broadcast rights. The National Collegiate Athletic Association [NCAA] recently sold broadcast rights to its annual men's basketball tournament for upwards of $770 million per season. And the Big Ten Conference has launched its own television network that sells air time to sponsors during the broadcast of its football and men's basketball

(10) games.

These college sports revenues are passed along to NCAA executives, athletic directors and coaches in the form of salaries. In 2011, NCAA members paid their association president, Mark Emmert, $1.7 million. Head football coaches at the 44 NCAA Bowl Championship Series schools

(15) received on average $2.1 million in salaries. The highest paid public employee in 40 of the 50 U.S. states is the state university's head football or basketball coach. At the University of Alabama, the head football coach, Nick Saban, recently signed a contract paying him $7 million per year—more than 160 times the average wage of a Tuscaloosa public

(20) school teacher.

Nevertheless, the NCAA member colleges continue to vote to forbid the sharing of revenues with student-athletes. Instead, they hide behind a "veil of amateurism" that maintains the wealth of college sports in the hands of a select few administrators, athletic directors and coaches. This

(25) "veil" not only ensures great wealth for athletic directors and coaches, but it also ensures sustained poverty for many of the athletes who provide their labor. A 2011 report entitled "The Price of Poverty in Big Time College Sport" confirms that 85 percent of college athletes on scholarship live below the poverty line.

(30) Not only are the NCAA rules that prevent colleges from paying student-athletes immoral, but they also are likely illegal. Section 1 of the Sherman Antitrust Act, in pertinent part, states that "every contract, combination ... or conspiracy, in restraint of trade or commerce ... is declared to be illegal." Applying this language, any agreement among

(35) NCAA members to prohibit the pay of student-athletes represents a form of wage fixing that likely violates antitrust law. In addition, the NCAA's no-pay rules seem to constitute an illegal boycott of any college that would otherwise seek to pay its student-athletes.

(40) The NCAA defends its no-pay rules on several dubious grounds. For example, it claims that compensating student-athletes would destroy competitive balance in college sports; however, it does not consider the possibility of other less restrictive alternatives to maintain competitive balance. In addition, the NCAA claims that compensating student-athletes would create a Title IX[1] problem; however, the average Division I men's basket-
(45) ball coach earns nearly twice as much in salary as the average Division I women's basketball coach. NCAA members have not suggested terminating the pay of college basketball coaches to resolve this concern.

The argument in favor of allowing colleges to pay their student-athletes comes down to economic efficiency, distributive justice and a reason-
(50) able interpretation of antitrust laws. By contrast, the argument against allowing pay to student-athletes arises mainly from greed and self-interest.

—Marc Edelman
excerpted and adapted from "The Case for Paying College Athletes"
http://www.usnews.com, January 6, 2014

[1]Title IX—law that prohibits discrimination based on gender in any federally funded education program or activity

Text 2

It's Time to Pay College Athletes

...The historic justification for not paying players is that they are amateur student-athletes and the value of their scholarships—often worth in excess of $100,000 over four years—is payment enough. But a growing number of economists and sports experts are beginning to argue for giv-

(5)   ing athletes a fair share of the take. The numbers are too large to ignore. College athletes are mass-audience performers and need to be rewarded as such. "The rising dollar value of the exploitation of athletes," says Roger Noll, a noted sports economist from Stanford University, "is obscene, is out of control." ...

(10)   Most scholarships are revocable, so if an athlete doesn't perform well on the field, he can, in a sense, be fired from college. But academic work for some athletes is secondary: top men's basketball and football players spend 40 hours per week on their sports, easily. During football season, former Georgia tailback Richard Samuel, who earned an undergraduate

(15)   degree in sports management in 2011, said he was an "athlete-student," not a "student-athlete," as the NCAA wants people to believe. "In the fall, we would spend way more time on sports than academics," says Samuel.

Players are essentially working full-time football jobs while going to school; they deserve to be paid more than a scholarship. Because even

(20)   full-ride athletic scholarships don't cover the full cost of attending school, athletes are often short a few thousand bucks for ancillary expenses on top of tuition, room and board, books and fees: money for gas, shampoo and, yes, maybe a few beers. Some athletes are on only partial scholarship or are walk-ons[1] still paying full tuition.

(25)   While many players scrimp, their head coaches don't. Average salaries for major college football coaches have jumped more than 70% since 2006, to $1.64 million, according to *USA Today*. For major-conference men's hoops coaches who made the 2012 March Madness tournament, pay is up 20%, to $2.25 million, over that of coaches who made the 2010 tour-

(30)   nament, according to the *Journal of Issues in Intercollegiate Athletics*. "It's nuts," says Michael Martin, chancellor of the Colorado State University system, who was chancellor at Louisiana State University from 2008 to 2012. LSU hired Les Miles to coach its football team in 2005; Miles now

---

[1]walk-ons—non-scholarship athletes

(35)   earns $4.3 million annually. "It's time for people to step up and say, We think this is the max that a football coach ought to get, and we ought to stick to it," says Martin. ...

The time is right to give schools the option to share their rising sports income with college athletes. Not every school would—or could—participate. Only the 60 or so schools in the power conferences, which have (40)   the football and basketball revenues to support such payments, would likely even consider such an option. With conferences and schools set to see record television payouts for the next decade and beyond, the idea of paying players is no longer just fodder for academic debate. It's an ethical imperative. ...

—Sean Gregory
excerpted from "It's Time to Pay College Athletes"
Time, September 16, 2013

Text 3

Sorry Time Magazine: Colleges Have
No Reason to Pay Athletes

...In its current issue that features [Johnny] Manziel on the cover, *Time* argues vehemently for payments to big time college athletes, even calling the issue "an ethical imperative." The magazine cites the usual laundry list—schools enjoying exposure while pulling in millions,
(5) coaches making big salaries and local bars thriving on game nights. All while the poor players get nothing.

John Rowady, president of sports marketing firm rEvolution, which has worked with many colleges, disagrees. He believes that paying the players as professionals carries a big risk of the public quickly tuning
(10) out. "It would create a massive unknown, you have to wonder if it would change the whole dynamic of what it means to be a student-athlete," he says.

There's also another fundamental issue that never seems to come up. It's called the free marketplace. Why don't schools pay? Because they
(15) don't have to. Recruits jump on the offer of tuition, room and board without hesitation. And let's not call them exploited—they aren't. Slaves were exploited. A scholarship athlete at a university can leave anytime he wants to, free to become a tuition-paying student like anyone else.

When you really think about it, many of us are just way too enamored
(20) with the word "should," as in a college athlete "should" be paid. It's shorthand for trying to impose our own sensibilities onto others, to stick our noses where they don't belong. The issue of compensation for college athletes really comes down to the colleges and the athletes. According to census bureau data, college graduates earn approximately $1 million
(25) more during their lifetimes than people whose highest educational attainment is a high school diploma. Most have to invest $100,000 to $200,000 to get that coveted college degree. A scholarship athlete doesn't.

Rowady sees another form of payment that gets overlooked, at least for the top players: brand building. A top notch football or basketball
(30) recruit isn't just getting the competitive experience he needs for launching a pro career. He's gaining exposure that's bound to pay off in endorsements and a nice contract the moment he turns pro.

"They perform in a high profile environment, and gain access to incredible networks of people," says Rowady. For those who aren't pro
(35) material: study. Your education is free, remember.

(40)   Few ever benefitted more from the exposure factor than the man behind an attention-grabbing lawsuit against the NCAA over player media likenesses, Ed O'Bannon. The former basketball player earned close to $4 million during a brief and disappointing NBA career after he was picked by the New Jersey Nets in the first round of the 1995 draft.[1] Why was O'Bannon drafted so high? Probably because he had just led UCLA to the 1995 national title in front of a massive March Madness audience. Sure, O'Bannon had talent, but there's little doubt that the big brands of UCLA and March Madness pushed his evaluation a bit out of proportion.

(45)   Add it all up, and the marketplace produces a collegiate athletic population that is generally happy with what it gets—a free education and broad sports exposure. That doesn't mean there's anything wrong adding some cash to college players' current benefits. Or to let Manziel and others make money signing autographs or doing commercials. If they can get organized and get more for what they do, good for them. ...

(50)

—Tom Van Riper
excerpted and adapted from "Sorry Time Magazine:
Colleges Have No Reason to Pay Athletes"
http://www.forbes.com, September 6, 2013

---

[1]draft—process by which teams select eligible athletes

Text 4

There's No Crying in College: The Case
Against Paying College Athletes

...Should college athletes get a piece of the $871.6 million pie the
NCAA brings in annually?

The answer is simple: No, absolutely not.

College athletes are already being paid with an athletic scholarship
(5)   that is worth between $20–$50,000 per year.

Oh, and that does not even begin to factor in the medical and travel
expenses, free gear, top-notch coaching, unlimited use of elite athletic
facilities and a national stage to audition for a job in the professional
ranks.

(10)   All of those perks are paid for in full by the universities these athletes
choose to attend.

Before attempting to discredit some of the cases for compensating
players at the college level, let's take into account all of the things they
already receive cost-free.

(15)   Athletic scholarships cover just about everything a student-athlete
needs to survive for four years at a major university. Campus housing,
daily medical care and free meals via training table are all included.
Tuition and books are covered as well.

None of those things are cheap. It costs $57,180 to attend Duke
(20)   University. The University of Texas charges $35,776 for out-of-state
enrollees. Even Butler University charges $31,496 per year.

This means many college athletes are being reimbursed with nearly as
much money as the average American makes per year.

Leaving a four-year college with a degree will help former players earn
(25)   more money than those who only have a high school diploma, regardless
of whether or not they move on to a professional sports career.

Students who attain a Bachelor's degree will make $1.1 million more
in their lifetimes than non-graduates.

Traveling around the world is another privilege these student-athletes
(30)   are afforded. ...

The Fair Market Value Argument

This is one of the more common stances pay-for-play supporters take. The idea that players are not being paid their "fair market value," however, is a complete myth.

(35)   The two sports impacted by this argument the most are football and basketball, because their revenue funds just about every other varsity team at most universities.

These athletes have to be worth millions, right? Wrong. College athletes are not worth a single cent on the open market, at least until they are eligible for the NBA or NFL draft.

(40)   Changes to the NBA draft eligibility requirements brought an end to high school athletes heading straight to the professional ranks. Now, NBA hopefuls must be one year removed from high school to enter the draft.

Meanwhile, NFL prospects have to wait three years before they can be drafted.

(45)   Every student-athlete knows they cannot get paid in college, but if they do not like it there are other options.

Brandon Jennings was the No. 1-overall basketball prospect in the country in 2008. Instead of attending college, Jennings opted to sign a $1.2 million deal with Lottomatica Roma, a professional team in Italy.

(50)   The Compton, CA product was drafted 10th by the Milwaukee Bucks after playing one season overseas.

Much like the foreign basketball associations, the Canadian Football League does not have an age requirement. High school graduates wishing to play pro football can head north and sign a contract right away. ...

(55)   Instead of choosing this route, though, NFL and NBA hopefuls take their talents to the NCAA. The media exposure, coaching and training provided by the universities is far better than the athletes will receive in foreign markets. Going to classes is simply the tradeoff for reaping these benefits. ...

Paying College Athletes Will Eliminate Scandals

(60)   Contrary to popular belief, the recent scandals involving the Ohio State Buckeyes, Miami (Fla.) Hurricanes and USC Trojans are not exactly anything new to college athletics.

Paying players will not eliminate any of the greed or determination to win at all costs that exists in today's society. Cheating will never stop, and
(65)   it existed at the NCAA level well before the era of modern technology. ...

The NCAA Has More Than Enough Money to Pay Players

Although the NCAA reels in over $800 million per year, 81 percent of which comes from television and marketing-rights fees, the organization continues to be non-profit.

How is this possible? An astounding 96 percent of the revenue the
(70) NCAA brings in annually is redistributed to its members' institutions.

This is done through donations to academic enhancement, conference grants, sports sponsorships, student assistance funds and grants-in-aid. A percentage of revenue is also added to the basketball fund, which is divided up and distributed to the NCAA tournament field on a yearly
(75) basis.

The universities themselves are not exactly rolling in wads of cash, either. Last year, only 22 athletic departments were profitable. Football and basketball bring in the dough, and every other college sport survives as a result.

(80) Remember this year's Cinderella story in March Madness, the Florida Gulf Coast Eagles? The university nearly lost money as a result of their run to the Sweet 16.

Two years ago, the Division I Board of Directors approved a $2,000 stipend for college athletes to cover the "full cost of attendance." Less
(85) than two months later, the NCAA's member institutions repealed the stipend, because they could not afford it.

College athletics may sound like a great business, but in reality only the top-tier programs are churning out a profit.

I do not agree with everything the NCAA does. However, the evidence
(90) shows it is not the booming business everyone thinks it is. ...

—Zach Dirlam
excerpted from "There's No Crying in College:
The Case Against Paying College Athletes"
http://bleacherreport.com, April 3, 2013

PART 3—Text-Analysis Response

Your Task: Closely read the text on pages 258 through 260 and write a well-developed, text-based response of two to three paragraphs. In your response, identify a central idea in the text and analyze how the author's use of *one* writing strategy (literary element or literary technique or rhetorical device) develops this central idea. Use strong and thorough evidence from the text to support your analysis. Do *not* simply summarize the text. You may use the margins to take notes as you read and scrap paper to plan your response. Write your response on a separate sheet of paper.

Guidelines:

Be sure to

- Identify a central idea in the text.
- Analyze how the author's use of *one* writing strategy (literary element or literary technique or rhetorical device) develops this central idea. Examples include: characterization, conflict, denotation/connotation, metaphor, simile, irony, language use, point-of-view, setting, structure, symbolism, theme, tone, etc.
- Use strong and thorough evidence from the text to support your analysis.
- Organize your ideas in a cohesive and coherent manner.
- Maintain a formal style of writing.
- Follow the conventions of standard written English.

Text

...And so the battle was staged between a crippled, sane boy and a hostile, sane, secretly savage though sometimes merciful world.

Can I climb man-made mountains, questioned Joseph Meehan. Can I climb socially constructed barriers? Can I ask my family to back me when (5) I know something more than they, I now know the heinous[1] scepticism so kneaded down constantly in my busy sad world. What can a crippled, speechless boy do, asked Joseph, my handicap curtails my collective conscience, obliterates[2] my voice, beckons ridicule of my smile and damns my chances of being accepted as normal. ...

(10) How do I conquer my body, mused the paralysed boy. Paralysed I am labelled, but can a paralytic move? My body rarely stops moving. My arms wage constant battle trying to make me look a fool. My smile which can be most natural, can at times freeze, thereby making me seem sad and uninterested. Two great legs I may have, but put my bodyweight on them (15) and they collapse under me like a house of cards. How then can I convey to folk that the strength in my legs can be as normal as that of the strongest man? Such were boy Joseph's taunting posers, but he had one more fence that freezed his words while they were yet unspoken.

But fate was listening and fate it was that had frozen his freedom. Now (20) could fate be wavering in her purpose? Credence[3] was being given to his bowed perceptions—could fate avow him a means of escape?

Writing by hand failed. Typing festered hope. The typewriter was not a plaything. Boy Joseph needed to master it for the good of his sanity, for the good of his soul. Years had taught him the ins and outs of typewrit- (25) ing, but fate denied him the power to nod and hit the keys with his head-mounted pointer. Destruction secretly destroyed his every attempt to nod his pointer onto the keys. Instead great spasms gripped him rigid and sent his simple nod into a farcical effort which ran to each and every one of his limbs.

(30) Eva Fitzpatrick had done years of duty trying to help Joseph to best his body. She told him everything she knew about brain damage and its effects. The boy understood, but all he could do was to look hard into her humble eyes and flick his own heavenwards in affirmation. ...

---

[1]heinous—hateful
[2]obliterates—blots out
[3]credence—belief
[4]gumption—perseverance, toughness

(35) Eva's room was crested by creative drawings. Her manner was friendly, outgoing, but inwardly she felt for her student as he struggled to typewrite. Her method of working necessitated that her pupil be relaxed so she chatted light-hearted banter as she all the while measured his relaxation. The chatting would continue, but when Joseph saw his teacher wheel the long mirror towards the typing table he knew that they were
(40) going to play typing gymnastics.

Together they would struggle, the boy blowing like a whale from the huge effort of trying to discipline his bedamned body. Every tip of his pointer to the keys of the typewriter sent his body sprawling backwards. Eva held his chin in her hands and waited for him to relax and tip another
(45) key. The boy and girl worked mightily, typing sentences which Eva herself gave as a headline to Joseph. Young Boyblue honestly gave himself over to his typing teacher. Gumption[4] was hers as she struggled to find a very voluntary tip coming to the typewriter keys from his yessing head.

But for Eva Fitzpatrick he would never have broken free. His own
(50) mother had given up on him and decided that the typewriter was no help at all. She had put the cover on the machine and stored it away. She felt hurt by defeat. Her foolish heart failed to see breathing destructive spasms coming between her son and the typewriter. But how was a mother to know that hidden behind her cross was a Simon[5] ready and willing to
(55) research areas where she strode as a stranger. How could she know that Eva brought service to a head and that science now was going to join forces with her. Now a new drug was being administered to the spastic boy and even though he was being allowed to take only a small segment of Lioresal[6] tablet, he was beginning already to feel different. The little seg-
(60) ments of Lioresal tablet seemed harmless, but yet they were the mustard seeds of his and Eva's hours of discovery.

Now he struggled from his certainty that he was going to succeed and with that certainty came a feeling of encouragement. The encouragement was absolute, just as though someone was egging him on. His belief now
(65) came from himself and he wondered how this came about. He knew that with years of defeat he should now be experiencing despair, but instead a spirit of enlightenment was telling him you're going to come through with a bow, a bow to break your chain and let out your voice.

At the very same hour fate was also at work on Eva. When it was least
(70) expected she sensed that music of which he sampled. She watched Joseph

---

[5]a Simon—Biblical reference to Simon of Cyrene who helped Jesus carry his cross
[6]Lioresal—a medication to treat skeletal muscle spasms

in the mirror as he struggled to find and tip the required keys. Avoiding his teacher's gaze, he struggled on trying to test himself. Glee was gambolling[7] but he had to be sure.

(75) Breathing a little easier, his body a little less trembling, he sat head cupped in Eva's hands. He even noticed the scent of her perfume but he didn't glance in the mirror. Perhaps it won't happen for me today he teased himself but he was wrong, desperately, delightfully wrong. Sweetness of certainty sugared his now. Yes, he could type. He could freely hit the keys and he looked in the mirror and met her eyes. Feebly (80) he smiled but she continued to study him. Looking back into her face he tried to get her response, but turning his wheelchair she gracefully glided back along the corridor to his classroom. ...

—Christopher Nolan
excerpted from *Under the Eye of the Clock*, 1987
Weidenfeld and Nicolson

---

[7]gambolling—skipping

Regents ELA (Common Core) Answers June 2015
English Language Arts

Answer Key

Part 1

1. **2**	9. **1**	17. **4**
2. **1**	10. **4**	18. **3**
3. **3**	11. **2**	19. **1**
4. **1**	12. **1**	20. **2**
5. **2**	13. **4**	21. **4**
6. **4**	14. **2**	22. **1**
7. **3**	15. **1**	23. **2**
8. **3**	16. **4**	24. **3**

Regents ELA (Common Core) Examination June 2016

English Language Arts

PART 1—Reading Comprehension

Directions (1–24): Closely read each of the three passages below. After each passage, there are several multiple-choice questions. Select the best suggested answer to each question and write its number in the space provided. You may use the margins to take notes as you read.

Reading Comprehension Passage A

...When the short days of winter came dusk fell before we had well
eaten our dinners. When we met in the street the houses had grown sombre. The space of sky above us was the colour of ever-changing violet and
towards it the lamps of the street lifted their feeble lanterns. The cold air

(5) stung us and we played till our bodies glowed. Our shouts echoed in the
silent street. The career of our play brought us through the dark muddy
lanes behind the houses where we ran the gauntlet of the rough tribes[1]
from the cottages, to the back doors of the dark dripping gardens where
odours arose from the ashpits, to the dark odorous stables where a coach-

(10) man smoothed and combed the horse or shook music from the buckled
harness. When we returned to the street light from the kitchen windows
had filled the areas. If my uncle was seen turning the corner we hid in
the shadow until we had seen him safely housed. Or if Mangan's sister
came out on the doorstep to call her brother in to his tea we watched her

---
[1]tribes—gangs

(15) from our shadow peer up and down the street. We waited to see whether she would remain or go in and, if she remained, we left our shadow and walked up to Mangan's steps resignedly. She was waiting for us, her figure defined by the light from the half-opened door. Her brother always teased her before he obeyed and I stood by the railings looking at her. Her *(20)* dress swung as she moved her body and the soft rope of her hair tossed from side to side.

Every morning I lay on the floor in the front parlour watching her door. The blind was pulled down to within an inch of the sash so that I could not be seen. When she came out on the doorstep my heart leaped. I *(25)* ran to the hall, seized my books and followed her. I kept her brown figure always in my eye and, when we came near the point at which our ways diverged, I quickened my pace and passed her. This happened morning after morning. I had never spoken to her, except for a few casual words, and yet her name was like a summons to all my foolish blood. ...

(30) At last she spoke to me. When she addressed the first words to me I was so confused that I did not know what to answer. She asked me was I going to *Araby*. I forget whether I answered yes or no. It would be a splendid bazaar,[2] she said she would love to go.

"And why can't you?" I asked.

(35) While she spoke she turned a silver bracelet round and round her wrist. She could not go, she said, because there would be a retreat[3] that week in her convent.[4] Her brother and two other boys were fighting for their caps and I was alone at the railings. She held one of the spikes, bowing her head towards me. The light from the lamp opposite our door caught the *(40)* white curve of her neck, lit up her hair that rested there and, falling, lit up the hand upon the railing. It fell over one side of her dress and caught the white border of a petticoat, just visible as she stood at ease.

"It's well for you," she said.

"If I go," I said, "I will bring you something."

(45) What innumerable follies laid waste my waking and sleeping thoughts after that evening! I wished to annihilate the tedious intervening days. I chafed against the work of school. At night in my bedroom and by day in the classroom her image came between me and the page I strove to read. The syllables of the word *Araby* were called to me through the silence in *(50)* which my soul luxuriated and cast an Eastern enchantment over me. I asked for leave to go to the bazaar on Saturday night. My aunt was sur-

---

[2]bazaar—fair
[3]retreat—a time set aside for prayer and reflection
[4]convent—religious school

prised and hoped it was not some Freemason[5] affair. I answered few questions in class. I watched my master's face pass from amiability to sternness; he hoped I was not beginning to idle. I could not call my wandering
(55) thoughts together. I had hardly any patience with the serious work of life which, now that it stood between me and my desire, seemed to me child's play, ugly monotonous child's play.

On Saturday morning I reminded my uncle that I wished to go to the bazaar in the evening. He was fussing at the hallstand, looking for the hat-
(60) brush, and answered me curtly:

"Yes, boy, I know." ...

At nine o'clock I heard my uncle's latchkey in the halldoor. I heard him talking to himself and heard the hallstand rocking when it had received the weight of his overcoat. I could interpret these signs. When he was
(65) midway through his dinner I asked him to give me the money to go to the bazaar. He had forgotten.

"The people are in bed and after their first sleep now," he said.

I did not smile. My aunt said to him energetically: "Can't you give him the money and let him go? You've kept him late enough as it is." ...
(70) I held a florin[6] tightly in my hand as I strode down Buckingham Street towards the station. The sight of the streets thronged with buyers and glaring with gas recalled to me the purpose of my journey. I took my seat in a third-class carriage of a deserted train. After an intolerable delay the train moved out of the station slowly. It crept onward among ruinous
(75) houses and over the twinkling river. At Westland Row Station a crowd of people pressed to the carriage doors; but the porters moved them back, saying that it was a special train for the bazaar. I remained alone in the bare carriage. In a few minutes the train drew up beside an improvised wooden platform. I passed out on to the road and saw by the lighted dial
(80) of a clock that it was ten minutes to ten. In front of me was a large building which displayed the magical name. ...

Remembering with difficulty why I had come I went over to one of the stalls and examined porcelain vases and flowered tea-sets. At the door of the stall a young lady was talking and laughing with two young gentle-
(85) men. I remarked their English accents and listened vaguely to their conversation. ...

Observing me the young lady came over and asked me did I wish to buy anything. The tone of her voice was not encouraging; she seemed to have spoken to me out of a sense of duty. I looked humbly at the great jars that

[5]Freemason—a fraternal organization
[6]florin—coin

(90)   stood like eastern guards at either side of the dark entrance to the stall and
murmured:

"No, thank you."

The young lady changed the position of one of the vases and went back
to the two young men. They began to talk of the same subject. Once or
(95)   twice the young lady glanced at me over her shoulder.

I lingered before her stall, though I knew my stay was useless, to make
my interest in her wares seem the more real. Then I turned away slowly
and walked down the middle of the bazaar. I allowed the two pennies to
fall against the sixpence in my pocket. I heard a voice call from one end
(100)   of the gallery that the light was out. The upper part of the hall was now
completely dark.

Gazing up into the darkness I saw myself as a creature driven and
derided by vanity; and my eyes burned with anguish and anger.

—James Joyce
excerpted from "Araby"
Dubliners, 1914
Grant Richards LTD.

1 The description of the neighborhood in lines 1 through 11 contributes to a mood of

  (1) indifference   (3) anxiety
  (2) gloom   (4) regret   1____

2 Which quotation from the text best illustrates the narrator's attitude toward Mangan's sister?

  (1) "we watched her from our shadow" (lines 14 and 15)
  (2) "We waited to see whether she would remain or go in" (lines 15 and 16)
  (3) "yet her name was like a summons" (line 29)
  (4) "She asked me was I going to *Araby*" (lines 31 and 32)   2____

3 Lines 30 through 39 reveal Mangan's sister's

  (1) disinterest   (3) disappointment
  (2) silliness   (4) tension   3____

4 Lines 45 through 57 help to develop the idea that the narrator has

  (1) recognized that his priorities have changed
  (2) determined the academic focus of his studies
  (3) eliminated distractions from his daily routine
  (4) reassessed his relationship with his family   4____

5 The description of the narrator's train ride (lines 70 through 79) supports a theme of

  (1) confusion   (3) persecution
  (2) isolation   (4) deception   5____

6 The description in lines 87 through 97 suggests that the bazaar symbolizes

  (1) excessive greed   (3) false promise
  (2) future wealth   (4) lasting love   6____

7 It can be inferred from the text that the narrator's behavior is most guided by his

(1) school experience
(2) family situation
(3) childhood memories
(4) romantic feelings   7____

8 As used in line 103, the word "derided" most nearly means

(1) taunted   (3) rewarded
(2) restrained   (4) flattered   8____

9 Based on the text as a whole, the narrator's feelings of "anguish and anger" (line 103) are most likely a result of his having

(1) ignored his opportunities
(2) defended his family
(3) realized his limitations
(4) denied his responsibilities   9____

10 Which quotation best reflects a central theme of the text?

(1) "Her brother and two other boys were fighting for their caps" (lines 37 and 38)
(2) " 'Can't you give him the money and let him go?' " (lines 68 and 69)
(3) "It crept onward among ruinous houses and over the twinkling river" (lines 74 and 75)
(4) "I lingered before her stall, though I knew my stay was useless" (line 96)   10____

Reading Comprehension Passage B

Assembly Line

In time's assembly line
Night presses against night.
We come off the factory night-shift
In line as we march towards home.
(5)   Over our heads in a row
The assembly line of stars
Stretches across the sky.
Beside us, little trees
Stand numb in assembly lines.

(10)   The stars must be exhausted
After thousands of years
Of journeys which never change.
The little trees are all sick,
Choked on smog and monotony,
Stripped of their color and shape.
(15)   It's not hard to feel for them;
We share the same tempo and rhythm.

Yes, I'm numb to my own existence
As if, like the trees and stars
(20)   —perhaps just out of habit
—perhaps just out of sorrow,
I'm unable to show concern
For my own manufactured fate.

—Shu Ting
from *A Splintered Mirror: Chinese Poetry from the*
Democracy Movement, 1991
translated by Carolyn Kizer
North Point Press

11 In the first stanza, a main idea is strengthened through the poet's use of

   (1) repetition   (3) allusion

   (2) simile   (4) understatement   11____

12 Line 17 contributes to a central idea by pointing out a parallel between

   (1) profit and industrialization

   (2) humans and nature

   (3) recreation and production

   (4) sound and motion   12____

13 The structure and language of lines 20 and 21 suggests the narrator's

   (1) bitterness   (3) selfishness

   (2) determination   (4) uncertainty   13____

14 The phrase "manufactured fate" (line 23) emphasizes the narrator's

   (1) resignation to life

   (2) desire for control

   (3) hope for change

   (4) rejection of nature   14____

Reading Comprehension Passage C

...Memory teaches me what I know of these matters. The boy reminds the adult. I was a bilingual child, but of a certain kind: "socially disadvantaged," the son of working-class parents, both Mexican immigrants. ...

(5) In public, my father and mother spoke a hesitant, accented, and not always grammatical English. And then they would have to strain, their bodies tense, to catch the sense of what was rapidly said by *los gringos*. At home, they returned to Spanish. The language of their Mexican past sounded in counterpoint to the English spoken in public. The words would come quickly, with ease. Conveyed through those sounds was the *(10)* pleasing, soothing, consoling reminder that one was at home.

During those years when I was first learning to speak, my mother and father addressed me only in Spanish; in Spanish I learned to reply. By contrast, English (*inglés*) was the language I came to associate with gringos, rarely heard in the house. I learned my first words of English overhearing *(15)* my parents speaking to strangers. At six years of age, I knew just enough words for my mother to trust me on errands to stores one block away— but no more.

I was then a listening child, careful to hear the very different sounds of Spanish and English. Wide-eyed with hearing, I'd listen to sounds *(20)* more than to words. First, there were English (gringo) sounds. So many words still were unknown to me that when the butcher or the lady at the drugstore said something, exotic polysyllabic sounds would bloom in the midst of their sentences. Often the speech of people in public seemed to me very loud, booming with confidence. The man behind the counter would *(25)* literally ask, "What can I do for you?" But by being so firm and clear, the sound of his voice said that he was a gringo; he belonged in public society. There were also the high, nasal notes of middle-class American speech— which I rarely am conscious of hearing today because I hear them so often, but could not stop hearing when I was a boy. Crowds at Safeway or at bus *(30)* stops were noisy with the birdlike sounds of *los gringos*. I'd move away from them all—all the chirping chatter above me.

My own sounds I was unable to hear, but I knew that I spoke English poorly. My words could not extend to form complete thoughts. And the words I did speak I didn't know well enough to make distinct sounds. *(35)* (Listeners would usually lower their heads to hear better what I was trying to say.) But it was one thing for *me* to speak English with difficulty; it was more troubling to hear my parents speaking in public: their high-whining vowels and guttural[1] consonants; their sentences that got stuck with "eh" and "ah" sounds; the confused syntax; the hesitant rhythm of sounds so

(40) different from the way gringos spoke. I'd notice, moreover, that my parents' voices were softer than those of gringos we would meet.

I am tempted to say now that none of this mattered. (In adulthood I am embarrassed by childhood fears.) And, in a way, it didn't matter very much that my parents could not speak English with ease. Their linguistic

(45) difficulties had no serious consequences. My mother and father made themselves understood at the county hospital clinic and at government offices. And yet, in another way, it mattered very much. It was unsettling to hear my parents struggle with English. Hearing them, I'd grow nervous, and my clutching trust in their protection and power would be weakened. ...

(50) But then there was Spanish: *español*, the language rarely heard away from the house; *español*, the language which seemed to me therefore a private language, my family's language. To hear its sounds was to feel myself specially recognized as one of the family, apart from *los otros*.[2] A simple remark, an inconsequential comment could convey that assurance.

(55) My parents would say something to me and I would feel embraced by the sounds of their words. Those sounds said: *I am speaking with ease in Spanish. I am addressing you in words I never use with* los gringos. *I recognize you as someone special, close, like no one outside. You belong with us. In the family. Ricardo.*

(60) At the age of six, well past the time when most middle-class children no longer notice the difference between sounds uttered at home and words spoken in public, I had a different experience. I lived in a world compounded of sounds. I was a child longer than most. I lived in a magical world, surrounded by sounds both pleasing and fearful. I shared with my

(65) family a language enchantingly private—different from that used in the city around us. ...

If I rehearse here the changes in my private life after my Americanization, it is finally to emphasize a public gain. The loss implies the gain. The house I returned to each afternoon was quiet. Intimate

(70) sounds no longer greeted me at the door. Inside there were other noises.

---

[1]guttural—throaty
[2]los otros—the others

The telephone rang. Neighborhood kids ran past the door of the bedroom where I was reading my schoolbooks—covered with brown shopping-bag paper. Once I learned the public language, it would never again be easy for me to hear intimate family voices. More and more of my day was spent

(75) hearing words, not sounds. But that may only be a way of saying that on the day I raised my hand in class and spoke loudly to an entire roomful of faces, my childhood started to end. ...

—Richard Rodriguez
excerpted from "Aria: A Memoir of a Bilingual Childhood"
The American Scholar, Winter 1981
The Phi Beta Kappa Society

15 The phrase "the boy reminds the adult" in the first paragraph establishes the narrator's

    (1)   mood   (3)   creativity

    (2)   perspective   (4)   disposition   15_____

16 The use of the word "counterpoint" in line 8 helps to develop a central idea by presenting

    (1)   differing memories

    (2)   opposing principles

    (3)   contrasting cultures

    (4)   conflicting philosophies   16_____

17 The use of figurative language in lines 19 and 20 demonstrates the narrator's

    (1)   eagerness to learn

    (2)   desire for recognition

    (3)   frustration with authority

    (4)   anxiety about adulthood   17_____

18 The use of the word "public" in line 26 emphasizes the narrator's feeling of

    (1)   accomplishment   (3)   satisfaction

    (2)   disillusionment   (4)   separation   18_____

19 The description of the narrator speaking English in lines 32 through 36 emphasizes his inability to

    (1)   communicate effectively

    (2)   understand the culture

    (3)   distinguish between languages

    (4)   express emotions   19_____

20 In lines 44 through 49 the narrator's reaction to his parents' "linguistic difficulties" (lines 44 and 45) reveals his

   (1) low expectations   (3) educational concerns
   (2) conflicting feelings (4) hostile thoughts   20_____

21 Lines 50 through 59 contribute to a central idea in the text by focusing on the

   (1) narrator's sense of security
   (2) family's economic status
   (3) family's traditional beliefs
   (4) narrator's feeling of confusion   21_____

22 Which quotation best reflects the narrator's overall experience with language?

   (1) "The words would come quickly, with ease" (lines 8 and 9)
   (2) "I'd listen to sounds more than to words" (lines 19 and 20)
   (3) "My own sounds I was unable to hear, but I knew that I spoke English poorly" (lines 32 and 33)
   (4) "Hearing them, I'd grow nervous" (line 48)   22_____

23 The phrase "the loss implies the gain" (lines 68 and 69) contributes to a central idea in the text by indicating that when the narrator speaks English comfortably he is

   (1) disconnected from his family
   (2) distressed by hearing English sounds
   (3) uninterested in his school work
   (4) undeterred from making new friends   23_____

24 The narrator's tone in lines 74 through 77 suggests

   (1) distrust   (3) confidence
   (2) respect   (4) intolerance   24_____

PART 2—Argument Response

Directions: Closely read each of the *four* texts on pages 277 through 287 and write a source-based argument on the topic below. You may use the margins to take notes as you read and scrap paper to plan your response. Write your argument on a separate sheet of paper.

Topic: Should celebrities become the voice of humanitarian causes?

Your Task: Carefully read each of the *four* texts provided. Then, using evidence from at least *three* of the texts, write a well-developed argument regarding whether or not celebrities should become the voice of humanitarian causes. Clearly establish your claim, distinguish your claim from alternate or opposing claims, and use specific, relevant, and sufficient evidence from at least *three* of the texts to develop your argument. Do *not* simply summarize each text.

Guidelines:

Be sure to

- Establish your claim regarding whether or not celebrities should become the voice of humanitarian causes.
- Distinguish your claim from alternate or opposing claims.
- Use specific, relevant, and sufficient evidence from at least *three* of the texts to develop your argument.
- Identify each source that you reference by text number and line number(s) or graphic (for example: Text 1, line 4 or Text 2, graphic).
- Organize your ideas in a cohesive and coherent manner
- Maintain a formal style of writing.
- Follow the conventions of standard written English.

Texts:

Text 1—The Celebrity Solution

Text 2—Ethics of Celebrities and Their Increasing Influence in 21st Century Society

Text 3—Do Celebrity Humanitarians Matter?

Text 4—The Rise of the Celebrity Humanitarian

Text 1

The Celebrity Solution

In 2004, Natalie Portman, then a 22-year-old fresh from college, went to Capitol Hill to talk to Congress on behalf of the Foundation for International Community Assistance, or Finca, a microfinance organization for which she served as "ambassador." She found herself wondering
(5)　what she was doing there, but her colleagues assured her: "We got the meetings because of you." For lawmakers, Natalie Portman was not simply a young woman—she was the beautiful Padmé from "Star Wars." "And I was like, 'That seems totally nuts to me,' " Portman told me recently. [*sic*] It's the way it works, I guess. I'm not particularly proud
(10)　that in our country I can get a meeting with a representative more easily than the head of a nonprofit can."

Well, who is? But it is the way it works. Stars—movie stars, rock stars, sports stars—exercise a ludicrous influence over the public consciousness. Many are happy to exploit that power; others are wrecked by it. In recent
(15)　years, stars have learned that their intense presentness in people's daily lives and their access to the uppermost realms of politics, business and the media offer them a peculiar kind of moral position, should they care to use it. And many of those with the most leverage—Bono and Angelina Jolie and Brad Pitt and George Clooney and, yes, Natalie Portman—have
(20)　increasingly chosen to mount that pedestal. Hollywood celebrities have become central players on deeply political issues like development aid, refugees and government-sponsored violence in Darfur.

Activists on these and other issues talk about the political power of stars with a mixture of bewilderment and delight. But a weapon that
(25)　powerful is bound to do collateral damage. Some stars, like George Clooney, regard the authority thrust upon them with wariness; others, like Sean Penn or Mia Farrow, an activist on Darfur, seize the bully pulpit with both hands. "There is a tendency," says Donald Steinberg, deputy president of the International Crisis Group, which seeks to prevent con-
(30)　flict around the world, "to treat these issues as if it's all good and evil." Sometimes you need the rallying cry, but sometimes you need to accept a complex truth. ...

An entire industry has sprung up around the recruitment of celebrities to good works. Even an old-line philanthropy like the Red Cross employs

277

(35) a "director of celebrity outreach." Oxfam has a celebrity wrangler in Los Angeles, Lyndsay Cruz, on the lookout for stars who can raise the charity's profile with younger people. In addition to established figures like Colin Firth and Helen Mirren, Oxfam is affiliated with Scarlett Johansson, who has visited South Asia (where the organization promotes girls'

(40) education) and is scheduled to go to Mali. Cruz notes that while "trendy young people" are attracted to the star of "Match Point" and "Lost in Translation," Johansson had "great credibility with an older audience because she's such a great actress." ...

Microfinance is a one-star cause. Though for some reason the subject appeals to female royalty, including Queen Rania of Jordan and Princess

(45)

Maxima of the Netherlands, Natalie Portman is the only member of Hollywood royalty who has dedicated herself to it. Perhaps this is because microfinance is a good deal more complicated than supplying fresh water to parched villages, and a good deal less glamorous than confronting

(50) the janjaweed[1] in Darfur. The premise of microfinance is that very poor people should have access to credit, just as the middle class and the rich do. They typically don't have such access because banks that operate in the developing world view the poor as too great a credit risk, and the processing cost of a $50 loan is thought to wipe out much of the potential profit.

(55) But small nonprofit organizations found that tiny loans could not only raise the incomes of the rural and small-town poor but also, unlike aid and other handouts, could help make them self-sufficient. And they found as well that if they harnessed the communities' own social bonds to create group support, repayment rates among the very poor could be higher than

(60) among the more well-off. (Indeed, commercial banks, apparently having recognized their error, have now begun to extend loans to the poor.) The idea of microfinance is thus to introduce the poor to capitalism. This is not, it's true, star material. ...

There's no question that causes do a great deal for the brand identity

(65) of the stars and the sponsors who embrace them. But what, exactly, do stars do for causes? They raise money, of course. But that is often less important than raising consciousness, as Natalie Portman has done. John Prendergast, a longtime activist on African issues and the chairman of Enough, an organization that brings attention to atrocities around the

(70) world, says: "Celebrities are master recruiters. If you're trying to expand beyond the already converted, there's no better way to do instant out-

[1]janjaweed—militia

reach than to have a familiar face where people want to know more about what they're doing in their personal lives." People come to see Natalie Portman, and they go away learning about microfinance. ...

—James Traub
excerpted from "The Celebrity Solution"
www.nytimes.com, March 9, 2008

Text 2

Ethics of Celebrities and Their Increasing
Influence in 21st Century Society

The global influence of celebrities in the 21st century extends far
beyond the entertainment sector. During the recent Palestinian presidential elections, the Hollywood actor Richard Gere broadcast a televised
message to voters in the region and stated,

(5)　　Hi, I'm Richard Gere, and I'm speaking for the entire world. (Richard
Gere, actor)
Celebrities in the 21st century have expanded from simple product endorsements to sitting on United Nations committees, regional
and global conflict commentators and international diplomacy. The
(10)　Russian parliament is debating whether to send a global celebrity to its
International Space Station. The celebrities industry is undergoing, "mission creep", or the expansion of an enterprise beyond its original goals.
There has always been a connection between Hollywood and politics,
certainly in the USA. However, global celebrities in the 21st century are
(15)　involved in proselytising[1] about particular religions, such as Scientology,
negotiating with the Taliban in Afghanistan and participating in the Iraqi
refugee crisis. The Hollywood actor, Jude Law's attempt to negotiate with
the Taliban in Afghanistan was not successful; but the mere fact that Jude
Law tried, and that it was discussed widely over the global internet, shows
(20)　the expansion of celebrities' domain in today's society. The global entertainment industry, especially based in Hollywood, has vastly exceeded
their original mandate in society. ...
How is it that celebrities in the 21st century are formulating foreign
aid policy, backing political bills or affecting public health debates?
(25)　Traditionally, the economic value or market price of the entertainment
industry and its various components was seen as intangible and difficult
to measure. Movie stars and films, artists and the quality of art is often
seen as difficult to measure in terms of value and price without the role
of expert opinions. But global internet-driven 21st century seems to be
(30)　driven by a general growth of the idea that celebrity can be measured in a
tangible way. ...

---

[1]proselytising—trying to persuade or recruit others

The 21st century's internet society seems to thrive on a harmonious three-way relationship among celebrities, audiences and fame addiction. The global internet in turns [*sic*] moulds this three-way relationship and
(35) accelerates its dissemination[2] and communication. This in turn allows celebrities in the 21st century to "mission creep", or expand and accelerate their influence into various new areas of society. This interaction of forces is shown in Figure 1. ...

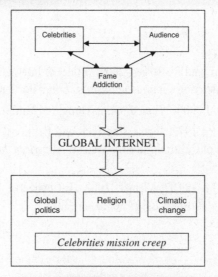

**Figure 1. Celebrities' mission creep
in the 21st century.**

In turn, the global popularity of internet-based social networking
(40) sites such as MySpace or individual blogspots all show the need to discuss events, but also things that are famous (Choi and Berger, 2009). Traditionally, celebrities were seen as people that needed to be seen from afar and while keeping one's distance. In this sense, celebrities were similar to art pieces, better to be seen from a distance (Halpern, 2008; Hirsch,
(45) 1972; Maury and Kleiner, 2002). This traditional distance has been reduced due to global technologies in communications. Celebrities, and famous people in turn, help to bring people, including adults, together in conversation and social interaction. The global role of the internet in the 21st century society will further accelerate such social and psychological
(50) trends throughout today's global knowledge-based society. Global inter-

---

[2]dissemination—wide distribution

net communications have increased the availability of "fame" and access to the lives of celebrities, which in turn will further accelerate the global influence of celebrities in the 21st century society. ...

—Chong Ju Choi and Ron Berger
excerpted from "Ethics of Celebrities and
Their Increasing Influence in 21st Century Society"
Journal of Business Ethics, 2009
www.idc.ac.il

References

Choi, C.J. and R. Berger: 2009, 'Ethics of Internet, Global Community, Fame Addiction', *Journal of Business Ethics* (forthcoming).

Halpern, J.: 2008, *Fame Junkies* (Houghton Mifflin, New York).

Hirsch, P.: 1972, 'Processing Fads and Fashions: An Organisation Set Analysis of Cultural Industry Systems', *American Journal of Sociology* 77 (1), 45–70.

Maury, M. and D. Kleiner: 2002, 'E-Commerce, Ethical Commerce?', *Journal of Business Ethics* 36 (3), 21–32.

Text 3

Do Celebrity Humanitarians Matter?

...Recent years have seen a growth industry for celebrities engaged in
humanitarian activities. The website *Look to the Stars* has calculated that
over 2,000 charities have some form of celebrity support. UNICEF has
dozens of "Goodwill Ambassadors" and "Advocates" such as Angelina
(5) Jolie and Mia Farrow. Celebrities have entered forums for global gov-
ernance to pressure political leaders: George Clooney has spoken before
the United Nations while Bob Geldof, Bono, and Sharon Stone have
attended summits like DAVOS[1] and the G8[2] to discuss third world debt,
poverty, and refugees. In the U.S. policy arena, [Ben] Affleck joins Nicole
(10) Kidman, Angelina Jolie, and other celebrities who have addressed the
U.S. Congress on international issues.[3] The increase in celebrity involvement has spurred debate in academic circles and mainstream media.
Celebrity humanitarianism is alternately lauded for drawing media
attention and fostering popular engagement and criticized on a number
(15) of ethical grounds. According to *Mother Jones*, Africa is experiencing a
"recolonization" as celebrities from the U.S. and UK lay claim to particular countries as recipients of their star power: South Africa (Oprah),
Sudan (Mia Farrow), and Botswana (Russell Simmons). As the involvement of American celebrities in humanitarian causes grows, let us consider
(20) the activities of Affleck and his Eastern Congo Initiative [ECI].

Celebrity Humanitarians

Affleck can be considered a "celebrity humanitarian," a celebrity figure
who has moved beyond his/her day job as an entertainer to delve into the
areas of foreign aid, charity, and development. These activities can involve
fundraising, hosting concerts and events, media appearances, and engag-
(25) ing in advocacy. Celebrities are distinguished by their unique ability to
attract and engage diverse audiences ranging from their fan base and the
media to political elites and philanthropists. Celebrity humanitarians
often play an important bridging role, introducing Northern publics

---

[1]DAVOS—an annual meeting of The World Economic Forum, hosted in Davos-Klosters,
Switzerland, on global partnership
[2]G8—A group of 8 industrialized nations that hold a yearly meeting to discuss global
issues
[3]ProQuest, "Quick Start: Congressional Hearing Digital Collections: Famous
(Celebrity) Witnesses," *http://proquest.libguides.com/quick_start_hearings/famouscelebs*

283

(30) to issues in the developing world. They also use their star power to gain access to policy-making circles to effect social and political change. Since 1980, the U.S. Congress has seen the frequency of celebrity witnesses double to around 20 a year with most celebrity appearances taking place before committees addressing domestic issues. Interestingly, fewer than 5 percent of celebrity witnesses testify before committees dealing with for-

(35) eign relations, where celebrity humanitarians push the United States to address global concerns.[4]

The rise and influence of celebrity humanitarians activate debates on the consequences of their involvement. For some academics and prac-titioners, celebrities are welcome figures in humanitarianism: educat-

(40) ing the public on global issues, raising funds, and using their populist appeal to draw attention to policy-making arenas. For others, celebrity humanitarians are highly problematic figures who dilute debates, offer misguided policy proposals, and lack credibility and accountability. Celebrity humanitarianism privileges and invests the celebrity figure

(45) with the responsibility of speaking on behalf of a "distant other" who is unable to give input or consent for their representation. Stakeholders in the developing world unwittingly rely on the celebrity humanitarian as their communicator, advocate, and fundraiser. Finally, celebrities are held to be self-serving, engaging in humanitarian causes to burnish[5] their

(50) careers. ...

Celebrity humanitarians should do their homework to earn cred-ibility while also respecting their bounded roles as celebrity figures. As a celebrity humanitarian, Affleck's proposals are based on serious preparation: spending years to gain an in-depth understanding, con-

(55) sulting with professionals, narrowing his advocacy efforts to a single region, and enduring the scrutiny of the cameras and the blogosphere. Besides this self-education, his credibility is based on ECI's dual mission of re-granting and policymaking. Since ECI has operations and partnerships in the DRC [Democratic Republic of the Congo], the content of Affleck's

(60) writings and Congressional testimonies are grounded in the realities of the DRC, peppered with first-hand accounts, and supported by statistics and other research. However, there are limits to his knowledge—Affleck is not a development expert or on-the-ground professional; his day job and main career lie elsewhere. And while the decision to found an organization

---

[4]See Demaine, L.J., n.d. Navigating Policy by the Stars: The Influence of Celebrity Entertainers on Federal Lawmaking. *Journal of Law & Politics*, 25 (2), 83–143
[5]burnish—improve or enhance

(65)   suggests that Affleck's commitment to the DRC will extend beyond his nascent[6] efforts, rumors that he may seek political office distort this image.

Celebrity humanitarians must find a way to avoid diverting resources and attention. Rather than bring his star power and ample financial support to existing Congolese organizations, ECI furnished a platform for
(70)   Affleck's advocacy and leadership that amplifies his voice over those of the Congolese. Nor was ECI crafted inside eastern Congo but in the offices of a strategic advisory firm based in Seattle. ECI is privately funded by a network of financial elites and does not rely on means-tested grant cycles or public support. While Affleck has received multiple awards in the short
(75)   period he has been a celebrity humanitarian, his star power also distracts us from the people who work in the field of humanitarianism on a daily basis and rarely receive such recognition.[7] And by concentrating attention and money for Affleck's issue of Eastern Congo, other causes and countries may go unnoticed. ...

—Alexandra Cosima Budabin
excerpted and adapted from "Do Celebrity Humanitarians Matter?"
www.carnegiecouncil.org, December 11, 2014

---

[6]nascent—beginning
[7]Marina Hyde, "Angelina Jolie, Paris Hilton, Lassie and Tony Blair: here to save the world," The Guardian, 27 November 2014 *http://www.theguardian.com/lifeandstyle/ lostinshowbiz/2014/nov/27/angelina-jolie-paris-hilton-tony-blair-lassie-save-the-children- award?CMP=share_btn_fb*

Text 4

The Rise of the Celebrity Humanitarian

...One of the most effective methods of attracting a wide, although perhaps not a deep, following is the use of a celebrity humanitarian: An A-Lister who has delved into areas of foreign aid, charity and international development. The United Nations is the leader in this attention-

(5)   getting ploy, with at least 175 celebrities on the books as goodwill ambassadors[1] for one cause or another. Some celebrities even leverage their star power to promote their very own foundations and philanthropic projects.

It's a mutually beneficial relationship, really. Hollywood's elite get

(10) to wield their unique ability to engage diverse audiences, and the power of celebrity is put to good use effecting change—whether it's out of the good of their hearts, or because their publicists insist.

There is some downside that comes with publicly linking a campaign to a celebrity. For some, celebrity humanitarians are problem-

(15) atic figures[2] who dilute debates, offer misguided policy proposals, and lack credibility and accountability. Take Scarlett Johansson, who became embroiled in a scandal after partnering with soft drink maker SodaStream, which operated a factory in occupied Palestinian territory. This alliance was in direct conflict with her seven-year global ambas-

(20) sador position for Oxfam, which opposes all trade with the occupied territories. In the end, she stepped down from her role with Oxfam, stating a fundamental difference of opinion.

Moreover, if the star's popularity takes a hit, it can affect the reception of the cause. For example, when Lance Armstrong's popularity

(25) plummeted in the wake of doping allegations, it tarnished the brand of the Livestrong Foundation,[3] the nonprofit he founded to support people affected by cancer. Livestrong does, however, continue today, after cutting ties with Armstrong and undergoing a radical rebranding.

Even so, the following big names substantiate the idea that celebrity

(30) involvement brings massive amounts of attention and money to humanitarian causes and that, usually, this [sic] is a good thing. ...

---

[1]Bunting, Madeline. "The Issue of Celebrities and Aid Is Deceptively Complex" *http://www.theguardian.com*, Dec. 17, 2010
[2]Budabin, Alexandra Cosima. "Do Celebrity Humanitarians Matter?" *http://www.carnegiecouncil.org*, December 11, 2014
[3]Gardner, Eriq. "Livestrong Struggles After Lance Armstrong's Fall" *http://www.hollywoodreporter.com*, 7/25/2013

(35) Bono participates in fundraising concerts like Live 8, and has co-founded several philanthropies, like the ONE Campaign and Product (RED). He also created EDUN, a fashion brand that strives to stimulate trade in Africa by sourcing production there. He has received three nominations for the Nobel Peace Prize, was knighted by the United Kingdom in 2007, and was named Time's 2005 Person of the Year. ...

(40) Popular singer Akon may not be as famous for his philanthropic work as Angelina Jolie or Bono, but he is in a unique position to help, as he has deep roots in the areas in which he works: He was raised in Senegal in a community without electricity, which inspired his latest project, Akon Lighting Africa. He also founded the Konfidence Foundation, raising awareness of conditions in Africa and providing underprivileged African youth access to education and other resources. ...

(45) In weighing the pros and cons of celebrity activism, perhaps [Ben] Affleck himself summed it up best in an essay reflecting on the constraints and possibilities of his own engagement:

(50) "It makes sense to be skeptical about celebrity activism. There is always suspicion that involvement with a cause may be doing more good for the spokesman than he or she is doing for the cause...but I hope you can separate whatever reservations you may have from what is unimpeachably important."

—Jenica Funk
excerpted and adapted from "The Rise of the Celebrity Humanitarian"
www.globalenvision.org, January 29, 2015

PART 3—Text-Analysis Response

Your Task: Closely read the text on pages 289 through 291 and write a well-developed, text-based response of two to three paragraphs. In your response, identify a central idea in the text and analyze how the author's use of *one* writing strategy (literary element or literary technique or rhetorical device) develops this central idea. Use strong and thorough evidence from the text to support your analysis. Do *not* simply summarize the text. You may use the margins to take notes as you read and scrap paper to plan your response. Write your response on a separate sheet of paper.

Guidelines:

Be sure to

- Identify a central idea in the text.
- Analyze how the author's use of *one* writing strategy (literary element or literary technique or rhetorical device) develops this central idea. Examples include: characterization, conflict, denotation/connotation, metaphor, simile, irony, language use, point-of-view, setting, structure, symbolism, theme, tone, etc.
- Use strong and thorough evidence from the text to support your analysis.
- Organize your ideas in a cohesive and coherent manner.
- Maintain a formal style of writing.
- Follow the conventions of standard written English.

Text

It was my father who called the city the Mansion on the River. He was talking about Charleston, South Carolina, and he was a native son, peacock proud of a town so pretty it makes your eyes ache with pleasure just to walk down its spellbinding, narrow streets. Charleston was my father's
(5) ministry, his hobbyhorse, his quiet obsession, and the great love of his life. His bloodstream lit up my own with a passion for the city that I've never lost nor ever will. I'm Charleston-born, and bred. The city's two rivers, the Ashley and the Cooper, have flooded and shaped all the days of my life on this storied[1] peninsula.
(10) I carry the delicate porcelain beauty of Charleston like the hinged shell of some soft-tissued mollusk. My soul is peninsula-shaped and sun-hardened and river-swollen. The high tides of the city flood my consciousness each day, subject to the whims and harmonies of full moons rising out of the Atlantic. I grow calm when I see the ranks of palmetto trees pulling
(15) guard duty on the banks of Colonial Lake or hear the bells of St. Michael's calling cadence[2] in the cicada-filled trees along Meeting Street. Deep in my bones, I knew early that I was one of those incorrigible[3] creatures known as Charlestonians. It comes to me as a surprising form of knowledge that my time in the city is more vocation than gift; it is my destiny, not my
(20) choice. I consider it a high privilege to be a native of one of the loveliest American cities, not a high-kicking, glossy, or lipsticked city, not a city with bells on its fingers or brightly painted toenails, but a ruffled, low-slung city, understated and tolerant of nothing mismade or ostentatious.[4] Though Charleston feels a seersuckered, tuxedoed view of itself, it
(25) approves of restraint far more than vainglory.[5]
As a boy, in my own backyard I could catch a basket of blue crabs, a string of flounder, a dozen redfish, or a net full of white shrimp. All this I could do in a city enchanting enough to charm cobras out of baskets, one so corniced and filigreed[6] and elaborate that it leaves strangers awed and
(30) natives self-satisfied. In its shadows you can find metalwork as delicate as lace and spiral staircases as elaborate as yachts. In the secrecy of its gardens you can discover jasmine and camellias and hundreds of other plants that

---

[1]storied—told of in history
[2]cadence—rhythmic recurrence of sound
[3]incorrigible—cannot be reformed
[4]ostentatious—showy
[5]vainglory—excessive pride
[6]corniced and filigreed—architecturally decorated

look embroidered and stolen from the Garden of Eden for the sheer love of richness and the joy of stealing from the gods. In its kitchens, the stoves are

(35) lit up in happiness as the lamb is marinating in red wine sauce, vinaigrette is prepared for the salad, crabmeat is anointed with sherry, custards are baked in the oven, and buttermilk biscuits cool on the counter.

Because of its devotional, graceful attraction to food and gardens and architecture, Charleston stands for all the principles that make living

(40) well both a civic virtue and a standard. It is a rapturous, defining place to grow up. Everything I reveal to you now will be Charleston-shaped and Charleston-governed, and sometimes even Charleston-ruined. But it is my fault and not the city's that it came close to destroying me. Not everyone responds to beauty in the same way. Though Charleston can

(45) do much, it can't always improve on the strangeness of human behavior. But Charleston has a high tolerance for eccentricity and bemusement.[7] There is a tastefulness in its gentility[8] that comes from the knowledge that Charleston is a permanent dimple in the understated skyline, while the rest of us are only visitors. ...

(50) I turned out to be a late bloomer, which I long regretted. My parents suffered needlessly because it took me so long to find my way to a place at their table. But I sighted the early signs of my recovery long before they did. My mother had given up on me at such an early age that a comeback was something she no longer even prayed for in her wildest dreams. Yet in

(55) my anonymous and underachieving high school career, I laid the foundation for a strong finish without my mother noticing that I was, at last, up to some good. I had built an impregnable castle of solitude for myself and then set out to bring that castle down, no matter how serious the collateral damage or who might get hurt.

(60) I was eighteen years old and did not have a friend my own age. There wasn't a boy in Charleston who would think about inviting me to a party or to come out to spend the weekend at his family's beach house.

I planned for all that to change. I had decided to become the most interesting boy to ever grow up in Charleston, and I revealed this secret to

(65) my parents.

Outside my house in the languid[9] summer air of my eighteenth year, I climbed the magnolia tree nearest to the Ashley River with the agility that constant practice had granted me. From its highest branches, I surveyed

---

[7]bemusement—bewilderment
[8]gentility—refinement
[9]languid — without energy

my city as it lay simmering in the hot-blooded saps of June while the sun
(70) began to set, reddening the vest of cirrus clouds that had gathered along
the western horizon. In the other direction, I saw the city of rooftops and
columns and gables that was my native land. What I had just promised my
parents, I wanted very much for them and for myself. Yet I also wanted it
for Charleston. I desired to turn myself into a worthy townsman of such a
(75) many-storied city.

Charleston has its own heartbeat and fingerprint, its own mug shots
and photo ops and police lineups. It is a city of contrivance,[10] of blue-
prints; devotion to pattern that is like a bent knee to the nature of
beauty itself. I could feel my destiny forming in the leaves high above the
(80) city. Like Charleston, I had my alleyways that were dead ends and led
to nowhere, but mansions were forming like jewels in my bloodstream.
Looking down, I studied the layout of my city, the one that had taught me
all the lures of attractiveness, yet made me suspicious of the showy or the
makeshift. I turned to the stars and was about to make a bad throw of the
(85) dice and try to predict the future, but stopped myself in time.

A boy stopped in time, in a city of amber-colored life, that possessed
the glamour forbidden to a lesser angel.

—Pat Conroy
excerpted from *South of Broad*, 2009
Nan A. Talese

---
[10]contrivance — invention

Regents ELA (Common Core) Answers June 2016
English Language Arts

Answer Key

Part 1

1. 2	9. 3	17. 1
2. 3	10. 4	18. 4
3. 3	11. 1	19. 1
4. 1	12. 2	20. 2
5. 2	13. 4	21. 1
6. 3	14. 1	22. 2
7. 4	15. 2	23. 1
8. 1	16. 3	24. 3

INDEX